# Inside Out

## The Practice of Resilience

### Dr Sven Hansen

Published by Dr Sven Hansen,
The Resilience Institute, PO Box 28-123, Remuera, Auckland 1050;
www.resiliencei.com

Copyright © 2015 Sven Hansen
All diagrams copyright © 2015 The Resilience Institute unless otherwise credited.

The copyright holder asserts his moral rights in the work. Concepts expressed in this work form the foundation of the Author's work as founder and director of The Resilience Institute. All diagrams are copyright The Resilience Institute unless otherwise credited.

This book is copyright. Except for the purposes of fair reviewing, no part of this publication may be reproduced or transmitted in any form or by any means, whether electronic, digital or mechanical, including photocopying, recording, any digital or computerised format, or any information storage and retrieval system, including by any means via the Internet, without permission in writing from the publisher. Infringers of copyright render themselves liable to prosecution.

ISBN 978-0-473-30689-2
Ebook ISBN 978-0-473-30690-8
Editorial services by Oratia Media, www.oratiamedia.com

First published 2015
Printed in China

# Contents

*Foreword*    5

## Part One: Foundations

1. Wake Up!    9
2. Altitude    17
3. Beyond Reasonable Doubt    28

## Part Two: Bounce

4. Response to Challenge    37
5. The Death Spiral    46
6. Get Brilliant at Bounce    61
7. Coherence    71

## Part Three: Courage

8. Prevent and Heal    91
9. Hunt and Gather    116
10. Sleep    138
11. Nourish    154

## Part Four: Creativity

12. Emotion    169
13. Mind    190
14. Mastery    205
15. Flow    217

**Part Five: Connection**

| | | |
|---|---|---:|
| 16 | Work | 231 |
| 17 | Love | 241 |
| 18 | Pray | 254 |
| 19 | Discipline | 262 |

*Notes*     275

*Glossary*     278

# FOREWORD

If we step back and look at the journey of humanity over the past 200,000 years, the singular feature that separates us from other species is creative adaptation. What we have achieved over this time is truly heroic, radical and terrifying. Heroism is built into our DNA. Humans take incredible risks to explore novelty. We are prepared to die for those we love — and sometimes those we don't. Radical refers to the cultural mutations we are able to provoke: populating the world, farming wilderness, language, war, transport, globalisation, and so on. Today we sit at a frothy edge where many of these radical mutations are finding ways to co-exist simultaneously.

Those who can engage and surf this surging wave are having an extraordinarily good time. For those with the skills to meet the challenges, things have never been better. The science of performance, advanced learning a click away, a world of opportunity, and like-minded souls ready to work as a team, create a virtuous and reinforcing upward loop. Work, love and meaning are in abundance. Creative expression flourishes.

On the flip side, fear walks hand in hand with change. When we witness the tsunami of change around us, it can be terrifying. A consensus among the wisest scientists alive is that they are deeply alarmed at the system-wide risk to the future of our species. It is hard for most of us to take a good look at the data and not feel the suck of despair. Yet for humanity it has always been a dangerous world in which to live. Tsunamis and terror groups replace food shortage and wild animals.

There is another form of fear that is inside us. Think of it as self-doubt. You can feel it as a tightness in your gut, as disturbed breath or as tension in your muscles. Feelings of anxiety, wariness or agitation surface into awareness. Thoughts of 'should I?', 'am I?', 'what if?', 'could this hurt?' and many other worries can swirl through our minds, disturbing sleep, work, intimacy and contentment.

Fear is a human braking mechanism. It prefers to operate below awareness. When opportunity or a connection arises in the presence of fear, you turn away. Heroic and radical options do not present as possibility.

Terror of imagined consequences replaces hope and enthusiasm. Life slips by. Moments of being fully engaged are replaced by nagging worries. The life we strive for slips by, becoming a downward spiral of suffering.

*Inside-Out* is written as a counter to fear. By finding out who we are and how we operate, we can still the doubt, cultivate our positive attributes, and discover an entirely new way to live.

Today, we know that all of us can learn:

- ▶ How to bounce from adversity.
- ▶ How to prevent resilience failure.
- ▶ How to build the sources of resilience into life.
- ▶ How to join the heroic and radical.

The solution is not a special white pill, or a magical diet, piece of equipment, surgery or falling in love. These are delusions of the consumer world. We are encouraged to believe that salvation comes from outside. Forget it! The solution is inside you. Success is a product of your lifestyle, your emotions, your thoughts and your actions.

You are the difference that directs life to abundant work, love and meaning, or allows it to spiral down into suffering. We have the resources and the knowledge, and the paths are well trodden.

The inside-out approach seeks to advance this critical dimension of being human. We are the most exquisite and complex organisms. We must learn how to understand and master the inside if we are to be happy, healthy and successful.

So, throw away the pills and join me on the journey of abundance and creative expression. It will test you and delight you.

*Dr Sven Hansen*
*January 2015*

# Part One

# Foundations

1  Wake Up!                         9

2  Altitude                         17

3  Beyond Reasonable Doubt          28

## Chapter 1

# Wake Up!

........................................................

### Practice

1. Sit upright, relax your face and breathe out slowly through your nose.
2. Stretch your arms behind your back, opening your chest and shoulders.
3. Dash up the stairs or take a brisk walk outside.
4. Consider three things you are really lucky to have in your life.
5. Say (or text) something appreciative to someone to whom you are close.
6. Send a pulse of silent kindness to someone you love.
7. Absorb the beauty of nature, love or art — feel the flow of creation.

........................................................

The concept of resilience is intuitive. While many variations exist, most people reach a common understanding of what resilience is and is not. It will help to deepen your thinking so that resilience makes good, trustworthy sense, supports your life practice, and helps you connect with others.

Resilience is learned. Many are quick to collapse into a fatalistic view that you were born to be either resilient or not. They are wrong.

The evidence is clear; it shows that everyone, no matter how blessed or cursed, can learn to demonstrate more resilience. Those who succeed gain measurable advantages, ranging from 50% less depression,[1] to more friends, better marriages, improved academic performance, sales success, and happier lives.² This wisdom rests in philosophies and spiritual paths of self-awareness, discipline and compassion. Science is embracing the journey.

Our optimism, built from experience with tens of thousands of people who enjoy the benefits of resilience from inside-out, is well founded. Small, targeted investments drive meaningful results.

By being alive you are Resilient. You can build more whenever you are ready. Welcome to our community, enjoy the fruits of practice and, if it works for you, spread the good word wherever you can.

Through this book we will explore, define and demonstrate the philosophy, principles, practices and supporting evidence for a life that embraces resilience. You will understand the logic and the clear, lasting benefits of getting started on your journey. The journey is influenced by our genetic inheritance, early upbringing, environmental shaping (epigenetics), culture and personal effort.

Let's consider the evidence that resilience is partly genetic.

The history of life on this planet is brutal. You had to be strong and flexible to survive. We are here thanks to evolution. Species that found a way to thrive in the hurly burly of life's lust for itself carved the genetic code that runs through each of us. This is deep inside and lusts for expression.

Resilience, defined as bounce, courage, creativity and connection, is embedded in our nature. Resilience is in each genetic translation, in every cellular process, in the function of organs, and in our response to change when novelty presents.

If resilience fails in any one of these trillions of instantaneous processes, the organism is subtly compromised. If too many processes fail — either instantaneously or over time — our viability is compromised. This compromise may present as disease, injury, pain or death. Our genes have been selected to protect us.

Some species have learned that it is advantageous to form social groups. They secure safety, resources, and reproduction, supporting survival of both the individual and the group. Insect colonies, hunting packs, herds and primates thrive through the sophisticated bonds of communication, specialisation and collaboration. Those that thrive in these social environments are more likely to propagate their genes.³

Evolution has shaped us through the resilience of the individual and the group. Resilience is an intrinsic part of life embedded in our genetic code and our predisposition to learn. At a superficial level height, blond hair, facial symmetry and body shape have measurable advantages, even today. Intelligence and social skill have profound benefits in today's world. Nature and nurture create a virtuous loop.

The prevalence of the serotonin transporter gene (STG) in its long forms nudges a person towards optimism, steadiness under pressure and confidence. Conversely, the short form predisposes its owner towards depression, anxiety disorders and some forms of mental illness. Where Occam's razor is sharp, such as in conflict, natural disaster or in competitive pursuits such as business, war or sport, the owners of long forms of STG are more likely to succeed. Not surprisingly, they hang out together and mate further, concentrating genetic advantage.[4]

Intelligence — specifically the 'g' factor or processing speed — is genetic, as shown in twin studies and evolutionary genetics. Intelligence is a reasonable predictor of success. Smart people tend to go to good schools, get good jobs, then marry and produce smart kids. However, if a smart person has deficiency in empathy (high functioning Autism) there may be disadvantages.[5]

These examples may cause a degree of genetic drift towards more successful and less successful communities. In the hurly burly of the free market, we see this drift when we compare Harvard alumni with those who are third-generation welfare beneficiaries. These crunchy challenges must be faced. We cannot afford to put our heads in the sand or crucify the researchers. We must understand these forces if we are to shape a fair and Resilient society. But genes are a small, and perhaps diminishing, element of the story.

Epigenetics, the study of environmental and behavioural effects on genetic expression, has thrown a curve ball. We can change the expression of the DNA in our genes without changing the actual sequence. The environment and state in which we live switches our genes on or off. For example, genes responsible for diabetes switch on in the presence of refined and processed carbohydrate, and off in lean times or in the presence of high-fat/high-protein diets.

The environment and lifestyles we choose affect the genes that protect or predispose us to disease. These changes to gene expression can cross generations, conferring the advantage or risk to the next generation. Distress, poor nutrition, smoking, substance abuse and inactivity impact the genes of the next generation.

So when smart people behave stupidly, their community shifts downwards. When less fortunate people behave cleverly, their community shifts upwards.

We will examine more about how lifestyle choices — including where we live and work, who we live or work with, what we eat, how we exercise and patterns of sleep — all have molecular effects on our physiology, biochemistry and, ultimately, our genetic code.

Finally, the clear conclusion from multiple trusted resources is that resilience can be learned, cultivated or undermined by what we do every day of our lives. This is clearly signalled by thousands of studies that include the following subject matter.

- ▶ **Parenting**  Secure bonds within our early family experience code for success.
- ▶ **Fitness**  Exercise improves our physical, emotional and cognitive performance.
- ▶ **Relaxation**  Regular deep relaxation and mindfulness build resilience.
- ▶ **Sleep**  A good night's sleep is essential to resilience at all levels.
- ▶ **Nutrition**  Sound eating habits reverse disease and liberate wellbeing.
- ▶ **Positivity**  Happy, contented and kind people secure better lives.
- ▶ **Optimism**  Constructive and positive thoughts about life secure better lives.

## Summary

1. Elements of resilience are sourced in the evolution of our genetic structure.
2. Our environment and lifestyle choices shape genetic activity — personal and offspring.
3. Our daily activities, emotions and thoughts have profound impacts on resilience.

Let's examine each of the four perspectives on resilience.

## Bounce

Life delivers serious adversities from time to time. These may be of our own making or a result of external forces. For 50 years we have recognised that some of us respond constructively to adversity, finding ways to bounce back and emerge stronger and more effective. Others react negatively, losing confidence and acting in ways that undermine their wellbeing, vitality and effectiveness.

Those who bounce back effectively focus on what they can achieve rather than blaming, they maintain and engage supportive networks, and display a bias to take action. When in trouble, focus inward, connect and act — inside-out. These characteristics can be learned and practised. In fact, adversity may be exactly what we need to realise these strengths and master the ability to bounce back.

Some recommend the administration of small, repeated shocks to train people and society to exercise their capacity for bounce and adaptation.[6] This has been missing in modern parenting and education. We are 'killing people with kindness'. Adversity triggers adaptive responses. As comfort-seeking creatures, we are quick to remove the experience of adversity. Excess safety reduces exploration, medication counters natural healing, tolerance encourages destructive behaviour, and social welfare undermines individual resourcefulness. We are afraid to let people learn.

Depression is increasing despite gains in wellbeing, and it now competes with heart disease as the major disease of our time. Depression rates in children have increased tenfold over the past 40 years, and the age of a first episode has dropped from 29.5 to 14.5 years.[7] With an enormous weaponry of modern medicine and psychiatry, we frequently turn to medication and therapy rather than teaching the skills of bounce.

Bounce is the base camp for a good life in a dynamic world.

## Courage

The second element captures our orientation to change, including the daily challenges of life. Based on the work *Learned Optimism* by Martin Seligman,[8] we learn helplessness or optimism from our interactions with circumstance. We always hold the option to engage constructively or to collapse, flee or fight. The difference is courage. We have removed many of the daily challenges of survival. To thrive we must now go out and seek challenge with courage. We can do this through exercise, fasting, exploring, connecting and creating.

Sometimes we resent novelty and resist change. We retreat into thoughts (ruminate) on how things were and should be, or worry about the future. Resistance to change focuses our attention on external causes. This provokes anger, sadness (past) or fear (future). Change becomes a risk to be feared and fought.

At other times we take an energised, optimistic and constructive stance to change and challenge. We focus on the goal and leverage resources to engage creatively. This leads to mastery and success, and stimulates an upward spiral of competence and confidence. Our attention is focused on our own actions.

While chasing change for its own sake has risks, someone who takes an engaged and optimistic stance to the turbulence of modern life will be more likely to succeed. Courage embraces the future with a curious mind, an open heart, and the will to take action. It is displayed by positive physical action towards meaningful goals.

## Creativity

The third element of resilience pushes beyond difficulty and tenacity. Bounce and courage provoke learning and growth. Creativity is expansive and ambitious. While our capacity to develop is immense, it is not for everyone. Reaching our full potential requires deep self-awareness, skill mastery and perseverance. Often experiments will fail. Fearing failure, many settle for mediocrity.

Evidence shows that those who discover and stretch their talents experience increased life satisfaction, joy, health and longevity.[9] Aligning our talents and skills with a meaningful challenge enriches life. As we live longer in an economically insecure world, it will be necessary to find the skills to work well beyond traditional retirement. Our planet's resilience depends on the creative stewardship of humanity.

The world changes, our abilities mature, and what really matters evolves. It is important not to overstay a phase of life, a job or a role. As the challenge changes and our skills adapt, we can rejuvenate and find another layer of possibility. The creative impulse to advance into novelty is the story of humanity.

## Connection

There are people who meet the first three elements of resilience but fail at the fourth. Connection begins with a respectful engagement with our bodies, our emotions, our thoughts and our purpose. It extends to family, friends, community, workplace and beyond, to nature and our planet. Broken connections cause pain.

Connection requires respect inside and out. It is a measure of maturity — an impulse to goodness. It measures how we have lived and defines how we will be remembered. It is an onerous responsibility and mistakes will be made. Creativity is a core ingredient that works synergistically with Connection.

Provided we work with self-awareness, respect, tolerance and compassion, the work of relieving suffering and ennobling others is deeply rewarding at all levels — body, heart, mind and spirit. Our wellbeing, emotional state, cognition and contentment improve when we help others.

Targeted helping (altruism), embedded in our evolution, reaches its finest expression when compassion is discovered and practised by an enlightened human being.

Figure 1: An Integrated Model of Resilience

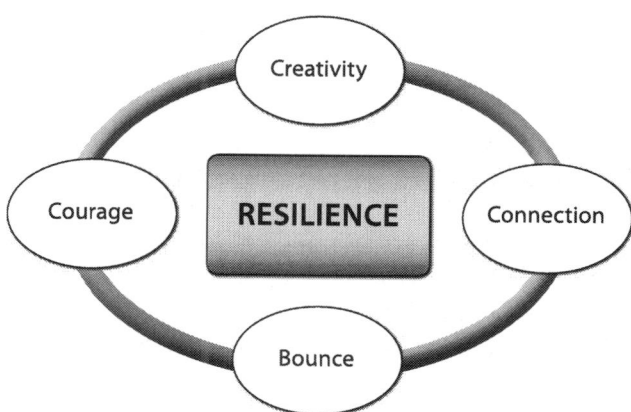

The integrated model of resilience is a closely woven system where bounce leads to courage, which leads to creativity and sometimes connection. The influence works in reverse and across all combinations. When all parts interact we create an integral reinforcing holon (whole greater than parts) that liberates far more potential than any single part. The impulse towards resilience begins inside and works outward. As we gain insight into who we are and how we function, we can select the practices and choices to master situations. In turn, mastery allows us to attune to others, connect and engage in skilful and compassionate work. This is the foundation of vitality, joy and a good life.

••••••••••••••••••••••••••••••••••••••••••••••••••••••••••••••••••

## Summary

Resilience is the ability to demonstrate:

1. **Bounce**
2. **Courage**
3. **Creativity**, and
4. **Connection**.

All four are relevant to you, your family, your business and your community. Enabling ourselves will relieve pressure on the planet and bring us into constructive engagement with the challenges of the future.

••••••••••••••••••••••••••••••••••••••••••••••••••••••••••••••••••

# Chapter 2

# Altitude

## The Dash for Cash

Modern life is addicted to speed. We are time paced — racing through phases of life and the moments of each day, packing in work, play, entertainment and distractions. Driven to mate, to work, to find a home and to broadcast our success, we spend much of our lives in a frantic 'dash for cash'. This is a powerful centrifugal force (pushing out). While this is important work in the real world of survival, it squeezes out recovery, reflection, joy and creative engagement. Without a counter-balance it will destroy resilience. This counterbalance is the centripetal force (pulling in) that builds resilience — inside-out.

Our economy and social structure are measured in this horizontal dimension. We measure numbers and physical relationships because we can 'trust' them. There is obsessive focus on the Gross Domestic Product (GDP), but this growth model is not delivering happiness and wellbeing. In fact it measures prisons, war, healthcare, planetary destruction and government bureaucracy as positive inputs.

The limitations of the GDP growth model are now obvious. Many academics, politicians and business folk are searching for alternatives. The January 2012 issue of the *Harvard Business Review* is devoted to the topic. Transformation is due.

Resilience operates on the vertical dimension of depth. It is an energetic and conscious dimension. As the capabilities of body, emotion, mind and spirit are activated, our energy increases (negentropy), countering the second law of thermodynamics (entropy says that everything loses energy). Our resources and behaviour become more complex, integrated and powerful. We thrive, becoming a force for good in the world.

When the resources of body, emotion, mind and spirit are depleted, we find our energy falling (entropy). Our resources and behaviour become more rigid, inappropriate and weak. We flail and problems become intractable. Our life can become suffering and a social liability. Centrifugal forces have pulled us apart.

With resilience we engage creatively with both opportunities and threats that arise in our life. This is possible only when we understand and master biological energy. This energy flows through body, heart, mind and spirit. Few know how to use this resource. It is a latent gift waiting to be activated. Our marvellous organism is not issued with an instruction manual. Inside-out is something of a human instruction manual.

The future may well belong to those who master biology. It a reasonable hypothesis.

Resilience begins with an awareness of depth (biological insight). By observing carefully the signals from our body, emotions and thoughts, we perceive the rich dimensions of our life experience. Depth opens the full experience of life right now. We can be fully connected to body, senses, feelings, thoughts, purpose and relationships. With practice we can hold our available resources on the process of being fully present and effective in every moment …

Now … and now … and now!

For example, right now take your attention into your body. Notice your posture and muscles. What feels strained and what feels good? Notice your breathing. Follow the flow of air through the nostrils. Watch where the air moves. Follow the change from inhale to exhale and back. See if you can smooth and soften the flow of breath.

Focus on how you are feeling right this moment. See if you can name some of the feelings (emotions). Then switch to the process of your thinking. What thoughts, images and chit-chat are going on in your head? Can you bring all of your attention into NOW? Has anything changed as you do this?

We waste time and energy ruminating on the past (how things should be) and the future (worry, doubt and magical thinking). Our resources are not available to enjoy the real game, which is thoughtfully called The Present.

Our life is right here, right now.

Being creative, decisive and focused in the moment is the experience of resilience. To achieve this state of being we have to understand and master our equipment — body, heart, mind and spirit. This takes time, careful reflection and practice.

Our parenting and education systems fail to devote enough time to this important work. Given all we know about resilience, it is alarming that most young folk leave school with no idea of how to breathe under pressure, take care of their spines, master destructive emotional impulses, or focus attention.

Mystics have used the metaphor of the cart, horse, driver and passenger to articulate this life challenge. The question: what does cart, horse, driver and passenger represent in your own life?

One explanation is that the cart is the physical body, the horse is the emotions and the driver is the mind. The contraption is designed to carry a passenger — the spirit — in safety and comfort. The spirit has purpose, a destination, and work to do.

Looking around — or perhaps in the mirror — it is easy to see some pretty messed-up contraptions. The cart is often broken or too heavy for the horses; the horses are in a rage, a panic or have simply given up; the driver is drunk or asleep; and the spirit is hiding in a local pub. Our life's purpose is vague, unrecognised and silent.

When we view ourselves through this lens, we can quickly bring an integrated perspective on our lives. The lesson:

1. Fix the cart and make it a comfortable ride: strong body.

2. Feed, water and gently encourage the horses: constructive emotion.

3. Wake up the driver and work out where you are going: clear, focused mind.

4. Invite your spirit aboard to find your life's work: realise purpose.

We will come back to this concept in a contemporary framework shortly. First, let's take a broad view of the Resilience Diagnosis and Development Model.

The medical model of diagnosis groups us as normal, diseased or 'nothing serious'. A career of work with serious illness, multiple states of 'normal' and those excelling in leadership and sport taught me that there are many states of being. There are many states of positive resilience and, equally, many states of resilience failure.

This learning lead to our Diagnostic and Development Model.

Figure 2: A Diagnostic and Development Model of The Resilience Institute

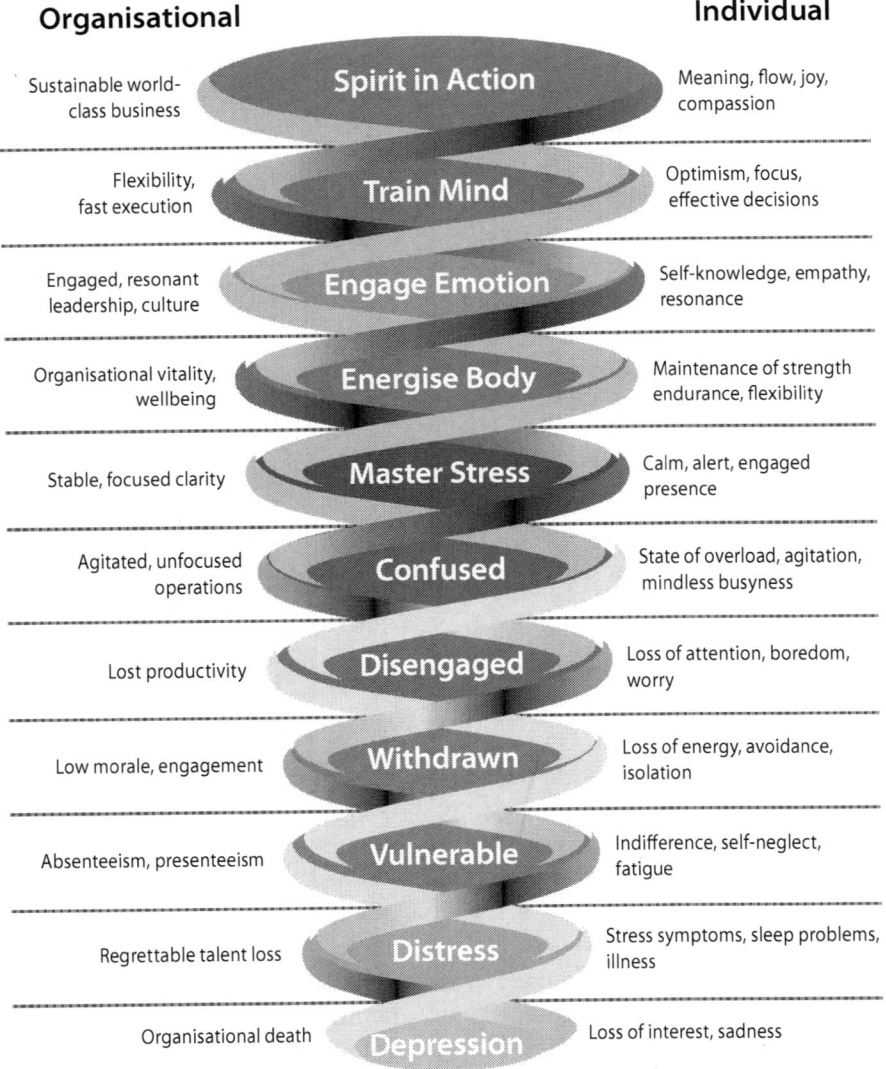

This model guides the inside-out approach to resilience. First, it is a just a model and not reality. It is one simple map of the complex realities of life. It attempts to describe the richness of states and stages we experience in life.

## Practice

To check your resilience with our Resilience Diagnostic, access it here: www.resiliencei.com/Shop_332.aspx

The lower half describes the progressive failure of resilience. This is what the philosophers call suffering, or dukkha. We call it the death spiral and will address it in part two on Bounce. As you slide down the spiral, you lose altitude. Mind, then emotion, and then body fail progressively. To be on the lower rungs is a sorry situation. Seeing this will encourage you upwards.

The top half shows how to gain biological altitude in a proposed order of progression. The right-hand side descriptions map the experience of an individual at each level. The left-hand side describes the organisation or group experience. Life energy expands, and choices and freedom increase. You learn to fly high. It is a good state to be in and we naturally want more of it.

'Master Stress' includes the ability to recognise threats to our resilience, to bounce quickly, and to regain a calm, engaged state — what we will call coherence. It builds on bounce and requires that we wake up to ourselves. Resilience depends on quick recognition and recovery when we slip downwards. 'Master Stress' builds the base from which we establish the higher disciplines.

We can all be much better at this. Frequently we tolerate hours, weeks and even years in the death spiral. This is crazy. There are so many ways to escape this suffering. The pace and uncertainty of modern life make this ever more critical. To be calm, alert, engaged and present is a huge plus.

'Energise Body' embraces the ability to build energy, strength and flexibility. Here we can achieve quick, powerful gains in resilience. We ignore it at our peril. The body is complex and self-regulating. It follows laws of physics, chemistry and biology. While clearly a product of our genes, the body is open to shaping with the right training. Left to run riot on bad habits, in due course it will self-destruct.

The body is our organ of perception, using the five senses of taste, touch, hearing, sight and smell. It is the canvas of emotion and a context for thought. The body communicates and receives the richness of social interaction. People assess us through signals our bodies send out. The global healthcare crisis is a failure at this level. The solution depends on more people taking responsibility for the well-researched practices that extend and enhance a healthy, productive life.

'Engage Emotion' embraces the awareness, regulation and alignment of our emotions with what we seek to achieve. Emotional competence (EQ, emotional quotient, or emotional intelligence) is an old idea reawakened. Emotion was neglected for most of the 20th century. It has been a surprising revelation that the gushy, 'soft' world of emotion is, in fact, a crucial determinant of our ability to thrive and perform in life and at work.

Emotion is central to alertness, attention, creativity, decision-making and execution. As our poets always knew and science now demonstrates, the heart leads.[10] In fact, when the links between experienced emotion and the forebrain are destroyed, a person drifts into chaos, unable to make effective decisions about personal wellbeing, activities or relationships.

Emotion is the most neglected aspect of our human equipment — an ignorance of which is the root of most suffering. We have been designed not to be aware of emotion, so this is a particularly challenging component.[11] However, the payback from small wins is huge.

'Engaged Emotion' is the gateway to relationship and social enterprise. Promoted as emotional intelligence, it is the source of 85% of what makes outstanding leaders great. It has repeatedly been shown to be at least twice as important as Intelligence Quotient (IQ) and technical skill in the arenas of business, sport and parenting.

'Train Mind' embraces the world of thoughts, attention, attitude and decision. It cannot be separated from emotion. We will work with both emotion and mind in the section on Creativity.

The higher functions of mind, intellect and creativity can operate only through the older and more primitive structures of the brain. Even the purest thought is brought into being with the assistance of animal instinct and a complex emotional milieu. Small shifts in physical and emotional state can cause wild fluctuations in the performance of mind.

Brain sciences take centre stage with an early understanding of the most complex structure in the universe. Proving to be surprisingly plastic, the brain gives us enormous scope for self-improvement.[12] The cognitive decline of ageing can be slowed. Many functions within the brain can be improved throughout life.[13] It will not be long before schools and organisations introduce targeted training of the mind.

'Spirit in Action' charts the domain of meaning and spirit with practical advice on crafting awareness, presence and resonance into life. Our whole being is in action. We recognise times when it all comes together and we achieve peak experiences. This may be in nature, on stage, in sport, at work, on canvas or in contemplation. These are the times that body, heart and mind work together to achieve, relate or experience in extraordinary ways.

In these times we are able to measure positive changes in physical parameters such as blood pressure, pulse and blood chemistry. The emotions felt are positive and the mind is measured as calm, focused and synchronised.

Antonio Damasio, a leading neurobiologist in the field of emotion and consciousness, uses the metaphor of the actress about to step through the curtains into the light of her first gala performance. It is in these moments that we feel the full alignment of self: our preparation and the challenge ahead emerges as 'spiritual'. We can participate in life with the lights of consciousness ablaze to show the way. These states are also often described as flow states and have been extensively studied.[14] From inside-out, body, heart, mind and spirit align and engage. It is a good altitude at which to lead your life.

## Reflection

Think back to the last time you were fully engaged with meaning. This is a time you may describe as your spirit being fully in action. Put your own words to each of the components we have just described.

### Practical Application of the Model

Simplifying the model down to the basics allows us to explore it from four clear perspectives: insight, mastery, empathy and influence. Each perspective is an opportunity for specific and lifelong practice. These are the keys to a good life, successful work and leadership, a good marriage and good parenting.

Figure 3: The Four Lenses of Resilience — Insight, Mastery, Empathy and Influence

We will address these in more detail as the journey unfolds. For now, let's understand the basics of each lens.

Insight, which is also referred to as self-awareness, self-knowledge or mindsight, is the ability to look inwards and sense ourselves in action. This can be both in the moment and over time. The question to ask of ourselves is, "Where am I on the spiral?" As we will learn, we can all improve our ability to sense our breathing, heart rate, posture, energy levels, emotions, thoughts and consciousness.

Mastery, or self-regulation, is the ability to know what to do to improve your position and how to do it. The question to ask is, "What do I need to do to calm myself?" You can replace 'calm' with 'energise', 'engage emotion', 'focus the mind' or 'be fully actualised'. We will learn how we can create quick and sustained adjustments to our state. This may be to bounce from depression or to strengthen our power of attention.

Empathy, or social awareness, is the ability to tune in to those around us. The question is, "How does this look or feel to her/him/them?" Empathy may be focused deeply on one person or expanded to understand the mood of an audience. Frans de Waal describes the Empathy Portal[15] as a neural system that we can open or close. Closely related is situational awareness, which is the ability to sense and understand the context within which action happens — human, technical and kinetic. Experts in every field become accomplished at this. For example, a doctor understands how the various components of an emergency unit come together to save a life. An elite soldier knows where to look for a sniper.

Influence, social skill or leadership is the ability to interact in a way that helps others be happier, healthier and more whole. The question to ask is, "How do we behave in a way that he/she feels respected, cared for and enabled?"

Simple to understand. Devilishly difficult to master on a consistent basis. The earlier we start, the more skilful we become. It is never too late. Each lens requires effort, energy and skill. To be resilient over time we have to build our fitness for resilience. A physical example of leadership can be seen in recent work at Harvard.[16]

At first we have no idea that we have slumped in the chair during a meeting. As the body slumps, we feel tired and despondent. This sends a 'closed' signal to others. We do not appear engaged and it is tough to influence constructively. Leadership development at this level requires that we devote energy to a series of steps. Energy is limited so we might work in small steps. Ideally, we would have insight switched on and would notice our posture slump. Immediately we would correct our posture, lengthening the spine and opening the shoulders. This takes physical/muscular effort, but we will immediately feel better. From the open posture it is easier to attend fully to others — and they notice this immediately. In fact, within minutes testosterone increases and cortisol reduces. You are more energised, focused, confident and relaxed. Your impact on others is positive.

Just as an athlete must build the basics of flexibility, strength, endurance, balance and speed, so we need to build the capacity to hold the lenses and skills of insight, mastery, empathy and influence.

The concept of depth is contentious, yet clearly some achieve more complex and appropriate patterns of behaviour. We can observe people with huge energy and passion and contrast them with those who wither from novelty. We have all had times when life is firing on all cylinders. We bound out of bed, engage in daily tasks with enthusiasm, tackle difficult issues, enjoy wonderful connections with others and generally have a superbly good time. At these times creativity, decision-making and execution come easily.

Remember the horse and cart? The cart is serviced and polished, the horses are fuelled and energetic, the driver has a clear destination and route, and perhaps the spirit is on-board.

We can examine these moments of optimal life experience using the Performance Supply Chain. This is a simple model we have developed to capture the dynamic interplay of body, heart and mind in moment-to-moment action.

To elaborate, let's take the example of sleep. If the resilient goal is 7.5 hours of unbroken sleep, the action of placing one's head on the pillow might deliver this performance. Unfortunately, only a small percentage of people are so lucky. To resolve the challenge, we can go back and examine some of the preceding actions. Did you check your e-mail, watch TV in bed, send a text, or start a difficult conversation before trying to sleep?

Figure 4: The Performance Supply Chain

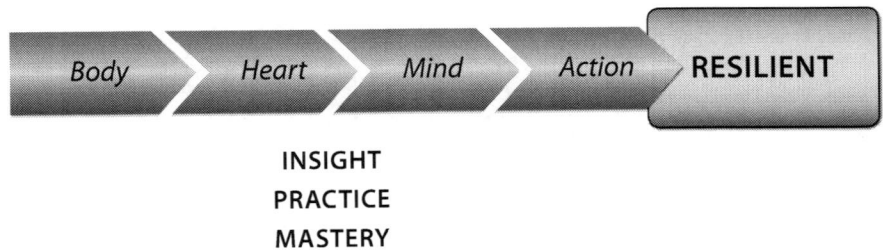

CRAFTING YOUR PERSONAL BRAND:

**INSIGHT**
**PRACTICE**
**MASTERY**

*God, grant me the serenity to accept the things I cannot change,*
*The courage to change the things I can,*
*And wisdom to know the difference.*

If not, we can look at the mind. What are you thinking? What is the quality and content of your thoughts? If you are worrying about the future or fretting about the past, the mind maintains wakefulness — it cannot relax. You might have to learn how to stop thinking. We can go further back and examine your emotions. Some emotions encourage sleep and others prevent sleep. Anger is a sure sleep stopper, along with fear.

Further back is the body. Did you exercise today, get enough light to produce melatonin, limit alcohol and heavy foods or spend some time cooling and quieting down? Is your bedroom too warm or too bright?

In this way we can use the Performance Supply Chain to analyse a situation for better outcomes. We can help the body, heart and mind work constructively and in alignment to secure the desired performance.

Behind each component is a range of mechanisms we can learn to understand and a set of skills that we can master. We will come back to this repeatedly as we continue our journey.

Inside-out will help you learn what works, train you in the practices of resilience and encourage you to develop your own daily routines. Enjoy the adventure of clambering up the resilience spiral and finding the confidence and the energy that is waiting for you at higher altitudes.

## Summary

- Balance the 'dash for cash' with quality and depth.
- Recognise the potential of body, heart, mind and spirit.
- Check your view with insight, mastery, empathy and influence.
- Understand the Performance Supply Chain.

# Chapter 3

# Beyond Reasonable Doubt

## From Boosterism to Resilience

By now you may be asking yourself if this is another 'positive thinking' trip, also known as 'boosterism'. While fully supportive of alternative approaches that work, resilience as articulated in *Inside-Out* is evidence based. All that we discuss and recommend can be quickly referenced in the writing of respected thought leaders, peer-reviewed journals and clinical practice.

Boosterism is a term given to the self-esteem movement that invaded our schools and communities in the late 20th century.[17] Boosterism is detected when kids are congratulated for a sloppy effort and certificates are handed out for mediocrity. The intent is for all to feel good, regardless of the performance. Boosterism has invaded our parenting, education and business.

Firstly, boosterism is dishonest, unrealistic and dangerously misleading to the recipient. It gives a distorted truth to the performer and fails to motivate towards improvement and mastery.

Secondly, we all — even young children — recognise a good effort. We need accurate, realistic and honest feedback. Without this we begin to doubt our own assessment and disregard the desire to improve. Just being positive or feeling good does not build true resilience. Positive feelings must be based on mastery: the ability to complete or accomplish a task to one's satisfaction.

Thirdly, it is important to remember the value of positive feedback when it is linked to a good effort and/or good results. Sometimes we need to break mastery down into small, manageable steps. Feedback must be given gently, firmly and consistently. It must be based on a clear understanding of what is expected.

Resilience is evidence based. Thinking and feeling is based on accurate self-awareness and self-assessment. Confidence must be based on performance against agreed standards. And, where generating a positive mindset or feeling is clearly shown in good studies to be adaptive, we should listen and find out how to do it with integrity.

## Integrity of Thought and Action

Biology, the study of life, informs inside-out. Biology is topical, both as an embracing life science and as a metaphor for organisational life. Biologists study from the bottom of the ocean to deep space, the history of life to genetic modification, and culture to biotechnology. Biology is fundamentally reductionist — by examining every whole in increasingly tiny, molecular detail, biology seeks to remove the ghost from the machine.

The detail of information embraced within modern biological science is vast and beyond the comprehension of any one mind. While Charles Darwin hinted at it 150 years ago, it is only in the past decade that we have really begun to explore the biology of optimal human physiology — physical, emotional, cognitive and spiritual. Biology is stretched thin at this frontier, but leading thinkers are shifting from reductionism to embracing holistic or integral models. Biology now seeks to find coherence and meaning behind complex systems such as the mind. We see this in the new physics, physiology, anthropology, psychology, neurobiology and medicine.

Edward O. Wilson (our modern Darwin) calls this integration of detail into complexity and coherence 'consilience'.[18] It is a captivating and compelling integration of many disciplines. With time we will inevitably develop much better models of how reality actually works.

Following are a few cautionary points from a practical biologist.

Biology is a hard science. Many implications of biology look compelling and intuitive, but are not absolutely proven. In the case of the human mind, it will be many years before a full picture emerges. For now, we can only extrapolate from existing work in animals and humans as to how the mind might actually work. Remember this when you commit to a philosophy or practice. It is essential that you maintain a critical stance and an open mind to new data. Biological science is rigorous. However, if we cannot prove something, it does not mean it does not exist.

Life is not hard science. Life is experience — a subjective perspective. No matter how detailed our understanding of a certain emotional process, we cannot describe the subjective experience from a brain scan. To do this requires listening, understanding and shared experience. We must always respect individual experience. While molecules, neurotransmitters, neural firing and convergence zones most certainly do underpin the experience of love, they are not love.

We cannot wait for all the facts before acting. The human mind is equipped to make decisions without the full set of information. We use experience, emotional judgement and reason to come to a decision. Life is action. If a certain practice makes sense, try it! With time you will learn to recognise the practices that change your biology (through your direct, subjective experience) for the better. Use them and fine-tune them as more data comes to hand.

No community has yet engaged the full power of modern biology. This is an exciting opportunity for those with Courage. It is an emerging reality. More and more people will live to 100 and more. Many will stay physically and economically competitive well into their eighties and nineties. Stay open to possibility. Imagine being part of a community that took resilience really seriously, supporting all of its members in the journey up the spiral.

Biology is a living science. It is growing and maturing at an extraordinary pace. The data and hypotheses will change but a philosophical approach can remain steady. I recommend the following hierarchy of thinking and action as you become a biologist studying your own experiences, relationships and life journey.

The diagram (next page) shows a rough hierarchy of knowledge and practice. The end game is the subjective experience. This experience emerges from what we do — our practices. Aligning our practices with carefully considered principles can lift your game markedly. The goal is to crystallise our principles and refine our practices. We support this effort with the best evidence we can find and the experience of those who have tested the limits.

Biology and medicine have documented many of the lifestyle practices that definitively improve life. All practices should be based on principles of action. Principles are longer-term concepts built from the philosophy of the sciences. They are there to guide us while we wait for the outcome of

Figure 5: The Hierarchy of Thought and Action

studies. Principles help us solve complex problems and should be studied and understood.

The philosophy and data are the domains of scientists. It is entertaining for the rest of us, but probably not essential. What is important is to find the 'biological guides' who can help us understand how to apply the principles that rest on the hard data and philosophy.

Keep this hierarchy of thought and action in mind as you build your resilience. The scientific approach can help us find the most logical and effective means to achieve our goals. The real test is in your life — body, heart, mind and spirit. Science still has a lot to discover. Don't wait — get started.

## Resilience Revealed

The invitation, should you accept it, is to build resilience. There are five objectives:

1. Be calm, alert and engaged in all that you do.
2. Protect, maintain and build your physical vitality every day.
3. Be aware, empathic and resonant in your various life roles.
4. Awaken your spirit to embrace the fullness of life.
5. Have a positive impact on others and your world at all times.

The aim of this book to help you achieve these objectives and realise your potential.

How you do this is up to you. You will have to explore and experiment. You will create your own journey. Whether at the beginning or close to the end of your journey in this body, the evidence is clear and compelling that you will enjoy many benefits should you succeed. Further, the world will be a better place. Your life will contribute to less suffering and more enlightenment.

There will be setbacks and stagnation. You might lose your way from time to time. Never forget the mission and never surrender your will to recover and grow. Sometimes you will make surprising and stunning advances. Your life will leap forward as certain components come together in just the right way for you. Celebrate but maintain your focus on the mission and the objectives.

This particular approach may not be for you. All I ask is that you give it a fair trial. You may find some parts particularly relevant while others miss the mark. Take what you find helpful. Challenge everything, double check what you learn, and satisfy yourself that what you do find helpful, is valid. Debate these ideas with others. If you find someone who can benefit from something you learn, share it with respect and compassion.

Today, for the first time ever in human history, we have access to all the world's major philosophies, religions, sciences and lifestyles. Even a hundred years ago a seeker of wisdom had to head off on expensive, dangerous and vague journeys to mysterious places. Today you can run a Google search from the comfort of your bed. There is more knowledge than you can ever consume.

Herein lies a trap for the unwary. It is easy to read, think, reflect, and talk too much and not take meaningful action. Resilience is action biased. Study until you have mastered the basic idea. Then put the concept into practice with passion, focus and tenacity. Practise repeatedly until your being feels the impact. Adjust, develop skill and learn how to apply the practice to your specific context and needs.

Resilience is designed to make the study of this vast philosophical and research field accessible. It will give you a rough road map and indicate where you can consult with experts and alternative approaches.

Inside-out is also designed to help you develop and perfect a range of safe and well-tested practices. Tackle the journey in bite-size chunks. Read a section at a time and if the practice seems relevant, stop, work out how to take some action and experiment. Get help where and when you need it.

Study! Practise! If you feel the urge, teach!

........................................................

### Summary

- ✴ Watch out for boosterism.
- ✴ Biological understanding is accelerating very fast.
- ✴ Seek knowledge, act courageously and respect others.
- ✴ Remember the integrity of thought and action.

........................................................

# Part Two

# Bounce

4 Response to Challenge — 37

5 The Death Spiral — 46

6 Get Brilliant at Bounce — 61

7 Coherence — 71

## Chapter 4

# Response to Challenge

### Beyond Stress

Stress is a sloppy word: loose, subjective and confusing. Is stress internal or external? Can it be both positive and negative? Once we use the word 'stress' we have slipped into confusing territory. It is unhelpful. Dismiss it. There is a much better way to understand and master the challenges of life.

### Response to Challenge

A more objective and useful way to understand resilience is to understand how we respond to a challenge. For example, another car bumps into the back of your car, pushing you across an intersection. We can be clear about the external challenge. You were hit at a certain speed, causing a certain amount of damage and moving you a certain distance. The police will describe this accurately. It is objective.

How we might respond to such a challenge is variable. Some might sail through the experience with slight surprise, quick evasive action and calm resolution. Others might be paralysed with fear or fly into a screaming rage. The external challenge (stressor) is the same but the response (distress caused) varies tremendously. We might consider what a resilient response might be.

Let's take another example. You are relaxing at home on a Friday night when the phone rings (challenge or stressor). Your response goes as follows: your heart jumps, you suck in air, feel a surge of fear and leap for the phone 'knowing' that your son has been hurt (high level of distress). The call is an automated reminder of a meter check tomorrow. Again, what might the resilient response be?

In both cases the biological response might have been roughly the same — surprise, surge of adrenaline, heart rate acceleration, rapid inhalations, raised blood pressure, blood shunting from brain and skin to legs, fear, catastrophic thoughts and reactive outbursts. In the first case, the challenge was physically violent and real. In the second, there was no challenge. It was entirely imagined — a product of our feelings and thoughts. The response can be measured.

We can map response to challenge on the curve below. As our biological response changes, our performance changes. At first biological arousal activates us and resources body, heart and mind to perform effectively in the situation. So if our car is hit and pushed across an intersection, you definitely want to be more alert, focused and able to steer, brake and get out of harm's way. This effective response requires increased heart rate, some muscle tension and increased brain blood flow.

Understandably, in most cases the biological response is extreme and we move into distress. Heart rate is too high, muscles become too stiff or collapse, there is too much adrenaline and not enough blood in the brain. Our ability to match the challenge declines steeply as we head into biological distress. We are unlikely to be able to move out of harm's way.

Figure 6: Mapping our Response to Challenge

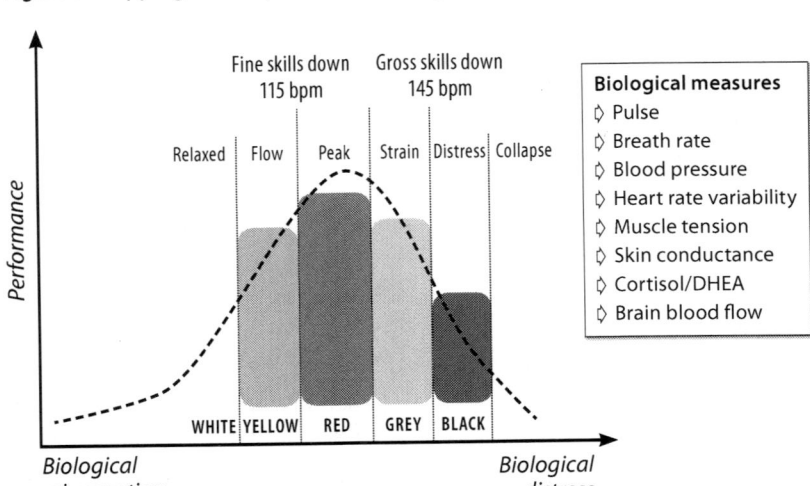

The curve that defines our response to challenge dates back to the work of Robert Yerkes and John Dodson, who first calibrated a pressure/performance relationship in 1908. This curve has been used in many ways to explore how a system — including human — responds and performs under varying levels of challenge or pressure. It is now at the heart of understanding expert performance in military and sport studies.[19]

When we perceive little challenge we tend to relax and rejuvenate (left-hand side or condition white). This is vital to our health and resilience. However, if we relax for too long we slide into apathy. This can happen to someone who is bed-ridden, bored or unemployed. As challenge is sought out or presented to us, we respond positively to find ways to engage with the challenge (condition yellow). This is optimal performance or flow, and takes us into higher performance states. Our performance is sustainable in condition yellow. We are activated biologically (but not too much) and respond constructively and efficiently. It feels good. We can maintain the effort over time and through the unexpected.

When facing a major challenge we can push the pedal to the floor and redline our biology. This is the zone of peak performance (condition red). We can use condition red in short bursts, but it quickly leads to exhaustion and declines in fine motor skills and decision-making. This is true as we approach our maximum levels of speed, force output, empathy or thinking complexity. The risk in condition red is that we are pumping so much blood and glucose to one part of the body or mind that other parts may blink out. We will explore this in future chapters.

As the challenge increases, our response is stretched past effective performance (condition grey). We are biologically compromised; the condition is not sustainable over time. With the flood of activity in our lives, many now live in this over-stimulated state. It is exhausting. We're now in strain. We may feel this when we work or train too hard and for too long. Strain or condition grey has become the norm in education, sport and business. As a result, children lose their health or creativity, athletes overtrain, and business people 'burn out'. We lose our physical wellbeing, insight, empathy and focus.

In controlled situations, such as elite sport or combat with a defined scope, feedback and coaches, it is possible to train into grey. Modern life has complex challenges over long periods. There is often little feedback, and people simply don't notice that parts of their life have dipped down the wrong side. It is often our health, marriage, friendships or hobbies that decline while we struggle to maintain work. Condition grey should be reserved for desperate situations — natural disasters, acute illness and survival.

Distress or condition black (right-hand side) occurs when we ignore strain signals and keep trying to meet a challenge. Performance falls fast. Biological activation has peaked and has started to decline into biological distress; our body, emotions and mind begin to fail. The signals are strong. We experience aches and pains, illness, emotional outbursts, relationship failures, headaches, sleep disturbance, confusion and anxiety. Condition black is unsustainable and dangerous. Experts might cope for short, focused bursts at critical moments, but this condition quickly leads to deterioration. Recovery disciplines are essential in order to recuperate and rebuild after periods in this state.

## Biological Measurement

Elite sport and the military have climbed all over the booming field of 'self-quantification'. While we have been able to track pulse and blood pressure for many years, the past decade has brought a flood of measures that we can track with relatively inexpensive and wearable devices. Increasingly, the public is reaching out to devices and manufacturers such as fitbit (www.fitbit.com), Jawbone (www.jawbone.com), iHealth (www.ihealthlabs.com), SleepTracker (www.sleeptracker.com), Garmin (www.garmin.com), Omron (www.omron-healthcare.com) and emWave (www.heartmath.com).

These devices provide real-time feedback on how our biology is responding to challenge. We are now able to map ourselves on the Response to Challenge curve. Apple Watch may be another step towards making this more commonplace.

Biological measurement has several key contributions to make to resilience:

- ▶ **Insight** — precise knowledge of how your biology is actually responding to a challenge,
- ▶ **Training precision** — the ability to know and target the training or rest required, and

▶ **Precise peaking** — designing training to meet the demands of specific events.

For those who have not embarked on the journey of self-quantification, here are some basic guidelines to what is available at a reasonable cost.

**Activity monitors (fitbit, Jawbone, iHealth, Garmin)** These devices are based on an accelerometer that tracks movement and indicates distance covered. Given that physical activity is the most powerful driver of resilience, it makes sense to try this out so that you at least understand what kind of activity levels you achieve through a standard week. Evolutionary evidence suggests that we should be moving briskly for 9 to 15 km per day. These monitors give you an indication of how much you have moved each day and may reward you for 10,000 steps.

You can use the activity monitor to track sleep, providing an indication of when you are in deep versus light sleep. So far the sleep feedback is a bit inconsistent in terms of reliability. My preference is to use SleepTracker, which provides a more precise and helpful reflection of sleep quality. Smartphone applications can do some of this, but we strongly recommend that you never take these devices into the bedroom — and most certainly don't leave them under your pillow.

**Blood pressure monitoring** is very helpful given how common and dangerous high or low pressure is. Simple wrist monitors (Omron, iHealth) can quickly provide you with feedback. So long as you use them precisely as directed, they are reasonably accurate. If you have high blood pressure or a family history, this is a key measure. It also gives you quick feedback when you are working too long in condition grey. More importantly, it will show you what reduces your blood pressure.

**Pulse monitors (Polar, Garmin, Nike)** are great monitors of your curve. You can very simply measure pulse with a finger to your wrist or neck, but the dynamic monitoring during physical training, recovery and messy human interactions can be instructive. If you wish to improve your fitness and train for racing this pulse feedback is important. Most of these devices will now map your speed to heart rate over the course of a training session or race.

**Heart rate variability (emWave/HeartMath)** is a superb measure of your position on the curve. We will come back to this one, but we have a clear 'buy' signal here. These monitors provide one of the best deep measures of your body's biology through the variation in heart rate. A regular, smooth alternating increase and decrease in heart rate variability (HRV) is a strong signal of your autonomic nervous system, or what we will discuss shortly as the vagal brake.

There are now a range of EEG-based **brainwave monitors** such as **Mindwave** (www.neurosky.com) or **Muse** (www.choosemuse.com) available at much reduced cost. These devices attach to your scalp and can provide an indication of dominant brainwave states. For those interested in training the mind or mindfulness, they provide wonderful graphical feedback on the performance states of the brain. My prediction is that this measurement will become mainstream in the next decade.

We will cover this curve in more detail over the next chapters. At this point, let's consider one example in the sporting world where performance is objectively measurable. The goal of sport is to win a game. In almost all sports we get several attempts (games, sets, rounds, or periods) to win. Peak performance appears the obvious goal, but in fact consistency usually wins out over a single great effort. Even the high jumper must pace him or herself so as to maintain performance through the elimination rounds and retain enough reserves for a final jump. The need to hold condition yellow is even more marked in sports such as soccer, tennis or endurance events. In tournaments the athlete must recover after demanding games to play again the next day.

Elite sport is unforgiving. Those who spend too much time in condition grey or (even worse) dip into black without adequate recovery are quickly eliminated through injury, emotional outbursts or mental fatigue. All of these lead to stiffness, poor timing, loss of focus and error. Not only does the athlete need to work skilfully with this curve during competition, but their training must follow the rules.

In preparation the athlete must train in yellow, grey and black as they have to build the skills and disciplines to cope with difficult competitive situations. On the one hand, athletes must create enough intensity (black) in training to stretch their resources, thus training muscle, heart, brain and

## Figure 7: The Impact of Resilience Training — Relaxed Yet Effective

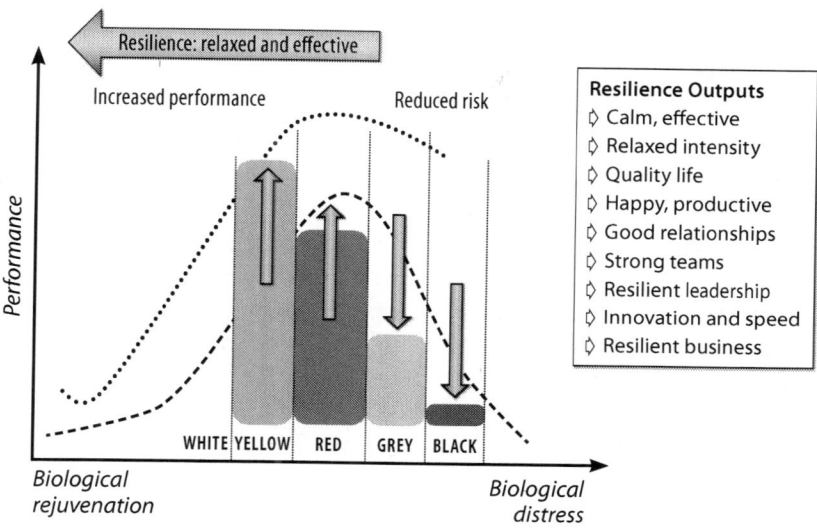

will. On the other hand, athletes who train too hard quickly get sick, injured or burn out. This is why athletes carefully plan their year and training schedules, so they can optimise the mix of training and periods of rest to get the best possible season. Skilful training, good coaching and smart science help the athlete shift the curve up and to the right. The performance boundaries in each condition are stretched — relaxed and skilful under greater pressure, but also capable of withstanding and bouncing back from extreme effort.

Elite performers master the response to the challenge curve. The athlete or warrior seeks to arrive at the top of the curve (physically, emotionally and mentally) for events. The training regime effectively and efficiently shifts this curve upwards and to the left. This allows us to achieve greater performance without excessive biological distress. Think of this as relaxed intensity.

This is rare in business or even our personal lives. Recently I coached a senior professional who was trying to press through a challenging job needing about 60 hours per week, parent two young children, sustain a marriage and follow a sport with passion — all while dealing with a major injury. This is a smart and skilful person. The first and last hours of the day are spent dealing with e-mail, sleep is a mess, wellbeing is compromised and guilt is pervasive. This is what living in condition black and grey looks like. Is this really achieving the right outcomes for family, employer and self?

What would this person's curve look like right now?

Remember that the curve can also shift downwards, reducing our tolerance to and performance under pressure. This happens when we neglect our resilience and the practices that support it. Note what happens after a couple of disturbed nights or when you stop exercising. Young people raised under parental and academic pressure, with laptops, texts, TV, fast food and late nights, have their resilience resources eroded.

Modern life has successfully removed natural pressures (hunger, hunting, cold, predators, and so on). The stimulation these challenges provided is gone. Consequently, our curves have downshifted. With a little insight we see how clearly we need to upshift our curves with sensible, safe and smart resilience training.

Here's a question for you. How do you run your life with regard to the curve?

Resilience training helps you master the curve. The practices of resilience in all areas of life — body, heart, mind and spirit — shift our curves, allowing performance to be maintained under increased demand. What was previously a condition black challenge can now be handled in yellow. In addition, this training gives us the motivation to engage without distress and the capacity to absorb adversity and bounce quickly.

Now, you are able to steer yourself out of the intersection and resolve the drama with calm effectiveness. And the phone call on Friday evening no longer triggers a panic response.

In short, resilience (a training effect) shifts one's curve up and to the left. You have deeper insight into your state. You can lift your performance in all conditions, and will build the confidence to tolerate extreme challenges with skill.

Keep in mind:

- ▶ living with no challenge leads to entropy (loss of energy), boredom and apathy,
- ▶ optimal challenge is not comfortable but does focus the mind and resources,

- ▶ in rising to challenge our physiology orchestrates positive adaptations,
- ▶ peak response cannot be sustained without rest and recovery,
- ▶ strain can be useful in short bursts to accelerate adaptation,
- ▶ periods of strain must be matched by periods of deep relaxation, sleep and recovery, and
- ▶ burnout, a state of biological exhaustion and failure, can sneak up on you.

### Summary

- ✸ Dismiss the word 'stress' from your thinking and vocabulary.
- ✸ Change and challenge ask us to respond skilfully.
- ✸ If we cannot respond skilfully we experience distress.
- ✸ Get to know your distress signals.
- ✸ Keep track of your response to challenge curve.

# Chapter 5

# The Death Spiral

## Know How Resilience Fails

The death spiral is a scary phrase, used to describe what happens when resilience fails. Once you understand the concept you will understand that it is a normal and common reality of human life. Many of us spend much of our time in various loops of this painful state of human suffering. Buddhist and yoga philosophy have always understood this well, and they have established sophisticated frameworks and practices to escape such suffering and achieve enlightenment.

The Cartesian split between body and mind dominates Western thinking. Emotion has only recently attracted attention and spiritual matters are relegated to another life. In our 'medicine', people are either 'normal' or afflicted by a sophisticated 'diagnosis'. Once labelled with the diagnosis their only hope is smart drugs, surgery or 'evidence-based' intervention. Isn't it safer to slip back to the 'stress' word?

Years of experience in hospitals, then in general practice, sports medicine and now resilience have shown me clearly that the medical model is not perfect. There are many gradations of 'normal' as resilience fails. We cannot collapse this to a physical disease model. Life is a complex web of connections between biological self, environment, social networks and higher aspirations of purpose, ethics and contribution.

The death spiral concept underpins our ability to bounce. It is also a powerful way to understand and explain some of the disconcerting experiences of a normal life. The death spiral is not a diagnosis. The experience of being in the death spiral is a fluid state. We may move from top to bottom in a single afternoon. Generally, though, we cluster around a centre of gravity. Psychologists used to call this the happiness set point, and argued that it is more or less fixed for one's life. We now know this to be incorrect. Certain practices can quite clearly move the set point up or down.

The Death Spiral Model organises the common experiences of life at a time when our biological coping strategies are not up to the tasks that face us. The stages of the spiral are drawn from the very real human experiences that clients have shared with me over the years. I am confident that there is enough coherence between the experiences we have at each level and our current scientific knowledge to proceed carefully.

## Stage 0: 'Normal'

The default state for a reasonable life is for nothing to be wrong. This is how many doctors will view a patient. If nothing wrong is found, we are pronounced normal. In resilience, the base camp is to be calm, alert,

Figure 8: The Death Spiral Model (individual symptoms are on the right)

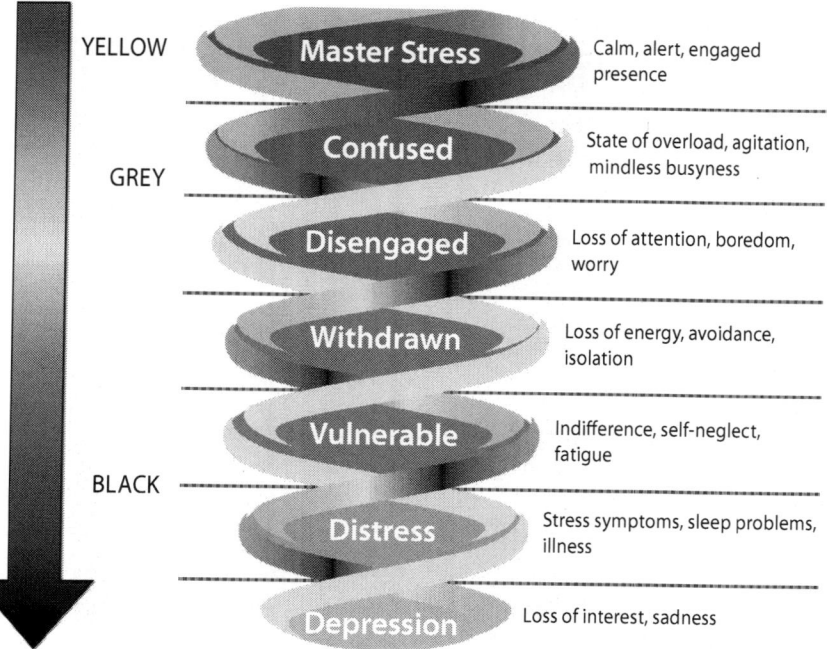

engaged and present in the experience of the moment (condition yellow on the Response to Challenge Curve).

Slipping down the death spiral destroys the experience of being calm, alert, engaged and present. It is here that suffering begins. It is also a very necessary life experience and one source of your resilience.

Without knowing the pain of the death spiral, it is hard to appreciate the optimal experience of life. It is insightful to go down the death spiral from time to time. If one is to live fully, love, have goals and seek growth, there will be challenges, setbacks and grief. A good life is one that embraces both the joy and pain with grace and intelligence. The resilient person will bounce out of the death spiral because they are fully aware of each stage and recognise what they must do to bounce, recover and re-establish joy.

Do not panic. Gently breathe out ... remember something positive ... focus on the task.

## Stage 1: Confused (cognitive risk)

When we slip into a confused state we lose the calm, alert and present state. It is a subtle shift in the way our mind (hence cognitive function) works and is rarely noticed by most of us. Therefore, it is very dangerous. Be vigilant for early evidence, which includes a sense of busyness, overload and arousal. From an objective view we look harassed and frantic. Resilience is failing.

Consider some of what we know about how we work:

- ▶ we switch tasks every three minutes,
- ▶ we turn to e-mail or texts 50 to 100 times per day,
- ▶ 85% of work e-mails are opened within two minutes, and
- ▶ it takes at least 24 minutes to get back on task after an electronic disturbance.

Gushing e-mail, online gossip and 24/7 availability of everything combine with high expectations to create an environment where a state of being confused is normal. Many of us are so accustomed to this information overload that we feel anxious and guilty when we manage to find small islands of calm relaxation.

Basic neurobiology helps put this in context. Behind the forehead is the prefrontal cortex (PFC), in which lies our short-term memory and executive attention network. This is where we pay attention and process moment-to-moment reality. Here we monitor inputs and activity from the rest of the brain for important signals. It directs our attention to critical issues. It also helps us to be aware of and master emotion.

This part of the brain is very expensive to run. It gobbles glucose and oxygen and works best on a single focus point at a time. In theory we can juggle four discrete ideas at any one time — perhaps a little ambitious for the male mind! Yet most of the time we are juggling hundreds of issues. Confusion is the result.

Some call this multitasking and even consider it a good practice — something to aspire to. This is misguided. Multitaskers are confused. Those who believe they are multitasking are much more likely to sleep poorly, fail in their exercise commitment and become impulsive. Confusion lowers productivity measurably.

With training, we can focus on a task to its completion and switch smartly to the next. In this way a trained brain can attend to many issues effectively. When we drift randomly from one task to the next we only partly resolve the task, wasting cognitive energy and becoming ineffective.

Boredom and lack of purpose will also lead to confusion. The mind wanders aimlessly, repeatedly checking e-mail or texts, discovering things to worry about, and procrastinating.

Activity overload or lack of purpose both weaken attention and invite confusion.

## Stage 2: Disengaged (cognitive failure)

The step from confused to disengaged is also subtle and seldom noticed. The executive attention network (PFC) is overloaded and simply fails to do its job. The body tries to save energy by shutting it down. Unfortunately there is no warning. Focused attention and short-term memory fails. We turn the page to realise that what we have just read has vanished. We 'zone out' or daydream (ruminate). We find ourselves missing chunks of time (the drive home or a child's story). Task performance declines and mistakes follow.

We can also disengage when the reptilian centres of the brain override the PFC. This happens during anxiety, worry, frustration, anger and sadness. It is more likely if we have not slept well, forgotten exercise or missed a meal. The lower and less fuel-demanding parts of the brain have taken control. Repetitive thinking and fidgeting replaces alert, goal-oriented action.

This is serious. Instead of attending to the task at hand, your attention has abandoned its job. You are distracted by thoughts and unhelpful emotions. You wander aimlessly into an imagined future or a preferred past. You are, quite simply, not present in your life. Life unfolds around you, yet you are not involved.

Some studies suggest that we spend 30–50% of our time in this disengaged state.[20] This is sometimes described as 'presenteeism' — present in body but not in mind — and it is thought to be at least six times more costly to business than absenteeism.

Neurobiologists describe this as attentional blink. Concentration is a scarce resource. Even when working hard at focus, our attention fails after two to five minutes. In other words, you begin to miss words in a conversation, paragraphs in a book or tasks to which you commit. The blink in attention is rarely noticed by you, and your mind attempts to fabricate a story to close the gap. It is prudent to maintain healthy scepticism of your powers of attention.

One study looked at how judges in Israel treated parole hearings. The key finding was that parole grants are strongly linked to time of day (see graph on next page). Prisoners presenting at the start of the day had a 70% chance of being released, but those presenting before lunch or in the afternoon had less than a 15% chance of being released. This is a massive miscarriage of justice, yet the judges were sure that they treated all cases the same.

This is clearly a serious misconduct of justice. If a parole hearing is held in the afternoon, the prisoner is likely to be sent back to jail. The judge fails to find the resources to think about the case. The default is not even to consider the merits of being released. Even in these finely trained brains, where every effort to be fair is made, justice fails. Is that meeting at 4 p.m. really going to deliver valuable outcomes? Should we really try to study or work late at night?

Nobel prize-winner, Daniel Kahneman has published on this phenomenon.[21] He describes Type One thinking as fast and easy. Type Two thinking requires careful consideration, calculation and reflection. The latter is biologically expensive and is shut down when we are tired or have low blood glucose. Remember, the judges were convinced every case was fully considered.

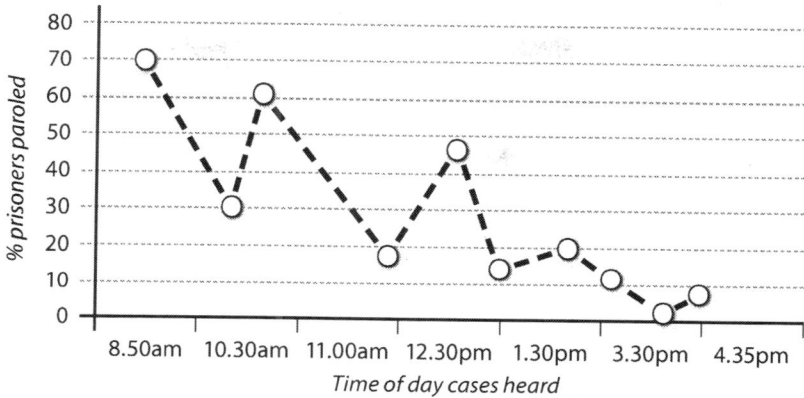

Figure 9: How the Likelihood of Parole Being Granted Varies Over the Course of the Day (For full report: Shai Danziger, Jonathan Levavb and Liora Avnaim-Pessoa, 2011)

If persistent, we describe the confused/disengaged cycle as Attention Deficit Hyperactivity Disorder (ADHD) or Attention Deficit Trait (ADT). It is increasingly prevalent in young people and adults. Elements of ADT are simply an early failure of resilience. Even in the milder, occasional form described above, being disengaged is a serious deficit in our efforts to be effective in our work, sport, families and communities.

## Stage 3: Withdrawn (emotional risk)

Disengaged behaviours (especially ADHD) result in performance failure, frustration or disapproval. If they are repeated, others become intolerant. Frequently it is our empathy (capacity to read emotions in others) that tunes out. We are distant and disconnected. If mistakes are made we lose self-confidence and stop trying.

We avoid the important but difficult calls, meetings and actions. Once we withdraw from the critical tasks, partly due to self-doubt and partly due to lack of purposeful structure, we lose energy and motivation. This is an emotional risk. We no longer have the strong drive to pursue a necessary task. We may well know what we have to do, but fail to find the energy to do it. Procrastination prevails.

In withdrawal, we avoid contact and engagement with others. We do not have the confidence to engage in complex human dynamics. We stop telling the truth. We tell people we are 'fine'. Relationship challenges are neglected. Skilful parenting, coaching and managing are avoided. Relationships, responsibilities and work suffer. Leadership fails. This is not as subtle as confused and disengaged — others now notice and you are unlikely to get desired results.

## Stage 4: Vulnerable (emotional failure)

At this stage we are numb and cynical. There may be deep fatigue. Self-neglect becomes the order of the day. Emotions that motivate us have failed. Exercise, relaxation and sleep are neglected. We might be susceptible to the 'drunk, alone, in front of TV on Monday night' syndrome. We have probably surrendered the activities that give us joy and keep us well. Laughter may be a distant memory.

"I am too busy" justifies the mind. Our cognitive and emotional resources have failed and we simply don't care. We are at risk of injury, relationship conflicts, illness and addictive behaviour such as overeating, smoking, drinking, gambling or drug taking. Sleep is disturbed.

One version of vulnerability is common in parents, caregivers and managers when diverting excess resources to taking care of others. Empathy slips into sympathy. While frantically rushing about to help others, they fail to recognise their own needs. Ultimately the others suffer.

Physiologically, we are in trouble. The immune system is compromised, muscle wasting and weight gain begins, and hormonal problems emerge. Testosterone and DHEA (dehydroepiandosterone), the hormones of vitality and confidence, fail. Cortisol, which can protect us in the short term, starts to compromise sugar metabolism, immunity and memory. Deep fatigue is the dominant experience. Life is fragile and we are vulnerable to illness, major work errors, relationship break-ups and accidents.

## Stage 5: Distress (physical risk)

In distress, symptoms break out where we are vulnerable — perhaps sleep disturbance, irritability, or gut, skin, muscle, lung and heart symptoms. Physical integrity breaks down. Physical signals combine over and above the emotional and cognitive deficits. We become aware that our resources are no longer adequate for the tasks we are facing. Distress can spiral out of control. This is very common and appears to affect about 40% of the population. The body is calling for help!

Self-doubt (loss of confidence) and anxiety are key themes. Self-doubt is subjective and may not reflect the actual situation. Some people can be clinically ill and measurably dysfunctional in their life and work, but will insist that they 'have it under control'. These folk repress their distress and it may manifest as inflammation, high blood pressure and immune disorders. Others fly into a panic at the first challenge. Their anxiety can manifest as hyperventilation, catastrophising (imagining the worst) and sleep deprivation.

Be careful of medication. The excessive use of anti-inflammatory, pain relief, sleep, digestive, and anti-anxiety medications might hide the symptoms but will not fix the source. We may feel better but the cause has not been addressed. What happens if the medication runs out?

See if you can befriend your symptoms of distress. Your body is asking you to pay attention and take care of yourself. Listen and respond with skill.

## Stage 6: Depression (failure of self)

Depression here is a state that may be transient. This is normal from time to time. However, if five or more of the symptoms below persist for more than two weeks, please seek qualified guidance:

- ▶ loss of joy (anhedonia), tears
- ▶ decreased energy
- ▶ persistent sadness and low mood
- ▶ social withdrawal
- ▶ sleep disorder (usually early waking)
- ▶ change of appetite and or weight
- ▶ loss of concentration
- ▶ persistent self-doubt and low self-esteem
- ▶ thoughts of self-harm.

Help is needed! Do not delay!

The lowest rung of the death spiral is a living hell and an invitation to personal disasters. The situation is easy to remedy in the early stages but it can be hard to action the appropriate remedies. The mind cannot figure out the answer and we lack the emotional and physical energy to take the action.

The medical diagnosis of depression is increasing in our society. It may affect up to 18% of the general population. At this stage the brain is dysfunctional in at least five critical areas involving attention, cognition, emotion and arousal. One's sense of self is dissolving. Life feels futile and suicide is a real risk. Depression is an emotional collapse.

Recently we have defaulted to anti-depressants en masse. There are many physical, emotional and cognitive skills that can help bring one out of depression — with or without medication. Make sure that you include these skills in any treatment plan.

I am exploring the possibility that the last stage of the death spiral could manifest as disease (physical collapse) and Post-Traumatic Stress Disorder (PTSD) and dissociation (a cognitive collapse).

Take some time to reflect on the death spiral with someone who you can trust.

For those who lead and manage others it is a powerful framework to understand where your people might be in trouble and why you are losing productivity.

The death spiral is a predictable and normal consequence of fast-paced lives. We are enticed by centrifugal forces (outward) including information overload, consumerism and appearance. Little exists to activate the centripetal forces (inward) of self-knowledge, reflection and personal vision. The death spiral is a consequence of this neglect. Resilience fails. Life is fragile. Bounce is the answer.

## A Note on Distress

It is important to differentiate between acute and chronic distress. Again, remember that this is not the challenge but rather our response to it.

Acute distress is the response to immediate and dangerous challenges such as an attack. The brain and body are flooded with adrenaline and rapid reactions of primitive emotional systems — the freeze (collapse), flight (fear) and fight (anger) responses. These are primarily sympathetic system reactions — fast and rarely controllable. Acute distress can sometimes be adaptive in a chaotic situation, but seldom is helpful in modern life.

Acute distress creates a wave of rapid reactions within the organism:
- the heart beats faster and harder: pulse and blood pressure increase
- blood floods the brain and muscles: mind and body prepare for battle
- blood leaves the digestive system: energy is diverted to organs of action
- the skin is drained of blood: bleeding is minimised
- hair follicles contract: hairy beasts appear larger
- the diaphragm contracts and chest expands, bracing body for action.

Acute distress will normally be followed by rapid recovery (parasympathetic activity). Provided we have time to recover, these short bursts of adrenaline can have positive adaptive consequences including increased speed, skill and complex coping tactics. However, if these waves of reactions are sustained without adequate recovery, they accumulate to create long-term destructive adaptations. This is chronic distress.

Chronic distress is a major cause of reduced productivity, chronic disease and death. It is chronic distress with which we are more concerned. Chronic distress is the response to unresolved, persistent challenges that are common in our lives. Rather than bursts of acute response and recovery, we face repeated, small sympathetic activations that accumulate over time, with profound effects on our long-term function. The relaxation or parasympathetic healing effect is overwhelmed by sympathetic overdrive. Some of the effects are listed below.

## Cardiovascular
- increased blood pressure and pulse rate (stroke, heart attack, heart failure)
- increased risk of irregular heart beat (arrhythmia)
- increase in arterial damage (specifically coronary arteries).

## Respiratory
- increased respiration, sighing and breath holding
- increased severity of asthma
- reduced immunity to common colds and flu.

### Abdominal/digestive
- ▶ increased risk of indigestion, heartburn and ulcers
- ▶ irritable bowel syndrome, diarrhoea and constipation
- ▶ poor metabolism, bone loss, disturbed hormone levels.

### Neurological
- ▶ slower reactions and reduced co-ordination
- ▶ reduced blood flow to executive attention network in front of brain
- ▶ disturbed sleep, concentration, memory and mood.

### Emotional
- ▶ chronic anxiety, burnout and depression
- ▶ poor coping skills and personality problems
- ▶ relationship difficulties including violence, impotence and divorce.

### Immune system
- ▶ decreased activity of protective cells (fight infections, toxins and cancer)
- ▶ increased activity of auto-immune cells (cause inflammation, arthritis, allergy)
- ▶ decreased rate and effectiveness of cellular repair.

### Skin
- ▶ increased eczema, psoriasis, rashes and itchiness
- ▶ increased risk of skin infections.

### Cognitive
- ▶ loss of optimism, confusion and decision failure
- ▶ loss of memory and creativity
- ▶ irritability and emotional reactivity.

There is no absolute measure of distress. The feeling is a complex state of physical, emotional and mental disintegration. We use the term homeostasis to describe the range of states in which life is balanced and responsive to change. In distress, homeostasis is disturbed. We are out of balance and not responding within the normal range. Complex central monitoring in the brain signals this loss of homeostasis with distress. Each person has distinct patterns of discomfort when distressed.

## Distress Questionnaire

Pages 58 and 59 contain a list of questions that can help you clarify whether distress might be an issue. To score yourself, consider the last three months and answer each of the questions honestly in terms of how frequently you notice them, using the following scoring guide:

| 0 | rarely or never | (less than once per week) |
|---|---|---|
| 1 | sometimes | (a couple of times per week) |
| 2 | regularly | (several days per week) |
| 3 | very often | (most days of the week) |
| 4 | all the time | (all days of the week) |

If your scores are in the 'rarely or never' or 'sometimes' boxes, you do not have a major issue with distress. A good life is in the 'rarely or never' category (total score 0). Sometimes we experience mild, occasional symptoms (score less than 10). This is normal and can be used constructively to remind you to pay attention to relaxation, integrating your life or relaxation skills.

When your scores are dropping into the 'regularly' box (scores of 10 to 19), pay attention. You are experiencing some strain — particularly if the symptoms extend for more than a week. Your ability to function in your life roles is compromised. You need to find resolution. A deliberate effort at relaxation practice, regular exercise and deep sleep will usually settle the symptoms. If they persist for more than two weeks you must discuss them with a health professional.

When your symptom scores are falling into 'very often' or 'continuously' (score over 20), it is worth getting some skilled help. You are at risk.

Depression and mood disorders are the most common manifestations of chronic, poorly managed distress and they must be taken seriously. Persistence of significantly lowered mood and loss of joy in everyday activity for more than two weeks indicates clinical depression. Please take a careful look at questions 1 to 9 again. These symptoms can indicate depression. Less than 50% of people with depression are diagnosed, and only 50% of those diagnosed are treated properly.

Figure 10: Distress Questionnaire

| I experience this problem | Rarely or never | Sometimes | Often | Very often | All the time |
|---|---|---|---|---|---|
| 1  Waking up early and unable to get back to sleep | | | | | |
| 2  Waking up tired and/or fatigue through the day | | | | | |
| 3  Decreased energy or feeling 'washed out' | | | | | |
| 4  Unable to organise thoughts or difficulty concentrating | | | | | |
| 5  Significant increase or decrease in appetite | | | | | |
| 6  Decreased interest in daily activities or hobbies/sports | | | | | |
| 7  Little pleasure or enjoyment from daily activities | | | | | |
| 8  Depression, persistent low mood or feeling sad | | | | | |
| 9  Tearfulness or suicidal thoughts | | | | | |
| 10  Feelings of nervousness, anxiety or worry | | | | | |
| 11  Trouble getting to sleep or restless sleep | | | | | |
| 12  Irritability, grumpiness or angry outbursts | | | | | |
| 13  Lump in throat or difficulty swallowing | | | | | |
| 14  Indigestion, reflux or stomach ulcers | | | | | |

| I experience this problem | Rarely or never | Sometimes | Often | Very often | All the time |
|---|---|---|---|---|---|
| 15 Irritable bowels, diarrhoea, constipation or pain | | | | | |
| 16 Headaches or migraines | | | | | |
| 17 Muscle tension, sore neck or shoulders | | | | | |
| 18 Wheezing or tightness in chest | | | | | |
| 19 Pains around left chest or irregular heart beat | | | | | |
| 20 Itching or persistent skin rashes | | | | | |
| 21 Working six or seven days a week | | | | | |
| 22 Too busy for family activities | | | | | |
| 23 Days are filled with deadlines | | | | | |
| 24 Unclear about your goals in life | | | | | |
| 25 Worried about 'work/life balance' | | | | | |
| *Total score by adding columns and multiplying* | x 0 | x 1 | x 2 | x 3 | x 4 |
| **Sum total** | | | | | |

**1–9:** Points towards depressive symptoms

**10–20:** Points towards physiological symptoms of anxiety

**20+:** High, and should be reviewed by your health provider

Chronic anxiety is captured in questions 10 to 20. These are more physical symptoms of distress. They have been called psychosomatic symptoms — symptoms in the body caused by emotional or cognitive distress. All too frequently we accept these symptoms as normal. This is a failure of resilience.

Vulnerability is indicated by questions 21 to 25. This is where our life loses balance and integrity. Our research indicates that 'Days are filled with deadlines' (no. 23) is not that critical, but high scores in the other four correlate strongly with depression and anxiety.

..............................................................................

### Summary

- ✸ Know your death spiral signals.
- ✸ Stay calm and remember, it's normal.
- ✸ Monitor your distress.

..............................................................................

## Chapter 6

# Get Brilliant at Bounce

Bounce restores our inner strength. In the death spiral, centrifugal (outward) forces have depleted you. Bounce is centripetal (inward), and we fill the reservoir. Resilience is rebuilt. Practice in bounce will build resilience capacity in all areas of your life. Little can build self-knowledge and confidence quite like a successful bounce from a major adversity.

Tolerating the lower rungs of the spiral is life denying. Many clients tell me they have felt tired for years, battle to get up, drag themselves through the day, crash in front of the TV at night and suffer restless sleep. Others trudge through work and life, without joy, for years. This should not be tolerated.

Understanding the process of how resilience fails is a great start. The complete picture of bounce provides context, logic and direction to recovery. Insight inspires hope and the upward steps become clear and achievable. There are many ways to work through bounce and the learning is immensely valuable.

We will examine bounce in a systematic way. We will start from the bottom and work upwards. No doubt your own life experience will help you recognise and tailor the steps to your own needs.

## Tackle Depression

First, let's focus on true depression, where you have been consistently down for more than two weeks. Recovery begins with acceptance. Denial and 'hard-man stonewalling' is an obstacle to recovery. In recent years, much has been done to make it acceptable to get help. Getting help is exactly what you should do. Start with your family doctor and make sure you have enough time to understand the options. Don't be afraid to seek alternative opinions, as ultimately you must be comfortable and engaged in your treatment plan.

Most approaches will offer a mix of:

- lifestyle improvement (sleep, exercise, diet, meditation, socialising)
- support groups and counselling
- anti-depressant medication
- cognitive behaviour therapy (CBT)
- positivity training.

Recovery usually begins within ten days to three weeks, and after six months of normal function you have recovered. Each case is different and you will need skilled medical guidance in most instances.

There is strong support for well-structured lifestyle discipline right from the beginning of recovery. While it can be hard to motivate oneself in depression, find a way to get regular exercise, eat well, practise relaxation and find joy, gratitude and appreciation in your daily activities. A coach or personal trainer is often the best solution to help you restructure your daily routines.

Secondly, short and temporary states of depression are common and natural following a major adversity. Recovery is usually assured and occurs over hours or days. Acknowledgement, acceptance, positive action and connection with others will help you move up fast. There is no need for medication or formal treatment.

## Dissolve Distress

First, understand how your body signals distress (see the Distress Questionnaire in the last chapter). These symptoms alert us to extreme overload and the beginning of body/heart/mind failure or disintegration. The goal is to have no symptoms, but many of us are so used to persistent symptoms that we consider them 'normal' and pay little attention. As we become aware, we begin to realise the suffering attached to the symptoms. Over time distress will become a gentle reminder to remedial action.

Distress must be treated with:

- deliberate, slow diaphragmatic breathing practice and facilitated relaxation (massage, yoga, tai chi)
- daily mindfulness and exercise
- stopping alcohol and drugs
- learning to be fully present in the moment.

At first you will need to be tenacious. Once again, skilled help is invaluable as you start to reactivate your parasympathetic activity and lower your sympathetic reactions. The first stage does not feel natural. It is weird, brings up guilt and frustration, and can be frustrating and boring. Persist because the second phase delivers surprising benefits. With a bit of help the parasympathetic system will kick in strongly and you feel much better. Again, persist so that your practices become a little more skilful and routine. You have built up your parasympathetic power (vagal brake). In stage three, distress resolves on a more permanent basis. Body, heart and mind start to reintegrate.

## Tactics to Get Beyond Distress

- **Reflective pause**  Take a moment to acknowledge, 'Hey, I need a breather.' Look inwards and notice the state of your body, emotions and mind. Simply noticing triggers recovery.
- **Stretch**  Get out of your chair and stretch. Do forward bends (hamstrings), back bends (extensions) and twists. Breathe consciously. Feel the stretch.
- **Switch tasks**  Stop your current activity and do something that you are comfortable with. Get out of the office or home. Take a drive or a walk, or do some other form of exercise. Go to a movie.
- **Exhale fully and pause**  A long exhalation reconnects you to diaphragmatic breathing, slows the heart rate and gives the mind a break. A couple of long out-breaths between tasks will refresh you.
- **Talk to someone**  Simply connecting to the emotional level will recharge you. Be respectful of who you disturb. Periodic tea or coffee breaks perform this function.
- **Music**  Music has an effect on emotions, distress chemicals and the

immune system. Classical music has been advocated but use what works for you. It can also be a distraction.

- ▶ **Exercise**   Exercise is always safe and effective if done within your capacity. Stretch, dash up stairs, do some resistance exercise, stand up and balance, and so on.
- ▶ **Powernap**   You will be surprised at the fast recovery following even a ten-minute nap.

## Beat Vulnerable

Self-neglect defines vulnerable. We no longer care to maintain ourselves. The core challenge is to look after ourselves. If you cannot get started, find a coach to help you get going.

This may begin with a good holiday, but must progress to re-establishing sensible daily practices of sleep, exercise, good nutrition and rest. Treat yourself to a massage, time with trusted friends, sunshine and nature. Action along these paths has a quick payback and sets the scene for resilience-building on the positive side of the spiral.

Taking a full weekend off with no phones or devices is my preferred practice. Experience has also reinforced the value of remembering activities that bring you joy and finding an appropriate way to reconnect with these activities. In a vulnerable state, joy and perhaps love have long been absent. Find a way to reignite the sources of joy, love, gratitude and awe. Nature can be a good friend.

If you cannot muster the energy or find the confidence to do this, hire a coach or join a gym or exercise group. Spend time with people who are working at this task. While the bounce effect below this takes time, remedial action at this level leads to a fast and rewarding response. Take the opportunity to formalise your communities and your time with key relationships.

## Reverse Withdrawal

In withdrawal we have lost the desire to reach out to others. Loss of confidence, pain or loss of self-respect can contribute to this state. It is easy to reverse by connecting to others. Most people naturally have a desire to be helpful and supportive. A well-developed network of friends and good communication within a family will generally arrest the spiral at this level.

The challenge is to re-establish your human connections at home, work and in recreation. Spending time with people stimulates healing and re-engagement. The impulse in withdrawal is to back away from others. The pivot is to reverse avoidance into approach. Choose your support network with some care. Don't underestimate the value of pets — particularly dogs. For most of our evolution, dogs have been our close friends.

To take the role of the person available for connection is a natural role for parents, leaders, managers and priests. Every good leader must be aware of this role. When one of your team becomes quiet and withdrawn, make time to check in and connect. Leaders who do this are described as 'affiliative' or 'coaching' style leaders. They have powerfully positive impacts on engagement, organisations and organisational performance.

## Prepare for Disengaged

In our overloaded world becoming disengaged is a reality of daily life. Assailed by information, tasks and stimulation, the executive centre of the prefrontal brain (PFC) is almost continuously stretched and has no choice but to blink out from time to time. The key is to recognise the overload and plan for breaks — both short micro-breaks and longer recovery breaks — during the day and the week.

Much is done naturally by the brain, such as automatically recovering between lines of reading or at the end of sentences. Make this recovery phase conscious and regular. This allows the brain to recover and recharge. Imagine that the neurons of concentration have fired themselves to death. There is no more neurotransmitter and the energy resources are depleted. Given regular breaks, the brain will recover naturally and effectively. Disengaged states are prevented.

Learn to take smart relaxation breaks during tasks, which can include:
- diaphragmatic breathing
- long, quiet nasal exhalations followed by a pause
- stretch or exercise breaks (consider a standing desk)
- getting out in the sunlight periodically

- taking periodic half-days off
- keeping protein (nuts, chicken), fatty snacks (nuts, avocado) and coffee/tea handy
- establishing a daily practice of relaxation or mindfulness.

## Resist Confusion

A calmly focused mind — often called mindful — is a central challenge for everyone. Focus that is driven by fear, anger and adrenaline shuts down the executive centre and sends us into reptilian reactivity. First we need a measure of calm and then we must learn to focus attention effectively. We will deal with this in more depth in part four in the chapter on Mind. For now, the following tips can help:

- focus on one task at a time
- delete what is not important
- delegate everything you possibly can

Figure 11: Bounce Back Practices

| Bounce Actions | State | Warning Signs |
| --- | --- | --- |
| Delete, delegate, short lists, select one goal | Confused | State of overload, agitation, mindless busyness |
| Recognise it, stretch, coffee, break, eat protein, get sun | Disengaged | Loss of attention, boredom, worry |
| Talk to someone, connect, shop, play sport, 'me' time | Withdrawn | Loss of energy, avoidance, isolation |
| Sleep, long weekend, wellness initiatives, massage | Vulnerable | Indifference, self-neglect, fatigue |
| Get help, counselling, exercise, meditation | Distress | Stress symptoms, sleep problems, illness |
| Get help, exercise, sleep, lifestyle, medication | Depression | Loss of interest, sadness |

- take frequent micro-breaks during intense work
- sharpen your priority list to no more than five issues — many say two per day!

Once you understand the spiral, its stages and the steps to prevent a slide, you can live your life with much more confidence. Further, you can manage periods of extreme challenge with intelligence. You will understand the risks and the signals prior to error. In the short run you can manage the strain. Remember to plan a proper restorative break once you have completed the challenge.

## Special Situations

### Bipolar disorder (manic depressive illness)

Bipolar disorder is a common biological hazard affecting 1 in 100 people — frequently leaders, entrepreneurs, artists, comedians and scientists. Sometimes these people go down the spiral in very destructive ways. At other times they soar to the heights of human exuberance, where they can be enormously productive, creative and entertaining. Living with or caring for someone with this disorder is very testing. When high, they take poorly considered risks — spending, gambling, driving fast or chasing sex. They put their lives, their families and their businesses at risk. When down, they become deeply depressed, morose and non-functional. Mood regulation is unstable.

Their contribution to business, art, science and other areas is in the upward spiral. The observed behaviour — early waking, huge energy, flights of ideas, pressure of speech (very fast talking), confidence and risk-taking activity — is similar to the activation of physical, emotional and cognitive circuits that we encourage in the top side of resilience. Unfortunately it is driven by complex overstimulation of certain neurotransmitters (serotonin and dopamine) and brain circuits. Symptoms include:

- inflated self-esteem or grandiosity
- decreased need for sleep (for example, feels rested after only three hours of sleep)
- more talkative than usual, or pressure to keep talking
- flight of ideas or a subjective experience that thoughts are racing

- ▶ distractibility (for example, attention is too easily drawn to unimportant or irrelevant external stimuli)
- ▶ increase in goal-directed activity (either socially, at work or school, or sexually) or psychomotor agitation
- ▶ excessive involvement in pleasurable activities that have a high potential for painful consequences (for example, unrestrained buying sprees, sexual indiscretions, or foolish business investments).

Milder forms — exuberance or hypomania — are more common.[22] This may be the case in many high performers. While a true manic depressive may end up in hospital, jail or under care, people with milder forms often thrive in business, sport and military. They love the thrill of competition and risk. The activation phase can be very energetic, effective and compelling. It is fun to work with them. They are major contributors to human progress in multiple fields.

There is encouraging evidence that the lifestyle practices of resilience can stabilise the emotional instability of a manic depressive person. Omega 3 oils, good sleep discipline, mindfulness and exercise combined with self-awareness and empathy can be helpful to shift their lives from chaotic and traumatic to powerful and creative.

## Condition Black Training

While our immediate response to the death spiral may be to run as far as possible, there is a case for using the concept skilfully to build resilience. We have long known, initially from swimming, that short periods of extreme training can lead to 'super compensation' or a powerful bounce response. The idea is now well used in sport. We see it in the enthusiasm for High Intensity Training (HIT).

Special forces specifically train to function under extreme duress. Using simunition (painful paintballs) they learn to 'suck up bullets' and continue fighting.[23] Rowers call this 'red lining' — learning to press past the point that one loses sight and even awareness. Military researchers have looked deeply into the idea to understand how to help combat soldiers deal with extremely traumatic encounters and also how to help them recover without developing Post-Traumatic Stress Disorder (PTSD).[24]

Figure 12: Combat Conditioning — Training for Condition Black

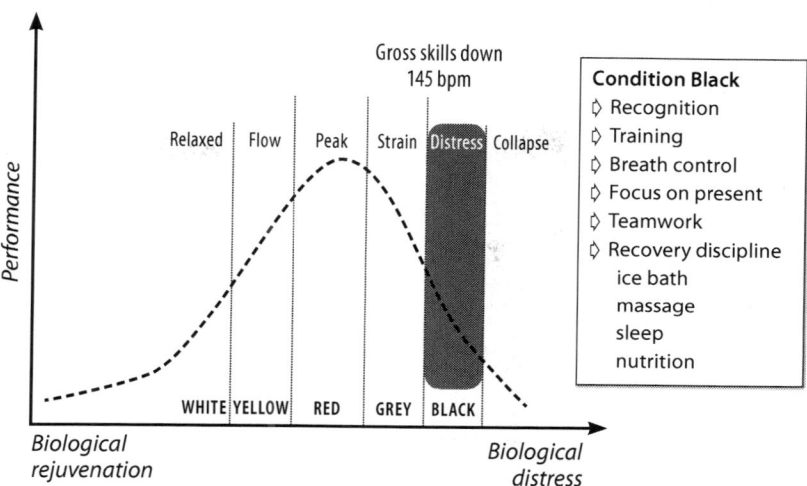

Richie McCaw's book, *Open Side*, tells the story of how the All Blacks applied this concept to beat the French in 2011, after their humiliating defeat in 2007.[25] The team rehearsed over and over how to execute effective play under extreme pressure. Not only did the All Blacks win the 2011 World Cup in Condition Black, they went practically unbeaten in the following seasons (once by England and once by South Africa).

We can think of this as combat conditioning or training in Condition Black.

Recovery discipline is absolutely essential.

The body/heart/mind cannot withstand repeated episodes of condition black. It causes micro tears in muscle and tissues, exhaustion of emotional resources and cognitive failures. We have to know how to facilitate adequate (although I want to say, full) recovery. In simple terms, this means being disciplined in taking rest days and slow days after intensity, knowing what we need to rejuvenate (massage, extra sleep, pizza …). Sport and military experience make clear that we almost always underestimate the recovery needed.

As we become more scientific and confident in our understanding of human limits, we will see more of this training application. I am a convert. This may be something to consider in your own life. How would you cope with an imminent car crash? What about an earthquake? How would you deal with the death of a loved one? Perhaps your children could be taught to deal with a disastrous exam? Or bullying?

Given the reality of the world we live in, and our high expectations, we could all give this careful thought. We have spent a lot of effort making things safe. But what about those times when we can't control things? Can we help ourselves and our children be 'more safe' by applying condition black training with care and wisdom? It works for soldiers, athletes and emergency workers. Why not start early?

At the very least an understanding of what happens when we confront adversity can help us recognise when we become less effective and less resilient in life. This recognition leads to faster activation of bounce and quick recovery. By training in condition black we rehearse for situations that might go awry. If things do go wrong we are prepared and ready to adapt and cope in adversity.

This is a big opportunity for all of us to build resilience and enjoy the benefits.

To conclude, the death spiral and bounce may at first be something you want to avoid. There is an upside. Periodically testing ourselves with adversity can help us learn how to function in very difficult times. Experts in sport, combat or theatre train systematically in this way. To achieve greatness we have to know how to function effectively when things fall apart.

## Summary

- ✴ Get help.
- ✴ Take a break.
- ✴ Reconnect.
- ✴ Relax and focus.
- ✴ Be fearless in adversity.

# Chapter 7

# Coherence

## An Emergent Idea?

Coherence is becoming central to resilience, both as a recovery tool and as a method of activating growth and performance. Coherence is the foundation of bounce. Along with physical exercise and sleep, it rates as one of the three leading factors that underpin resilience. On our Diagnostic and Development Spiral, it fits within Master Stress — the base camp of resilience. Ideally, it is a stage (more permanent) where we have mastered stress and secured a calm, stable base in life.

Figure 13: Locating Coherence in the Language of Resilience

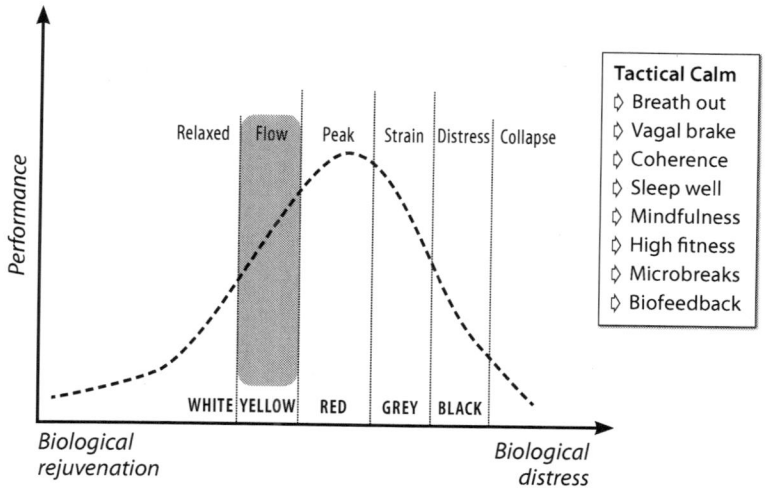

Coherence is the biological state of optimal homeostasis (balance). It is what happens when we relax effectively, rejuvenate and regain the resources to be effective. On the Response to Challenge Curve it means moving left, allowing for biological rejuvenation.

In figure 14, we see coherence as a state (temporary) where we are able to push ourselves into more relaxed states while preparing for or engaging in challenging situations.

Going deeper, coherence is a physiological measure of beat-to-beat heart-rate changes. It is called Heart Rate Variability (HRV), Respiratory Sinus Arrhythmia (RSA) or vagal tone. A healthy heart does not beat at one steady rate such as 70 beats per minute. Heart rate is always changing. This has long been noticed in medicine as sinus arrhythmia. It is linked to the autonomic system nerves that reach the heart and breathing.

The autonomic nervous system is automatic and largely unconscious. This part of your nervous system includes the lower parts of the brain and a set of nerve fibres running along the spine (sympathetic) and the vagus nerve (parasympathetic). The latter is associated with the organs and digestion. The two are either in a chaotic or coherent relationship.

Sympathetic activity triggers excitement, fear, anger and the chemicals of adrenaline and noradrenaline. It provides bursts of activation that accelerate the heart, increase blood pressure and shift blood from organs and skin to muscles. This is the flight (fear) and fight (anger) reaction of acute distress. This tends to create chaos in HRV (see figure 15, page 75).

Parasympathetic activity is linked to relaxation, recovery and pleasure. It slows the heart, lowers blood pressure and returns blood to organs, and promotes healing. The parasympathetic system works through the vagus nerve — the tenth cranial nerve. When active we see coherence in HRV (see figure 14).

The recording in this figure comes from a training session on emWave (www.heartmath.com). On the left we see chaotic variation of heart rate between 50 and 110 beats per minute. The person was anxious. Studies show this to be predictive of health risk, social disconnection and cognitive failure. This chaotic pattern results when vagal tone or the vagal brake is overwhelmed by our sympathetic system.

The recording to the right of three minutes shows a coherent HRV between 50 and 80. The sine curve (smooth alternation of acceleration and deceleration of pulse) is clear. The person training has become more relaxed

Figure 14: Heart Rate Variability — Patterns of Chaos (0–3 min) and Coherence (3–5 min) (The pattern is recorded during one of our coaching sessions on emWave)

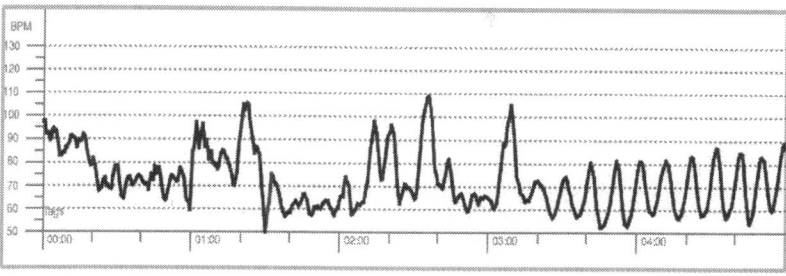

and her breathing is more even. The 'vagal brake' is on and is balancing the sympathetic activity. Coherence is a dynamic balance (homeostasis) of the autonomic nervous system. It is strongly linked to health, emotional resonance, better brain function, and bounce.

New research into our autonomic nervous system has given rise to the Polyvagal Theory.[26] This has advanced our understanding of how the two parts of the vagus nerve work. Stephen Porges has shown how evolution of the new or myelinated vagus allows us to access higher levels of function under challenge. He describes its role in both HRV and the 'vagal brake'.

The older part of the vagus slows the body and stimulates digestion and organ function — this part of the vagus nerve acts below the diaphragm. It facilitates rejuvenation and repair. When strongly activated we get the primitive immobilisation (freeze) response. The gut voids, blood pressure collapses and we can feign death. However, we become ineffective in a challenged situation. The newer part of the vagus nerve is myelinated (fast) and acts above the diaphragm — mainly on the heart and lungs. It supports efficient regulation of heart and lungs. It is referred to as 'vagal tone' and it counters and balances the sympathetic activation. A simplified description appears in the table on the next page.

If we can learn to activate the vagal brake, we become more calm, more focused and more connected. We are calm, in that distress is reduced and physiology rejuvenates; focused, in that blood returns to the prefrontal cortex (PFC) enabling complex thinking; and connected, in that our social engagement system (empathy portal) is on and we can focus on others. Coherence is good for us and it is good for others.

| Response | Experience | Mechanism | Evolution |
|---|---|---|---|
| New vagus (myelinated) | Safe, engaged and connected | HRV high<br>Vagal brake active<br>Alert and focused<br>Empathy active | Very recent |
| Sympathetic (adrenaline) | Moderate to extreme danger | Adrenaline floods<br>Acute distress<br>Fight and flight<br>Empathy off | Long ago |
| Old vagus (unmyelinated) | Life threatening to panic | Collapse<br>Void bowel or bladder<br>Freeze or feign death<br>Everything off | Very ancient |

## Assessing your Coherence

This critical physiological reality is neatly captured by the Institute of HeartMath (www.heartmath.com) and their emWave biofeedback system.[27] We are immensely supportive of their approach and tools, and strongly recommend you explore the system and order your own emWave for PC, Mac or other device. It is, quite simply, a life changer and a lifesaver. Every person interested in their wellbeing, resilience, leadership and life satisfaction should learn how to activate coherence quickly and confidently. There are other devices and smartphone applications that may suit you better.

## Calm, Focus, Connect

The shift from chaotic to coherent physiology is easily learned. There are many practices to shift from a chaotic, destructive physiology and vulnerable state to a coherent, constructive and resilient state. Many of these techniques have roots in the contemplative traditions of 2500 years ago. The evidence for practical benefits in our modern lives is now clearly demonstrated in research.

Figure 15: Increased Vagal Tone Shifts Your Performance Curve Up and Left and Leads to Relaxed Intensity

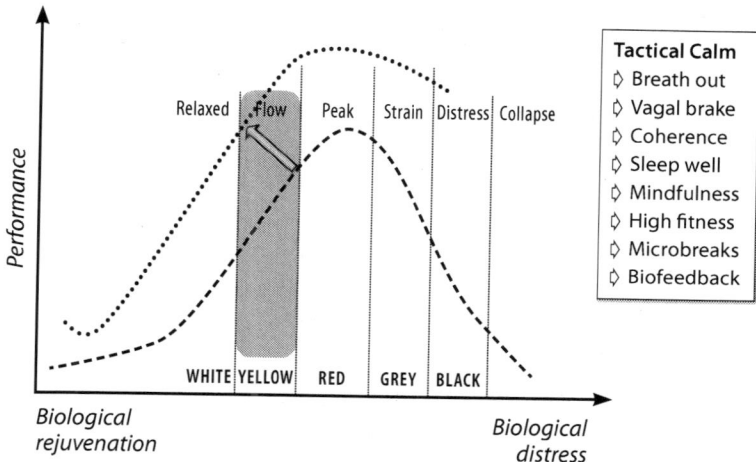

This move from chaos to coherence is the core change required. This change is easily measured through HRV. In the language that we have used above, this is the transition out of the death spiral and into creative resilience. It marks the move from challenge overload to the optimal performance states shown in the Response to Challenge Curve. Sustained practice shifts your curve up and to the left, as we see in the following diagram.

When you try to sense this shift, think of Roger Federer gliding across the tennis court. Federer was an explosive young player, but he learned early in his career how to play in condition yellow. This is one reason people love to watch him play. He appears calm, effortless, fluid and graceful. For over 15 years he competed as one of the world's top five players. This is what we strive to achieve, in different ways, by training the vagal brake and securing coherence in our lives.

As we transition from chaos to coherence, we reverse the effects of distress (both acute and chronic) and restore homeostasis. Excess adrenaline and cortisol is replaced by serotonin and dehydroepiandrosterone (DHEA), which is related to growth hormone. Breathing becomes slower and diaphragmatic. Pulse rate and blood pressure reduce. Blood flows back into the prefrontal cortex (PFC) and we restore conscious control over destructive, reactive behaviours.

This shift towards prefrontal activation restores calm focus and allows us to reframe our emotional state and thinking. Emotional intelligence is liberated and the mind is returned to a clear, optimistic and decisive state.

Many older contemplative and philosophical traditions put coherence at the centre of a good life and spiritual development. Meditation and mindfulness are common terms that describe the practice of sitting quietly, directing attention away from the distractions of life and focusing on the inner world of breath, emotion and thought. The goal is to develop a moment-to-moment awareness of the changes in our internal world.

As a practitioner develops awareness of these inner fluctuations, the tendency of distressed body, emotion or mind to throw us out of coherence is reduced. The practitioner is able to observe these distractions as objects, thereby learning to reduce and master their impact. The coherent state becomes more stable. We are training body, heart and mind.

We will start with practical and tactical paths and move towards a scientific approach to mindfulness. The benefits you can expect from these practices include:

- muscular relaxation, tension release through to reversal of fibromyalgia
- slowing of breathing leading to optimised physiology and brain function
- improvement in digestion and reduction of digestive/abdominal disorders
- better blood flow to organs, particularly the skin
- reduction and ultimately removal of distress symptoms
- reduced blood pressure and heart rate
- improved immune system function and resistance to disease
- reduction in adrenaline, cortisol and cholesterol
- improved recovery from illnesses including heart disease, cancer and asthma
- better brain function, alertness, reaction time and perception
- reduction in anxiety, worry and greater likelihood of a good night's sleep
- reduced low mood, increased optimism and sustainable happiness
- improved concentration and memory.

## Basic Relaxation Practice

Basic relaxation practice is simple and easy to learn, and the benefits can be experienced immediately. A first step is to create a period of at least five minutes when you can reduce external demands. The goal is to:

- ▶ reverse accumulated tension and fatigue,
- ▶ rejuvenate your physical, emotional and cognitive function, and
- ▶ master the technique for quick and effective impact.

••••••••••••••••••••••••••••••••••••••••••••••••••••••••••••••••••

### Instructions

1. Lie flat on your back on the carpet or on a firm bed.
2. Tense each muscle group on the inhalation and relax them fully on the exhalation.
3. Progress from face to chest to arms to belly to hips to legs and then to feet.
4. Check that your entire body is soft and relaxed into the carpet or bed.
5. Focus on the skin between the ribs and the umbilicus (belly button).
6. Watch five breaths, observing pace, flow and depth.
7. Lengthen the exhalation to about five seconds and soften the exhalation to three seconds.
8. Soften the transition between exhalation and inhalation.
9. Relax and pause on the exhalations.
10. Attend to your inhalation with alertness and clarity.
11. Let your breathing be natural, soft and unforced.
12. Release all anxiety, worry or frustration on the exhalation.
13. Enjoy, with gratitude, the freshness and oxygen of each inhalation.
14. End by extending the inhalation and stretching fingers and toes.

••••••••••••••••••••••••••••••••••••••••••••••••••••••••••••••••••

Taking time to relax in our frantic lives never seems reasonable. Yet the science is clear, and the benefits follow quickly. So get over your resistance and build it into your day. Initially, five minutes at the end of the day — perhaps in preparation for connecting with family — is ideal. It is also a great way to recover after strenuous sport. Perhaps join a yoga class where Savasana (lying flat in deep relaxation) is done at the end of every practice. Progressive Relaxation and Autogenic Training are well-known variations of this practice.

As you develop more skill, experiment with practising relaxation as you wake up. Then try the process sitting in an upright posture. One can do this at regular intervals through the day to maintain optimal performance. Having access to a biofeedback device will accelerate your learning, confidence and the benefits you can achieve.

## Breath Training

A normal, diaphragmatic breathing pattern is one of the power levers for bounce, coherence and resilience. The more challenging work of resilience — EQ and brain training — depends on sound breathing. Eliminating destructive breathing and establishing rock-solid diaphragmatic breathing is a foundation for a good life. Few people recognise how prevalent poor breathing has become in our society.

Breathing is the most natural and intuitive living process. Breathing is usually unconscious and mediated within the brainstem in much the same way that temperature and blood pressure are controlled. While one can voluntarily stop breathing, once loss of consciousness comes, breathing will start again — a resilient drive.

When all is well, we have little awareness of breathing. We breathe 12 or fewer times per minute. Most of the activity comes from the diaphragm — a domed muscle running between our chest and abdominal cavity. As we inhale, the diaphragm contracts and pulls down, sucking air into the lower lungs. From the outside it appears as if the belly is expanding with air. In fact, it is the diaphragm flattening and compressing abdominal contents.

The air comes into contact with blood in the small alveoli of the lungs. Oxygen is absorbed into the blood for the production of energy and carbon dioxide diffuses back into the lungs for removal. The diaphragm then relaxes and domes up into the lungs, pushing air out on the exhalation.

The desire to breathe comes from increasing carbon dioxide levels in the blood that reduces the pH (acidosis). Increased ventilation follows and the carbon dioxide moves quickly out of the blood and into lungs for removal on the next exhalation. Hold your breath out for 30 seconds and notice how strong the desire to inhale becomes.

Before we go further, examine your own breathing with the following exercise. Lie flat on your back. Place your right hand on your upper chest and the left hand between your belly button and lower ribs. Breathe normally and feel the flow of air. Notice how the chest and belly expand, and the relationship between their movements. Pay attention to the smoothness of airflow. Soften the breath and extend the exhalation.

Many things influence breathing: high carbon dioxide, increased use of oxygen in exercise, blood pressure and pulse rate. The most important in our day-to-day lives, however, is a perception of excessive challenge. Under pressure we change to shorter, sharper breaths that emphasise the use of the upper chest. This is helpful in the short term to galvanise the body into action. Sustained, it becomes a serious disability.

Many of us have ongoing breathing-related difficulty. Most of us have it from time to time. The huge increase in asthma is one effect, but the second, hyperventilation, is less well recognised. Hyperventilation, or over-breathing, is triggered by anxiety and overload. It is a classic case of a useful,

Figure 16: Distressed Breathing and the Hyperventilation Pattern

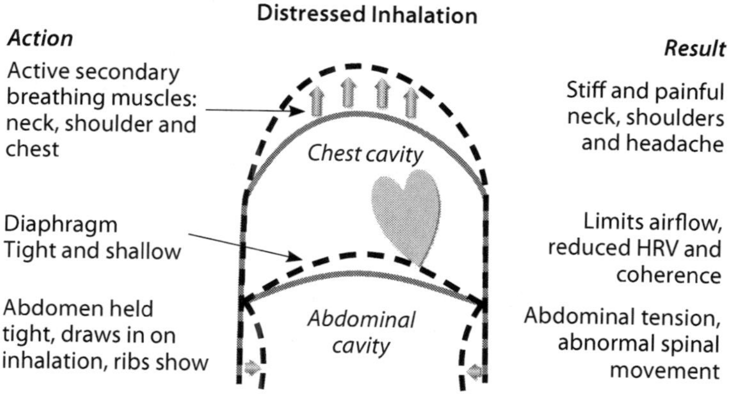

**Distressed Inhalation**

| *Action* | | *Result* |
|---|---|---|
| Active secondary breathing muscles: neck, shoulder and chest | Chest cavity | Stiff and painful neck, shoulders and headache |
| Diaphragm Tight and shallow | | Limits airflow, reduced HRV and coherence |
| Abdomen held tight, draws in on inhalation, ribs show | Abdominal cavity | Abdominal tension, abnormal spinal movement |

acute distress symptom (prepare to run) becoming a debilitating chronic distress symptom. When our breath rate increases above 12 per minute we are over breathing. When we reach 18 or more breaths per minute we have hyperventilation.

It is easy to notice distressed breathing in others and much harder to notice it in ourselves. It is an excellent way to assess distress or resilience. When we are relaxed and in our optimal performance zone, breathing is slow, low, even and deep. Under pressure, breathing can become irregular, high, fast and shallow. Poor breathing can exacerbate distress and fatigue and cause illness. It also makes asthma symptoms worse. We will hear long sighs and breath-holding ('pah' on exhale) while typing, and we will see neck tension.

In distressed breathing, the diaphragm loses its natural rhythmical movement. The neck muscles lift the upper ribs causing strain in the neck, fast or irregular breathing, and increased activation of the 'freeze, flight, fight' response. Over time, the accelerated respiration rate (more than 12 breaths per minute) causes carbon dioxide to be blown off through the lungs.

Reduced carbon dioxide levels increase the alkalinity (pH) of the blood. This causes increased fatigue, headaches, poor concentration and irritability. Activating the sympathetic system causes fast pulse, increased blood pressure, pale and dry skin, irritable bowels, sleep disturbance, and anxiety. Oxygen availability to cells and organs is reduced. Some studies show that blood flow to the executive centre in the prefrontal cortex (PFC) of the brain can reduce by half.

| Distressed Breathing | Healthy Breathing |
|---|---|
| ▷ upper chest and collar bone lifts and falls | ▷ lower ribs and belly expand and contract |
| ▷ uneven, sharp and chesty airflow | ▷ low, slow and even airflow |
| ▷ sharp inhalation — air grabbing | ▷ slow, smooth and quiet inhalation |
| ▷ deep, audible sighs on exhalation | ▷ long, slow, quiet and complete exhalation |
| ▷ tight belly and puffed chest | ▷ relaxed, soft belly and chest |
| ▷ stiff 'military' or slouched posture | ▷ neutral posture, long and light spine |
| ▷ tight neck muscles, Dowager's hump | ▷ light, relaxed neck, ears over shoulders |

Often when we start exercise such as running, the first ten minutes feel like hard labour. Breathing is hard and strained. Then, suddenly, we find our rhythm and pace. Breathing becomes easier, the body relaxes and the experience of exercise is markedly more enjoyable. The diaphragm has activated a 'second wind'. Exhausted secondary muscles of the neck and upper chest relax and the diaphragm engages.

Diaphragmatic or healthy breathing will reverse the chaotic and destructive state of distressed breathing. It will reduce distress, induce a calm, focused state and improve physical, emotional and intellectual performance. Good breathing uses a steady, smooth and full movement of the diaphragm. It is one of the simplest ways to activate your vagal brake.

Figure 17: The Correct Movement of the Diaphragm on Inhalation (above) and Exhalation (below)

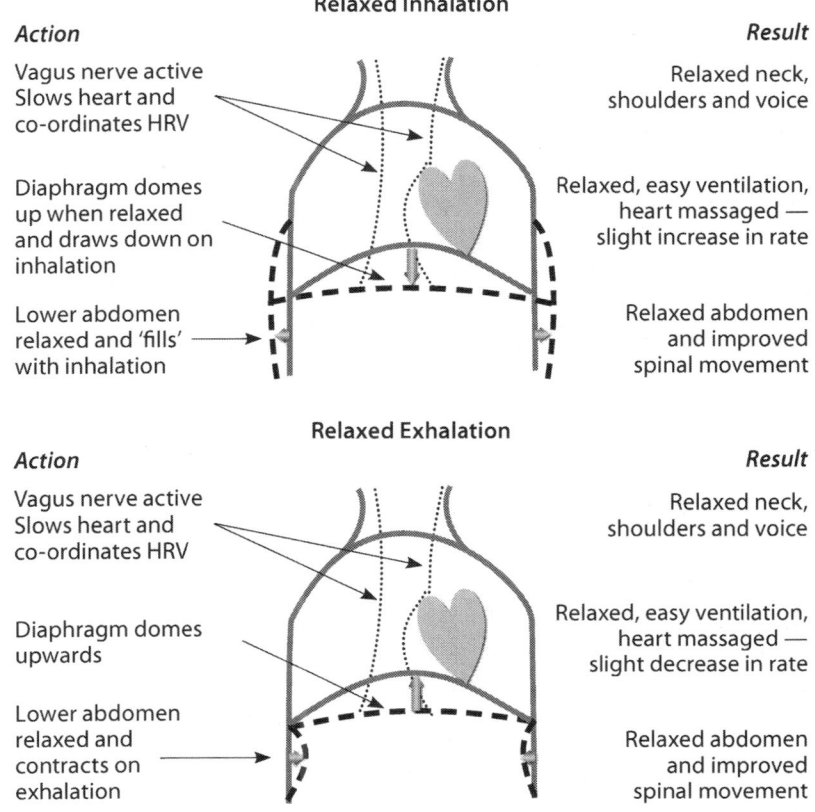

The diaphragm is a specialised muscle that domes upwards into the chest when relaxed and pulls flat into the belly when contracted. It is a very resilient and efficient muscle. It keeps the body well oxygenated and balanced. It also helps to promote the relaxation response by stimulating the vagus nerve (parasympathetic system). Vagal tone slows pulse, lowers blood pressure, increases blood flow to the skin and bowel, and promotes healing. Aim for six to ten breaths per minute.

Note that your pericardium (the sac around the heart) is attached to the top of the diaphragm. Correct movement of the diaphragm helps shift HRV into coherence by applying a massaging action to the heart.

## Diaphragmatic Breathing Practice

Practise diaphragmatic breathing by doing the following.

1. Keep your spine light and long.
2. Let your shoulders roll backward and down.
3. Breathe through your nose.
4. Relax your chest and let your sternum sink downward.
5. Exhale completely over 5 seconds and pause for one or two seconds.
6. Inhale slowly and evenly aiming for about three seconds.
7. Keep your chest, neck and face relaxed
8. Allow your belly, side ribs and loins (over kidneys) to expand.
9. Keep your face and neck relaxed.
10. Notice your pulse, muscle tone, and skin.

Take a few minutes, morning and night, to practise good breathing. Begin by sitting quietly in a chair with your back upright. Watch your breathing first. Observe where your muscles are tight, where you feel tension and how your breath moves. Then slowly adjust your breathing practice to follow the instructions. Maintain your attention on the even flow of breath. Try to feel rather than think the breath. Perhaps imagine your mind sinking into your breath.

If you have the emWave, you can watch how exhalation slows and inhalation increases the pulse rate. When you hyperventilate the pattern becomes chaotic. As you restore a smooth, even diaphragmatic breath, coherence returns.

If you are struggling to understand this or you are having difficulty getting a smooth diaphragmatic breath established, I recommend seeking out a specialist for help. Usually it is a specially trained physiotherapist who can do this, but you may find a skilled yoga teacher can help you get started. Even if you are competent, the investment in specialist assessment and guidance may be very useful.

Once you are comfortable with your diaphragmatic breathing, return to this pattern regularly. Specifically, remind yourself of it when sitting at traffic lights, in meetings, when feeling anxious or before an important event. As you improve you will find that it is a powerful way to relax, calm anxiety, focus your attention and beat off fatigue. It is also very helpful before falling asleep.

This way of breathing should become a lifelong habit. Athletes, artists and elite soldiers are continuously using their breath to achieve their goals. You can do this, too. Once you have achieved a slow, even, diaphragmatic breath, focus your attention on the movement. Keep your mind calm and still. When your mind wanders, bring it back to the movement of the breath.

## Breath Variations

For thousands of years the practice of yoga has worked with breath as a focus for personal and spiritual development. In almost all types of yoga the practitioner is expected to be aware of the breath. It is used in the vigorous postures, in meditation and in specific breathing practices (pranayama).

The yogis view the breath as life force and the connection between mind and body. They strongly promote the benefits of full, relaxed and diaphragmatic breathing. In yoga philosophy, the inhalation is associated with increased mental activity and the exhalation with a quietening of mental and neurological activity. Long exhalations followed by a short pause are promoted as a powerful way to calm the mind.

This idea of full exhalations followed by a pause has been utilised by most breathing experts. These approaches have had significant success in treating asthma, hyperventilation, anxiety and sleep disorders.

More recently, combat science has introduced and widely advocated the practice of tactical breathing.[28] Also called square breathing, the idea is to develop a robust, quick, calm and focused practice. The practice begins with four seconds of exhalation, holding for four seconds, inhaling smoothly for four seconds and holding for four seconds. This is based on yogic breath, and is simple and powerful. It has been shown to be highly effective when faced with deeply confronting challenges such as combat, sport or stage performance.

## Mindfulness

Mindfulness is also called meditation, contemplation and prayer. My preference is to call it 'Training the Mind'.

The first step in cultivating mindfulness is to learn how to pay attention. Simply pausing to notice what you are paying attention to starts the process. Often we are so caught up in activity that the mind is endlessly scanning, thinking, arguing, worrying, blaming or regretting. Mindfulness asks us to choose what we want to pay attention to, and to focus on that choice fully. For example, follow three cycles of slow, even nasal breaths and give your full attention to the movement of air at your nose. Equally, we can choose to focus on a feeling, another person, the process of eating or walking. This can also be called 'Being Present'. When our mind is rushing about worrying and fretting, we are distressed. When it slows down and is focused we immediately feel more calm and engaged. The mind is also more effective.

Today there is enormous interest in meditation practice. In meditation we choose to devote a longer period to training attention. One can start with a minute twice daily and progress to longer periods of up to an hour per day. Advanced practitioners may spend several hours a day in meditation. We will explore this more deeply in the Mind chapter (page 190).

There are many forms and styles, but in general we can distinguish three paths. The first is to focus on an object such as the breath, a word, a feeling or an image. This builds attention with stability, clarity and focus. The second is a state of open awareness, where one simply watches and witnesses the flux and flow of body sensations, emotions and thoughts. This develops an open awareness. The third is actively to generate feelings of loving kindness — first to those close to you and then extending to all living creatures.

All forms of meditation show impressive benefits to body, emotion and mind.[29] Coherence and vagal tone increase.

Today, scientific approaches to these techniques are common and actively promoted by many highly credible scientists.[30] Mostly based on the older traditions of Yogic or Buddhist meditation methods, they have been simplified and placed into a modern secular language. The research on mindfulness is extensive, encouraging and well understood in medicine, psychology and modern spiritual practice. It is estimated that 10–15% of people in developed economies are practising mindfulness.

## Maintain Perspective

It can be safely asserted that most of us are way too distressed, as recently described by Arianna Huffington in *Thrive*.[31] Embarking on a practice that helps you find coherence is one of the most useful steps you can take. But there is a need for balance. In a professional life or in achieving educational excellence, we need to be able to restore relaxation but not get too relaxed. We don't want to become apathetic. Just as the heart rate accelerates and slows to a regular rhythm (HRV), so must our engagement with life. There are times for deep relaxation and times for active, focused engagement.

Many of us slip too far in one direction — we are super-stressed out, hyperkinetic workaholics or conversely, we are apathetic, disengaged freeloaders. The answer is to seek out a rhythm that works for you. By testing both dimensions we train coherence and resilience in our biology. This includes the autonomic (vagus and sympathetic) nervous system, heart, lungs, hormones, emotions, brain and mind.

Stephen Porges' polyvagal theory and recent work by Richard Davidson demonstrate that the optimal capacities of human function require the focused engagement of deeper hidden resources of physiology, neurology and mind. Biology adapts and our faculties will rise to the challenge. We need both stretch and relaxation. We can expect more pleasure and impact when we are rhythmic.

The simple concept of rhythmic stretch and relax can radically enhance life experience. Deep in our physiology this rhythm nurtures the ebb and flow of sympathetic and parasympathetic activity, accelerates and slows the heart and lungs, and rejuvenates and focuses the mind.

Remember the Performance Supply Chain:

Figure 18: Performance Supply Chain

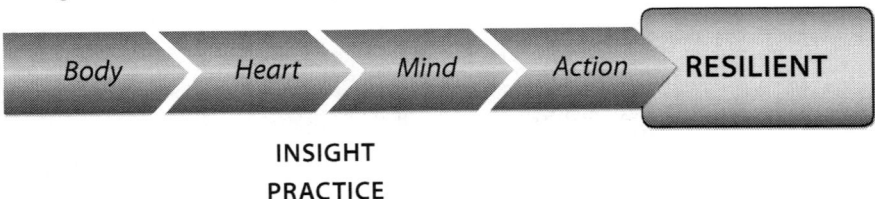

**INSIGHT**
**PRACTICE**
**MASTERY**

We introduced this model as one way to represent optimal life experiences. To thrive at the top end of resilience we aim to engage all of our faculties — body, heart and mind — when we are called to the stage of life.

Each of these faculties loves to be stretched and rejuvenated. As we discover in the next chapters, skilful stretching of body, heart and mind lead to measurable growth. This skilful development is a source of tremendous enjoyment. When body, heart and mind flourish together, we unleash optimal performance, achieve our goals and contribute to others.

The trick is to embed the discipline of relaxation, recovery and rejuvenation into the pulse of life. Just as the body needs — and usually gets — a great night's sleep after a strenuous day of physical work or sport, so the heart and mind also need time out. Some lucky souls get this idea, but in our 24/7 lifestyle it is tempting to try to sprint the marathon of life. The goal is to periodise, that is, to know when to go hard and when to relax.

Sleep is a powerful source of resilience and thus gets its own chapter. Stretching, progressive relaxation and massage are other options. We have seen the impact on the heart — HRV — from skilled diaphragmatic breathing. We could also use appreciation, gratitude and kindness. We will return to the benefits of meditation practice on the mind, but here we note you could also use reading, art or nature.

Sports medicine has clearly articulated the benefits of periodisation. This is a disciplined phasing of training to coach the athlete to optimal performance. Periods typically include phases of conditioning for the optimal development of each faculty required in competition. Thus, a runner may have periods of long-distance training for cardiovascular endurance, strength training for injury prevention and speed work for acceleration. In each of these periods, coaches often develop very specific recommendations for the right mixture of different training regimes, nutrition, rest and sleep.

Most of us need not be so intense, but we can all derive huge benefits with a little experimentation in periodisation. Two simple practical actions will immediately deliver payback. First, introduce some intense physical activity to the day and watch your sleep improve. This could be a brisk walk up a hill, repeating a series of strength exercises or doing a few short sprints. The metabolic effect of short intense bursts of exercise improves the quality of sleep. Indeed, it has also been shown to reduce weight, prevent diabetes, improve cognition and recharge your hormone status.[32]

Second, establish four short relaxation breaks in your work day. Select one of the above relaxation practices — even just a minute of diaphragmatic breathing, or a short stroll in the sun. Leave your gadgets off. These short breaks will allow your breathing to normalise, refresh your physical energy and recharge your capacity for attention[33] and productive work. Repeated experiments at Boston Consulting Group have shown that when periodic breaks are imposed on consultants, productivity and teamwork improve.

You may like to consider other forms of periodisation that may fit your own life and goals. We will return to this idea in the final chapter as it appears increasingly in the literature as a signature of those who succeed and perform. At the very least try to enhance and deepen your experience of rest and, when you do stretch for a goal, give it all you have — body, heart, mind and spirit.

## Summary

- ✷ Clarify what coherence means to you.
- ✷ Exhale slow and smooth.
- ✷ Breathe diaphragmatically.
- ✷ Take periodic breaks.
- ✷ Be mindful.
- ✷ Experiment with your own engage–relax rhythms.

## Part Three

# Courage

| | | |
|---|---|---|
| 8 | Prevent and Heal | 91 |
| 9 | Hunt and Gather | 116 |
| 10 | Sleep | 138 |
| 11 | Nourish | 154 |

# Chapter 8

# Prevent and Heal

## Body Rules

The flow of life happens through the physical body. We want to be energised, strong, flexible, balanced, and resilient enough to carry us through old age. Your physical vitality is a key anchor for resilience in the journey of life. There is evidence that every level of the death spiral can be countered by exercise, sleep and nutrition. Physical wellbeing underpins the top end of the spiral—particularly the cognitive elements of memory, attention and decision-making.

Our physical body is immediately tangible. We are partly aware of its state and needs. This is not true for emotions and thoughts, where 95% is below conscious awareness. The body is very real. We immediately recognise a fit body versus a fragile body. Most of us know what we should do to improve wellbeing. We feel the positive effects of change in days or weeks. Over time the benefits are so marked and our lives are so enriched that it is hard to relapse. Never forget that the human body is magnificently resilient and has been shaped over evolution to survive and thrive through all kinds of challenges. Health and vitality is truly our natural state.

Traps abound. The media assails us with images, information and products for the body. Changing research and professional recommendations keep shifting the advice. Commercial interests will often press us to make poor choices. Many profit from the fear of decline and death. Our generation is frequently anxious about health. Many pursue 'health objectives' with a level of psychological imbalance that is clearly not good for us or those around us.

Healthcare spending in the USA has boomed in the last hundred years from less than 1% to a whopping 18% of Gross Domestic Product (GDP). Physical vitality is an immediate and pressing issue for individuals, business and government. The cost of sickness multiplied by an ageing population is not sustainable. Our lifestyles, driven by greed, technology, and the food and entertainment industry, make short work of the good health we start with.

All governments are facing healthcare systems that simply cannot be funded into the next generation. Right now many of us confront the suffering of our parents who face limited income and healthcare rationing. We must plan for our own wellbeing in old age. We will probably live into our nineties, carrying the accumulated penalties of sloth, sleep deprivation, distress and fast food. We have not produced enough children or jobs to provide for this 'retirement'. Governments have spent their savings baling out our banks. The burgeoning tsunami of preventable disease will choke an already underfunded health system. Suffering on waiting lists for heart, joint and abdominal surgery is already common.

Medicine has, until recently, focused exclusively on a physical approach to treatment. Yet we know that in primary care, three-quarters of doctor's visits have no organic (physical) cause. Health is a primary global concern. We are waking up and lifting physical wellbeing to the top of our agenda. This is where it belongs. It is the next step for your resilience.

The tangibility of our physical being creates a perfect crucible for all resilience practices. The body can be touched, seen and measured in many ways. When we effect change we can see objective evidence of improvement or decline. We can really feel the benefits in emotions, mind and life when we get it right. A trained body supports constructive emotion, effective thinking and connection — inside-out.

Remember the metaphor of the carriage? The body is the home of the passenger or spirit. The body provides protection, comfort, a smooth ride and, if well cared for, can be a work of art for the passenger to appreciate. A well-designed and maintained carriage makes the work of the driver (mind) and the horses (emotions) much easier.

Sadly, when we look around us we see a world littered with damaged carriages.

## Sickcare: Our Healthcare System Failure

For the last hundred years healthcare has focused on treating illness. The global sickness industry captures US$6.5 trillion; each person on the planet consumes on average US$948 per year. In the OECD it is US$4,380, while in the rest of the world it is less than US$100. It is a classic 80/20 split, with 20% of the world consuming 80% of the resources. Healthcare consumes just under 10% of global GDP and that is expected to double by 2050.[34] Prevention and promotion accounts for less than 3% in the most progressive countries and less than 1% in many others.

The system rewards illness and punishes wellbeing by shifting resources from the well and productive to those who are sick. The intention is sound. We are compassionate humans who take care of each other. The problem is that the commercial incentives favour sickness over health. Millions of jobs depend on sickness and its remedies. We depend on an unsustainable system with endless demand and very limited supply. We have to change it.

The diagram below frames the scope of the current healthcare system as it impacts our lives from birth to death. There are three zones: wellbeing (where we want to be); acute illness and risk (including temporary illness, injury and risk factors); and chronic disease and suffering, which is where most of our resources are spent.

Figure 19: Mapping the Preventable Disease Burden

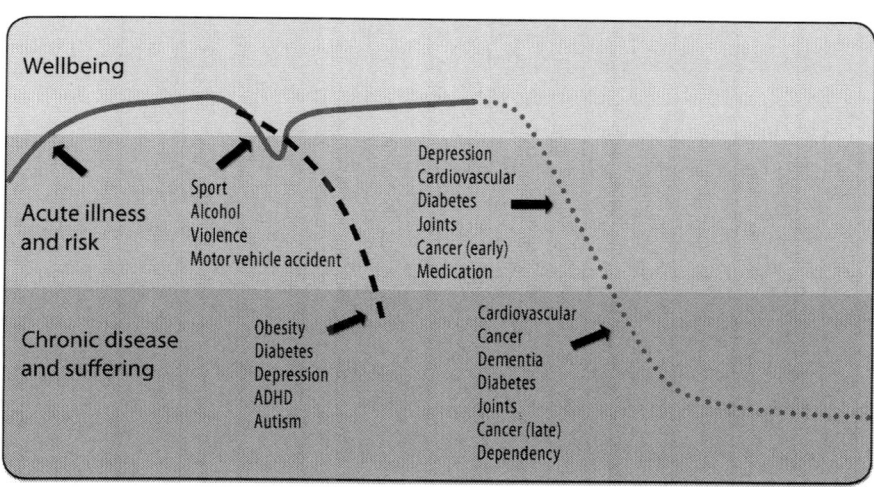

The curve maps how we might traverse these zones of health. Our journey has two parts: the first 45 years of life when health is largely a free gift, and the last 45 years when it is painful and expensive. Some are lucky and live a blessed existence without illness until dying quietly in sleep in their nineties. Others are less fortunate and suffer genetic and birth challenges that can burden their lives.

Birth can be messy and children have their challenges, but things tend to go reasonably well until teenage hormones stimulate risk-taking. In the first dip many young people get to know their doctors, or hospitals. Unfortunately some die due to motor vehicle accidents (MVA), violence and suicide.

Getting married reduces risk, and through our thirties wealth and wisdom nudge us to good health. For some this continues while others crash headlong into preventable disease processes. We all know of friends or relatives who have suffered a heart attack, a stroke, discovered diabetes, started anti-depressants or developed cancer in their late forties and early fifties.

The combination of increased longevity and expensive treatment leaves many of us suffering with chronic disease for years. It is humbling to talk to an older person who has survived a stroke, bowel cancer surgery, joint replacements or multiple drug therapy for chronic conditions such as heart failure, blood pressure, diabetes, and joint pain.

While in the chronic disease zone, people consume the resources of our medical system — including hospitals, doctors, nurses, medicines, surgery, prostheses, insurers and truckloads of administration. The cost of preventable disease is estimated by most healthcare systems to be at least 75% of total cost.

In other words, we could reduce healthcare cost and suffering by 75% through preventive action.

Note the dotted line in figure 19. A percentage of teenagers, particularly in certain sub-populations, are developing metabolic syndrome, obesity, diabetes, and depression that belong in old age. This will drive the preventable disease burden for 60 years.

The National Health and Nutrition Examination Study (NHANES)[35] study of teenagers in 2008 showed:

▶ diabetes and pre-diabetes levels at 23% (up from 9% in 1999)

- obesity at 16–18% (steady)
- high blood pressure at 14%
- high LDL cholesterol at 22%.

For parents, this is frightening news. These numbers indicate a massive issue for future generations as billions of young people in developed nations follow in the path of America.

Yet many of us — parents, schools and governments — appear paralysed. We see the collapse of wellbeing in ourselves, our children and our community but we are unable to provoke change. What do we need to know and do?

## Square the Function Curve

We know that a preventive approach delivers. Thousands of studies describe the benefits of exercise, relaxation, sleep, chocolate, coffee, broccoli, low carbs, sunshine and fish — to name a few currently attracting attention. In essence, we know what to do to prevent almost all chronic diseases. We

Figure 20: Square the Function Curve — The Power of Prevention

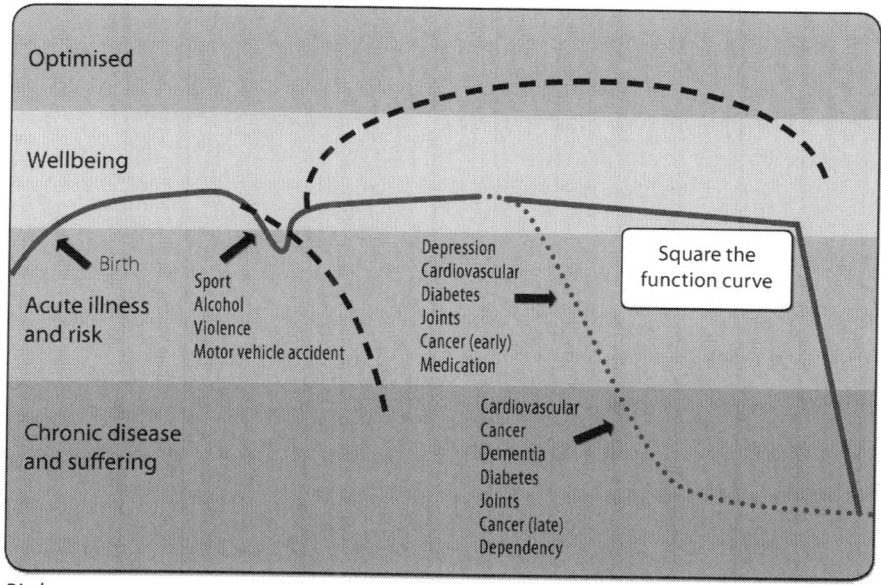

have the capacity to identify risk factors and early markers in tests that can identify illness before it is present. For example, raised insulin signals a high risk of diabetes developing. A raft of non-medical resources is available to reduce the impact of disease. We can liberate billions of people from unnecessary suffering and release trillions of dollars of productivity.

You are the source of where the action needs to happen!

In 1980, in the *New England Journal of Medicine*,[36] J.F. Fries coined the phrase 'morbidity compression' to describe our ability to push the onset of illness out by around 15 years. The article described how lifestyle changes in midlife reduce your risk of illness. Specifically, by changing diet, increasing activity and improving mental and emotional states, we can delay the onset of cardiovascular disease, diabetes, cancer, arthritis and many other diseases by 15 years and more.[37]

Figure 20 shows both a dotted and a solid line in the second half of life. The solid line is the goal and probable result of prevention and a sound lifestyle. Instead of suffering the effects of preventable illness listed, we can maintain wellbeing and function well into our eighties. It is called both 'morbidity compression' and 'squaring the function curve'. We know that around 80% of heart attacks, stroke, cancer (in particular the common lung, colon and prostate types), osteoporosis, diabetes, depression and dementia could be prevented.

What does this mean personally? Let's say you are middle-aged with a family or personal risk factors, and cancer, stroke, diabetes or heart disease is expected to hit you in five years. If you assess your risk and design a simple programme to introduce exercise, relaxation, sleep and good nutrition into your life, you can push the onset of disease away by approximately 15 years. You have just 'squared the function curve'. How much is 15 years of healthy life worth to you?

...........................................................................

### Case study: Prevention in action

I have a friend who lives on a beach where we holiday. He is 76. Lifesaving, swimming and paddling are his passions. He had a successful career running a chain of restaurants. Now he is mostly retired, apart from some property investment. I met him walking with his wife on the beach recently. He still has a powerful torso and well-defined muscles with an absolutely flat belly. His wife is in equally good shape. That morning he had been out on the ocean, fishing off his outrigger. He had brought home two fish and that evening was off overseas. He was a picture of vitality.

A year before he had felt chest pain while on his kayak and went to see his doctor. The exercise ECG showed major coronary blockage. He was sent immediately into angioplasty, where cardiologists plumbed out the blocked arteries and sent him home the same day. He could have died with a major heart attack in the waves. A lifetime of fitness and quick medical preventive action put him back into life with arteries that will feed his heart for the next 20 years.

..................................................................

Despite the data on the benefit of prevention, we spend a tiny 3% or less of the healthcare budget on prevention and public health.[38] Imagine what we could achieve if we invested 50% of our health budget in prevention and wellbeing. The payback to individuals, families, communities and governments would be massive.

Unfortunately, at the individual level, the hit of immediate gratification — digital entertainment, 'bliss spot' fast food, gambling or alcohol — overwhelms our desire for long-term benefits. This is particularly true in less fortunate communities that need preventive approaches the most. Balancing the principle of freedom with the risk and cost of self-abusing behaviours will test social policy. This is currently being tested with sugared drink controls.

The debate needs to be held courageously and soon. Nature drew the line ruthlessly in our past. As recently as a hundred years ago we simply could not survive chronic, preventable disease states. Today we can survive for decades utilising expensive care solutions. The impact on quality of life and productivity is substantial. Sports, military, performing arts and businesses are increasingly requiring compliance to good preventive behaviours, vitality and performance science. When optimal performance is required at the lowest possible cost, this is the only way forward.

The challenge of pushing back against the interests of the food industry, passive entertainment, alcohol and the traps of poverty is significant. Yet the curve described in figure 20 shows the huge upside to humanity if we can get this right. It is a tough challenge, but one we have to tackle.

## The Language of Vitality

Prevention can scare people with information on the consequences of disease (for example, images on cigarette packets and sunscreen advice). This is prescriptive about what you cannot do and what you have to do. This works well for those who are motivated by fear. Others rebel.

Aspirational approaches include wellness, lifestyle management, wellbeing and optimal health. Popular writers flood the market with their own particular biases. Paul Zane Pilzner[39] has famously predicted that wellness will become the next trillion-dollar industry.

We will simply use the word 'vitality' to describe the rich rewards of squaring the function curve. Vitality is integral, as per our principles in part one. Vitality is not simply going gluten free or running a marathon. It embraces medical, nutritional, physiological, psychological and emotional fields of expertise. The goal is to be healthy, feel good, function well and have confidence in healthy ageing. There are many legitimate ways to start and a raft of practical steps for prevention, nutrition, sleep, optimism, exercise, meditation or positive emotions. The parts can be progressively cobbled into your own life practice in a way that suits you.

Vitality strives to be evidence based. It is a honeypot for charlatans, so be cautious. Embrace sensible risk assessment, engage proven practices, use medical treatment when needed, aspire to optimal Vitality, and prolong optimal health. It is the best fit to the 'square function curve' on the morbidity compression diagram (figure 20). Be discerning, stay open to learning and experiment with curiosity in your own life.

The past decade has seen the rise of Longevity or Healthy Ageing Medicine. It is led by medical doctors and specialists who have embraced Vitality without abandoning the rigour of clinical practice, supervision, peer review and evidence-based science. They have recognised how the science, methods and tools of medicine can be applied to prevention and wellbeing.

The promise of 'the fountain of youth' has always captured the rich, famous and insecure. As a consequence, one needs to enter this field with eyes wide open. Abuse of hormones, surgery and cosmetic manipulation is widespread. The results may be grotesque and tragic. Vanity, insecurity and fear of death are easily tempted. However, the best models have fully embraced the preventive paradigm and offer an exciting future for old age.[40] We will be leaning on this work as we move through this section.

By committing yourself to the basic practices of vitality, you will begin to square your function curve. The payback is so profound that if it were a pill, we would all be on double doses. Consider the following:

- practically removing the prospect of cardiovascular stroke or heart attack
- ensuring you do not get diabetes or carry unnecessary weight
- maintaining and building your brain, memory and creativity
- being able to do the things you love into your eighties
- being able to work and do sport well into your eighties
- substantially driving down your risk of cancer
- saving a fortune in health insurance, doctors and hospital care
- enjoying greater happiness, life satisfaction and travel
- being able to enjoy the pleasures of life without guilt
- securing the benefits within weeks.

Our understanding of what supports and undermines vitality is vast. Much is common sense, but recent advances in biology and medicine make it exciting. The information changes as new research comes to light. Rather than being frustrated by this, try to see the excitement and the drama. Seek your own pearls of wisdom but don't grasp too tightly. Seek meaning and encouragement in your own practices. Some things are clearly good for us, some are very bad, several may go both ways, and some things we simply don't know. In this chapter we will do our best to help you secure vitality and prevent illness.

Six factors have a pivotal influence on vitality:

1. **Genetics**   Inherited, acquired and lifestyle-induced effects on genes
2. **Oxidation**   Free-radical damage to cell tissue
3. **Sugars and Glycation**   Effects of quick-release sugars and insulin
4. **Inflammation**   Overactive and misguided immune responses
5. **Plaque**   Accumulation of vulnerable plaque (atherosclerosis) in arteries
6. **Chronic distress and negative emotions.**

The body is made up of about 37.2 trillion cells (estimates range from 5 billion to 200 trillion).[41] Every single one has the same basic structure of cell wall, nucleus and various metabolic organelles. These cells group into specific organs and parts of the body, acquiring a vast range of specialisation from long-lived neurones in the brain, to rapid turnover fragile cells located in the gut.

The parts of the cells, the cells and the tissues they make up are all subject to wear and tear. Eventually cells stop dividing and die. A hundred-year lifespan is a true miracle. Usually we deteriorate and die well before then. We know a lot about how to care for our cells. There are hundreds of risk factors we could worry about. We will focus on six.

## The Six Factors

The six factors operate independently and together to influence how we travel the morbidity curve. Knowledge and recommendations will develop and change, but these factors are solid contributors and their importance is likely to persevere. Each factor is described here in detail. In the chapters following we will link lifestyle recommendations to them.

## 1. Genetics

Health and longevity are linked to our genes. There are a few rare genetic diseases that shorten life dramatically, and there are combinations of genes that contribute to common conditions such as cardiovascular disease, cancer and diabetes. It is also accepted that some families enjoy extreme longevity — sometimes despite bad habits. Overall, genetics play a relatively small role in our health outcomes — usually less than 20%.

In chapter one we introduced epigenetics: that is, how the environment and lifestyle choices change the way our genes express themselves. Genes provide the source code for the production of proteins that are the building blocks of cells and the interaction between them. We can influence gene action by blocking and unblocking different parts of the genetic code.

Epigenetics help us understand how someone with a genetic predisposition may develop or prevent an illness such as diabetes, heart disease, obesity, stroke, dementia, depression or schizophrenia. We know that these conditions have genetic correlations, but the genes don't always mean disease.

To simplify, genetics load the gun and lifestyle pulls the trigger. It is complex and uncertain. We strive to lean the odds in our favour. So, if your family has heart disease, please don't smoke. If you know your family has diabetes and obesity, stay away from processed carbohydrates and keep fit. If there is mental illness in your family, work on your happiness, stay connected and be super calm and relaxed. If you have asthma, try to avoid living in places that set it off.

Genetic engineering may open new avenues to 'excise dangerous genes'. I think it is over-rated and prefer not to mess with the laws of nature. We are playing God in many ways, but there is little evidence we are helping ourselves.

### Practice

▷ Good environments and lifestyles will nudge your genes towards more favourable outcomes.

## 2. Oxidation

Oxidation is an output of biological reactions that build and maintain life. Oxidation is like rust in living tissue. It begins with free radicals or reactive oxygen and nitrogen species (RONS). Free radicals are missing an electron and will steal from whatever tissue with which they make contact. For example, inhaling on a cigarette draws a flood of free radicals from the burning tobacco into our mouths, bronchi and lungs. These pass into the bloodstream and oxidise molecules such as cholesterol, damage cell walls, and even genes. The inhalation has triggered a flood of oxidative stress, and cellular damage and disease ensues.

Exercise is another form of oxidative stress. All metabolism, in burning oxygen and glucose to produce energy, releases free radicals. Exercise is accelerated metabolism where we suck in oxygen at massively increased rates. Fortunately, regular exposure to the oxidative stress of exercise leads to up-regulation of our antioxidant protection.[42] In other words, those who exercise are protected from oxidation.

Once a free radical hits part of a cell it causes an oxidative chain reaction, spreading like rust through the tissue. Oxidative damage leads to a cellular damage. First, it damages cell walls causing leakage, poor maintenance of cellular integrity and dehydration. Cells can repair this damage, but over time oxidation will lead to increased fragility, shrinkage, loss of function and death. An example is the skin wrinkling seen in older people, smokers and those with sun damage.

Oxidative damage can continue into cellular organelles such as the mitochondria, which produce energy. This will lead to loss of energy, reduced cellular recovery and faulty repair. Oxidative damage that penetrates the nucleus of the cell can cause chromosomal damage at the tips (or telomeres), which will accelerate ageing and may trigger cancer. This is why high antioxidant foods are linked to lower rates of common cancers and heart disease.

Every one of our 37.2 trillion or so cells receives over 1000 hits of oxidation per day. Those who exercise, smoke and otherwise burn brightly in life will oxidise faster. Be particularly alert to the risk of oxidation. One group of anti-ageing practitioners engages in extreme calorie restriction (CR) and fasting. This massive reduction in food intake slows the body and cellular processes down, thus reducing oxidative stress. There is evidence in worms, flies and fish that a starved cell cleanses itself from many of the cellular ageing factors. For most of us this practice is too disciplined to sustain.

A multi-billion dollar industry wants you to believe that antioxidants come in a bottle of multivitamins. While it is known that many of these isolated vitamins, such as vitamin C, E and B-carotenes, have antioxidant properties, large-scale studies on supplementation with such vitamins have not demonstrated improved health outcomes. In fact, a number of these studies have shown that those who take multivitamins suffer worse health outcomes. In some, the studies have been abandoned as the risk to the vitamin takers was so obvious. Current recommendations are to avoid supplements.[43]

For now, prudent people should stick to increasing their vegetable and fruit intake. Some, such as blueberries and other red/dark berries, broccoli, carrots, beetroot and tomatoes, are particularly valuable in delivering high-dose antioxidant protection to the body. We should also recognise that coffee, most teas and red wine provide an abundant source of naturally occurring antioxidants with measurable health benefits.

Remember that the protective benefit needs regular topping up. Include sources in all meals and snacks, aiming for an antioxidant cocktail every three hours or so. Reward yourself with your morning coffee or tea, and a glass of red wine at night.

## Practice

▷ Reduce oxidation by reducing: smoking, midday sun, excessive pollutants, processed carbohydrates and fried foods.

▷ Eat lots of fresh vegetables (nine servings a day) and loaded fruit such as blueberries, kiwifruit and apples.

▷ Build the protective effects of exercise, relaxation, sleep and not over-eating.

▷ An occasional fast might reduce oxidative strain and byproducts.

## 3. Sugars and Glycation

The role of processed carbohydrates in our food supply, health and disease is pivotal to understanding and mastering your life. In sharing these ideas among family and friends over the recent past, I have had dozens of responses from people who have lost significant amounts of fat and feel much better after cutting out processed carbohydrate. These well-informed people spent a life trapped by the belief that bread, pasta, grains and cereal are good for you.

There is a complex debate unfolding. This section will be short and as clear as possible. To do this we have to recognise the role of science (medicine), politics, profit and reasonable practice. I will reference the key concepts to leading thinkers and useful books for those who seek a deeper understanding. Here is the drama:

1. Our food environment is packed with processed grains, cereals and mass-produced carbohydrates. Think bread, muffins, cakes, cookies, chips, cereals, pastas and sugar — including all sugar drinks. These carbohydrates (or sugars) are heavily marketed, engineered to trigger the bliss point in your mouth, cheap, and

incredibly convenient. The processed carbohydrates are packed into almost everything you buy on a shelf, unless it is fresh, snap frozen or recently alive.

2. The human body has not evolved for this type of food. We are designed to hunt and gather. The carbohydrates we evolved on were tough tubers, raw and gritty fruits and occasional vegetables.[44] When exposed to processed carbohydrates (or sugars) our blood sugar spikes (hyperglycaemia), insulin rises (insulin resistance) and tissues glycate (caramelise). Over time these processed carbohydrates drive weight gain, fat storage, type 2 diabetes (adult onset, which is about 95% of all diabetes), cardiovascular disease, dementia, cancer and maybe ADHD.

3. When farming started in the Middle East/North Africa around 13,000 years ago, we started to shift to farmed carbohydrate. Human health and life expectancy crashed. In 1977 The US Dietary Goal for Americans unleashed processed carbohydrates on the world as 'healthy', getting most medical bodies to support them. Within five years obesity and diabetes exploded on the scene to become a leading health concern today.[45] Not only are sugars packed into our foods in millions of creative ways, but we have genetically modified our grains, vegetables and fruits to be sweet, loaded with quick release calories, and soft. In *The Real Meal Revolution*, Tim Noakes calls it Carbageddon.

## Basic science

Carbohydrates are one of the three primary food groups, along with protein and fat. Humans are adapted to eat carbohydrates from natural and scarce sources such as tubers, fruit and occasional honey. Carbohydrates break down into simple sugars in the gut — primarily in the form of glucose and fructose. Naturally sourced carbohydrates are released slowly due to the structured fibre content. Processed carbohydrates such as grains and cereals (wheat, corn, rice and soy) rapidly release glucose into the blood. This release is measured by the glycaemic index, where 100 is the speed at which pure and simple glucose is released. Most foods have now been measured for their glycaemic index.[46]

Fructose, the second simple sugar, is found in vegetables and fruit.

Sugar (sucrose) is 50% glucose and 50% fructose. High fructose corn syrup (HFCS) has a higher percentage of fructose and tastes very sweet. Being cheap and sweet, it finds itself infused into many processed foods. Fructose is not released directly into the blood and has to be processed by the liver. In small amounts, say eating an apple, fructose is released slowly. Sugar and high fructose food (including fruit juice) release large amounts quickly. This strains the liver, causing fatty liver and increasing our fat storage.

There is no argument that our processed, carbohydrate-laden diet leads to glucose spiking, fatty liver, obesity and, in time, diabetes. When glucose spikes the pancreas releases insulin. Insulin triggers storage of both glucose and fat. Over time the insulin overload leads to resistance (pre-diabetes). Then blood glucose rises and we develop diabetes. Type 2 diabetes is fully preventable, and in most cases reversible by reducing the glycaemic load — or removing processed carbohydrate. Most academics now accept that processed carbohydrate contributes to heart disease, stroke, dementia, cancer and perhaps attention disorders (ADHD).

The flood of glucose in our blood and cells accelerates glycation. In the presence of glucose our proteins and fats caramelise into Advanced Glycation End-Products (AGEs). Glycation does tremendous damage to our physical structure and has been implicated in accelerated ageing as well as in heart disease, stroke, dementia, and other neurological diseases. This is called endogenous (internal) glycation.

Glycation also happens to our food. This is called exogenous (outside) glycation. When sugar, protein and fat are browned and caramelised they become very tasty. This is the secret to our desire for bacon, barbecues, crème brûlée and pastries. Thus AGEs are now added to many foods. Infant formula milk contains a hundred times the AGEs of cow or human milk — yet another reason to be cautious of processed food. The AGEs will have the same effect once in your body.

Both glycaemic spiking and glycation are linked to accelerated oxidation, inflammation, plaque formation and the damage found in cardiovascular disease, diabetes, dental plaque and Alzheimers. Some of us are able to tolerate more processed carbohydrate and others will be very sensitive to its effects.

The current obsession with gluten is probably not important for most of us. Gluten is a protein in wheat that can cause coeliac disease. This gluten intolerance is rare, affecting only 1% of the population. It is possible that a higher percentage react to gluten with excess inflammation. The concentration of gluten in wheat has increased markedly. Some good books have been written on the topic.[47] My recommendation is to focus on the processed carbohydrate. If you truly are sensitive to gluten, removing processed carbohydrate will remove gluten. Having said that, removing bread anecdotally makes a big difference to some. If that is true for you, stick to a bread-free diet.

It is safe to recommend that carbohydrates should come from nature — vegetables, fruit, beans, nuts, and perhaps oats and rice, with minimal processing. Once the food industry gets involved, profits trump your health.

## Medical politics

The enthusiasm for carbohydrate began with biochemist Ancel Keys in the late 1950s, who 'showed' incorrectly that high saturated-fat diets correlated with high rates of heart disease. The opposite is now known to be the case. Countries such as France and Switzerland, with very high saturated-fat diets, have very low rates of heart disease.

Nevertheless, during President Nixon's reign, it was decided that American farmers needed subsidies and help to promote their grain and cereal products. The Nixon government co-opted the American Heart Association to support the initiative. By 1977 the US food pyramid appeared and quickly spread across the developed world. Wheat, soy and corn products boomed.

The food pyramid was based on grains being the large base of a healthy and nutritious diet. Within a few years, eggs, meat and dairy (sources of saturated fat and cholesterol) were blacklisted as causes of increased LDL cholesterol, which was named a major risk factor for heart disease. Bread, rice, cereals, baked foods and corn became staples. The food industry learned how to process, package, store and promote cheap, high-energy foods. The money flowed to farmers, but even more swiftly to the food industry.

Processed and carb-packed foods line aisles of our supermarkets — just think about the rows of cereals, rice, pastas, corn and potato chips, muesli bars, biscuits and snacks. The vast majority are based on grains. The food industry noticed that desire, consumption and profit were increased by adding sugar, high fructose corn syrup, salt and vegetable oil. Initially, large amounts of trans fats were used. Now it is mostly soy oil (vegetable oil = inflammation) and sugar (or HFCS), plus salt.

Even better, the food industry has been able to advertise the health benefits of grains, low cholesterol and low saturated fat (Carbageddon 2). Obesity, diabetes and the food industry have flourished ever since.

While some respected researchers cling to this disastrous view, science shows that saturated fat and cholesterol DO NOT lead to higher blood cholesterols and heart disease. The success of the Atkins diet (low carb–high protein) has been superseded by low carb–high fat diets.[48] Sadly, many doctors and nutritionists have not bothered to update their recommendations.

Most of us still eat far too much processed carbohydrate. We nurture our obesity (which has doubled), diabetes (which has tripled), heart disease, stroke, cancer, dementia and attention disorders with processed carbohydrates and sugar-soaked foods and drinks. The processed food industry laughs all the way to the bank.

## Practice

▷ A simple step everyone agrees on is that we should avoid the rapid release of glucose, or the glycaemic spike after carbohydrate food. A respected source for glycaemic index (GI) is from Professor Jenny Brand-Miller, University of New South Wales (www.glycemicindex.com). The table on the next page is a small sample of the GI scores of some common foods drawn from this publicly available and free website. Switch from high-glycaemic (right-hand column) to low-glycaemic foods (left-hand column). The benefit of a shift from processed grains and cereals to natural vegetable sources is clear.

▷ If you move to a low carbohydrate diet, remove the simple processed grains first and replace them with vegetables. A little more fish oil, monounsaturated fat (avocado, olive, nuts) and saturated fat is a safe way to access the additional calories an active person will need without processed carbohydrates. Replacing processed carbohydrates with protein (as in the Atkins diet) or fried foods is not supported by the science.

▷ Seek out low glycaemic options to enrich your diet. These are listed at top left. Adding low glycaemic foods such meats, eggs, beans, dairy or nuts will reduce the index of a meal. For example an egg, butter, peanut butter, cheese, chicken or avocado added to bread will significantly lower the GI score.

Figure 21: Simplified List of Glycaemic Index for Common Foods
(drawn from www.glycemic.com)

| Low GI <50 | | Moderate GI 50-69 | | High GI >70 | |
|---|---|---|---|---|---|
| Eggs, fish, meats | 0 | Potato – boiled | 49–56 | White bread | 70–75 |
| Hummus | 6 | Blueberry muffin | 50 | Potatoes – new | 70–78 |
| Yoghurt – natural | 11–16 | Rye bread | 50 | Cornflakes | 72–77 |
| Dhal, chickpeas | 11–31 | Pineapples | 51 | Toast – jam & pnb | 72 |
| Peanuts | 13–23 | Coca-Cola – US | 53-63 | Sultana bran | 73 |
| Beans | 14–24 | French fries | 54 | Honey | 74 |
| Carrots – raw | 16 | Raisins | 54 | Yam – boiled | 74 |
| Lentils – boiled | 18–30 | Vogel bread (honey & oat) | 55 | Bran flakes | 74 |
| Cherries, plums – raw | 22–24 | Rice – white | 56 | Mashed potatoes | 74 |
| Peas – boiled | 22 | Macaroni | 56 | Maize porridge | 74 |
| Milk, skim – whole | 24–40 | Baked beans | 56 | Swiss Rye bread | 74 |
| Grapefruit – raw | 25 | Muesli (Sanitarium) | 57 | Corn chips | 74 |
| Apples, peaches – raw | 28–34 | Weet-bix – bran | 57 | Pumpkin – boiled | 75 |
| Bananas – ripeness | 30–46 | Porridge (Hubbards) | 58 | Doughnut | 75 |
| Smoothie drinks | 30–32 | Rice – long grain | 58 | Grapenuts cereal | 76 |
| Butter/Navy Beans | 30 | White bread & butter | 59 | Coco-Pops cereal | 77 |
| Oranges – raw | 31–48 | Just Right cereal | 60 | Kumara | 77 |
| Dates – dried | 31–36 | Vegetable soup | 60 | Gatorade | 78–89 |
| Apricots – dried | 32 | Bran muffin | 60 | French baguette | 78 |
| Spaghetti | 32–44 | Paw paw | 60 | Rice milk | 79 |
| Carrots – boiled | 33 | Raisin bran | 61 | Broad beans | 79 |
| Pears – raw | 33–41 | Hamburger bun | 61 | Potato Instant mash | 80–96 |
| Peas – cooked | 35–39 | Porridge, organic oats | 63 | White bread – gl free | 80 |
| Milo, full fat milk | 36 | Beetroot | 64 | Pizza – ch & tom | 80 |
| Burgen bread (s&l) | 36 | Muesli – toasted | 65–67 | Fried rice | 80 |
| Ice cream, yoghurt | 36 | Cornflakes & milk | 65 | Rice bubbles | 81 |
| All bran cereal | 38 | Pancakes | 66 | Potato – microwave | 82 |
| Rice – long grain | 38–41 | Beer (Tooheys) | 66 | Oat cereal – instant | 83 |
| Muesli – natural | 40 | Nutrigrain | 66 | Sugar | 84 |
| Mangos | 41 | Raisins | 66 | White bread – wheat | 88 |
| Rye bread | 41–48 | Potato – mashed | 67 | Fruit bars (U Toby) | 90 |
| Apple juice | 41 | Shredded wheat | 67 | Rice cracker | 91 |
| Oat porridge | 42–49 | Fanta | 68 | Rice Milk – low fat | 92 |
| Rice – parboiled | 42 | Pita bread | 68 | Cornflakes (US/UK) | 92–132 |
| Up & Go breakfast | 43–46 | Ice cream (chocolate) | 68 | Potatoes – boiled | 96 |
| Multigrain bread | 43 | Potato (baked) | 69 | Potatoes – baked | 98 |
| Muesli – toasted | 43 | Bagel | 69 | Fruit bar – processed | 99 |
| Sweet corn | 46 | Special K cereal | 69 | Pancakes – buckwheat | 102 |
| Wholegrain breads | 47–51 | Weet-Bix | 69 | Jasmine rice (Thai) | 109 |
| Salmon sushi | 48 | White fibre bread | 69 | Maize porridge | 109 |
| Grapes – raw | 49 | White rice – boiled | 69 | | |

Another interesting reference is *Sugar, the Bitter Truth*, by Professor Lustig on YouTube http://www.youtube.com/watch?v=dBnniua6-oM.

In summary, some practice guidelines:

| Low GI foods: beans, nuts, lentils, meats and fats | High GI foods: white bread and cereals |
| --- | --- |
| Release glucose slowly over time | Release glucose quickly, in spikes |
| Reduce insulin and risk of diabetes | Increase insulin and risk of diabetes |
| Are filling and facilitate weight loss | Are not filling and risk weight gain |
| Improve cholesterol and halve CVD risk | Raise lipids and heart disease |
| Slow ageing and protect from cancer | May accelerate ageing and cancer |
| Generally come from natural food | Generally come from processed food |

## 4. Inflammation

Inflammation is the means by which the body tackles external invaders such as infection, tissue damage and cell death. The immune system keeps the inside calm and ordered by removing damaged tissue and facilitating efficient repair (the police). It also protects us from external attack by bacteria, viruses and poisons (defence force). A healthy immune system has a polite and persuasive police force and a deadly defence force.

Inflammation is the consequence of the immune system swinging into action.

Damage, infection, dead tissue and foreign bodies such as splinters trigger messages that activate the immune system. One of the messengers is histamine, which leaks from the cells and causes redness, swelling and itching. The immune system elevates its activity specific to the trigger. Vaccination against the common cold uses this mechanism. The body is pre-armed with the right immune cell for the expected flu. Immune cells flood the targeted area by leaking through blood vessel walls and 'eating' up the damage.

The entire process of inflammation includes redness, swelling, heat and pain. If minor and quickly controlled, the swelling reduces and the immune reaction is reabsorbed into the body through the blood or lymph. In a major battle, many of the immune cells can die and this results in the formation of pus and spreading infection. The body must seal off this battle damage and remove the dead cells (pus). This is what happens when a pimple bursts.

Early in life we activate the immune system — particularly from breast milk. The exposure of infants to dirt, bugs and community infections leads to further activation of the immune system. This early exposure is essential for the correct functioning of both the 'police' and the 'defence force'. Children brought up in very clean and sterile environments have a higher incidence of asthma and allergy than those exposed to crowded and more natural environments. In addition, there is evidence showing that children treated with antibiotics also have higher rates of asthma and allergy. In this case the police are running amok.

The immune system requires careful arming, maintenance and balancing. Excess inflammation within the body can trigger the inflammatory reactions of asthma, allergy, joint pain and arthritis, irritable bowel, skin conditions, rheumatoid conditions and, of particular concern, the inflammation of fatty plaque in artery walls that causes heart attacks and most strokes. By contrast, if there is not enough inflammation the body is vulnerable to external attack such as viruses and bacteria, or internal attack from cancer cells.

For example, asthma is a massive inflammatory response to cold air or pollens in the airways. The tightened muscle wall and inflammatory response would be appropriate if the lungs were exposed to a seriously toxic gas, but it is inappropriate and an enormous cause of suffering and preventable death when it is triggered by common, unavoidable stimuli. Treatment of asthma involves corticosteroid inhalers, pills and injections that powerfully suppress inflammation.

In the case of heart disease or stroke, it is inflammation that converts stable plaque in the arteries to unstable or vulnerable plaque. Inflammation in the plaque is vulnerable and unstable material that can rupture, like a boil, into the artery (see driver 5: Plaque).

Excess inflammation is also a significant factor in joint and rheumatoid disease, Alzheimer's, muscle pain, abdominal conditions, skin conditions and dental disease. In fact, every tissue in the body can become inflamed and suffer the short-term effects of heat, redness, pain and swelling. The long-term consequences are scar tissue, stiffness and dehydration of tissues.

Inflammation is difficult to measure. An indication can be found from a blood test called sensitive C-reactive protein. It should be very low. Raised levels suggest inflammation and are associated with increased cardiovascular risk. We can also get a measure from the balance between arachidonic acid (AA) and eicosapantenoic acid (EPA). Arachidonic acid comes from vegetable and Omega 6 fats and EPA comes from fish or Omega 3 fats. Symptoms of irritation, pain, swelling, rash, stiffness, asthma abdominal discomfort may give us early signals.

While exercise, relaxation and sleep are key to good immune function, nutrition has many factors worth listing that improve or exacerbate inflammation.

............................................................

## Practice

▷ **Engage with things that decrease inflammation**
Exercise, relaxation and quality sleep
Long chain Omega 3 oils (fish and flaxseed)
Olive oil, vegetables and fruit
Weight loss
Turmeric, ginger
Stretching and massage

▷ **Avoid things that increase inflammation**
Inactivity, distress and disturbed sleep
Short chain vegetable oils (soy, sunflower, corn)
Processed and refined carbohydrates and sugars
Abdominal obesity
Fast foods
Postural pain and fibromyalgia

............................................................

## 5. Plaque

Plaque is generally understood to be the collection of fatty acids, cholesterol, fibrous tissue and inflammatory cells in the artery wall. Called atherosclerosis, it is the underlying process of cardiovascular disease — heart attacks, strokes and other circulatory events. All of these events and the related 'disease' are linked to the deposit of fatty plaque in the arteries. This process damages the endothelium (inner lining) of our arteries, disrupting normal function of the artery. Over time it becomes a fatty streak that can be seen in children and then begins to bulge into the artery space, blocking blood flow. When plaque becomes inflamed it can rupture into the artery provoking a clot that causes a heart attack and most strokes.

Oxidation, low nitric oxide, excess blood glucose, inflammation and the metabolites of distress all increase the vulnerability of the endothelium. Good nitric oxide levels are emerging as a key preventive factor in reducing inflammation, lowering blood pressure, and enhancing sleep and arterial blood flow (performance, cognition and sexual function). It can be increased by regular exercise, relaxation practice, sleep and leafy greens. Caldwell Esselstyn, a cardiovascular surgeon famous for his work with Bill Clinton, has promoted a diet that appears to reverse plaque dramatically.[49] His approach is based on protecting the endothelium of artery walls through a plant-based diet that optimises nitric oxide function.

The early plaque is safe as the obstruction is minimal and the plaque is stable. In vulnerable plaque, inflammation has increased with a risk of rupture. If plaque ruptures, releasing the plaque contents into the blood stream, rapid clotting and thrombus (clot) formation follows. The clot gets stuck at an arterial branch or where the artery narrows. In the coronary arteries of the heart this is called a coronary thrombosis — heart attack. Blood flow to the heart muscle distal to the block stops. The starved heart muscle triggers chest pain and the symptoms of heart attack. In a large blockage the heart muscle simply fails or goes into arrhythmia, leading to sudden death.

Stable plaque on the right can accumulate until it restricts blood flow, causing angina. In this case treatment involves opening the arteries with devices inserted into the blocked part of the artery, or with a bypass graft.

Plaque rupture in the carotid arteries supplying blood to the brain cause strokes. Depending on the size and location of the blockage, there are mild to fatal strokes. Stroke survivors have specific loss of function depending on the location of the blockage. This can be left, right, motor, sensory, speech, and so on. Plaque rupture is the cause of about 75% of strokes. The remainder are ruptures linked to high blood pressure or congenital weakness in the arteries of the brain.

Together, stroke and heart attack remain the single biggest killers and major causes of morbidity. Globally, the two still account for 30% of mortality (preventable death) and morbidity (preventable illness, suffering and loss of function). The cost of cardiovascular disease in the US is estimated at US$500 billion despite an almost 50% decline in the past 30 years. Just under half of the decline is attributed to medical intervention and the rest to lifestyle and risk factor modification.

Other types of plaque also form in the human body. Plaque forms on teeth leading to inflammation of the gums, which may lead to more widespread inflammation. Plaque also forms as part of Alzheimers and in other tissues where proteins are damaged. There is an association between the damage caused by glycation (AGE) and plaque.

••••••••••••••••••••••••••••••••••••••••••••••••••••••••••••••••••

### Practice

▷ Check your family history and consider a CT scan or carotid ultrasound if concerned.

▷ When you check cholesterol, make sure you measure the little atherogenic LDL particles.

▷ Keep your HDL cholesterol high and triglycerides low.

▷ Keep fit and eat well — vegetarian and pescatarian (fish) diets show promise.

▷ Drive your processed carbohydrate intake down.

••••••••••••••••••••••••••••••••••••••••••••••••••••••••••••••••••

## 6. Distress and negative emotion

Distress as described in the death spiral and the associated negative emotions of fear, anger and sadness are strongly associated with increased risk of most preventable diseases. The increased sympathetic tone (distress response) and chemicals such as cortisol contribute to all of the five factors listed above. Both coherence and positivity are strongly linked to good health outcomes and measurable improvements in physiological parameters such as blood pressure, cholesterols, arrhythmias and chronic diseases. We have discussed coherence previously and will address positivity in part four.

The past decade has seen increased attention to distress and negative emotion as a key factor for poor health. Some evidence even shows that trauma in early childhood has serious lifelong consequences.[50] Taking time to activate the vagal brake (parasympathetic system) and to generate an increased number and frequency of positive emotions is at least as important as eating well.

························································

## Practice

▷ Check your distress symptoms again and resolve to overcome them.

▷ Refer to Emotions in part four, Creativity.

▷ Practise relaxation daily.

▷ Savour every positive emotion and optimistic thought.

························································

Over the past decades, the explosion of new research allows you and your doctor to take control of cardiovascular disease and reduce this number one killer. We can, with confidence, say that no one under 75 should succumb to a heart attack or stroke. The same idea holds for reducing diabetes, depression, immune diseases, bowel disease and lung disease. Prevention starts in the womb. Most of us wait for the first chest pain. By that time it is either too late, or it is a grim, uphill battle.

Your key to prevention and vitality is to understand the basic factors that determine vitality or illness and find your own way to master them in your life. As you master these six factors, your natural health and vitality will flourish. This is what your body is marvellously designed to secure.

In summary, here is a list of top ten actions:

1. Stay lean and fit — this benefits mind and emotion as much as your body.

2. Relax each day and sleep well — all systems benefit.

3. Eat between nine and 13 servings of vegetables and fruit a day.

4. Eat fish three times a week or take Omega 3 supplements.

5. Reject processed food containing added sugars, vegetable oils and salt.

6. Cultivate and build positive emotions — body, mind and relationships benefit.
7. Keep HDL cholesterol above 1.5 mmol/l and blood pressure below 115/75.
8. Add beans, soy, nuts, tomatoes, blueberries and garlic to your diet.
9. Enjoy moderate amounts of red wine (its benefit may be overestimated).
10. If at risk, discuss the value of a preventive CT scan or carotid ultrasound.

In the next three chapters we will explore the practical elements of exercise, sleep and nutrition.

## Summary

- ✹ Never underestimate the importance and gift of the human body.
- ✹ Square your function curve.
- ✹ Understand and master the six drivers of dysfunction, disease and early death.
- ✹ Allow your body to flourish.

# Chapter 9

# Hunt and Gather

## The Social Athlete

Humans evolved to run down their prey, climb, dig, gather, carry and fight. It was only through the unique development of our physical abilities that Homo sapiens survived the savannah and emerged to conquer the planet. We have evolved to run or walk an average of 9 to 15 km a day, climb, dig and carry.[51]

By mastering the body, children develop the power of emotion and mind. An active childhood is a stimulus to a happy and successful life. Through life it is physical fitness that takes care of health and supports our ability to work effectively. As we age it is physical fitness that can keep us engaged, active, employable and happy.

Physical fitness is by far the most tangible reflection of resilience. We feel it inside ourselves and in every movement. Others see it in us expressed through our posture and movement. In essence:

- ▶ physical resilience is the opposite of death
- ▶ half a century's research confirms it as the leading solution to chronic disease
- ▶ it is so good for the brain that if it were a pill, we would all be taking it
- ▶ the benefits of activity reach from the womb into very old age
- ▶ physical fitness makes you calmer, richer, sexier and happier
- ▶ high intensity training has surprising benefits including youth, sleep and thinking.

Relaxed activity calms us, vigorous activity energises us, social activity engages enormous passion and connection, and exercise enables and builds the brain and creativity. Exercise can be a passion or a joyous expression of your higher self. Some will work on fitness because they believe it will stop them suffering and some because they love it. Some exercise because they are addicted to the process or the results. Whatever your motivation, this chapter will lay out a practical guide and explain the benefits of your journey.

The body is the most basic reflection of your being. You can touch it, feel it, see it and (mostly) control it. At all stages in life (even in your nineties) the body will respond positively to training. If you fail to master your physical being you will fail to manage your self. Evolution has crafted us to survive and prosper on the planet. Before we could master our mind and social skills, humans had to learn how to hunt, gather and find protection.

The body is made to move. The non-negotiable fact is that active people enjoy better health, wealth and happiness than inactive people. Here, we use the term 'fitness' to embrace all of the components of physical resilience. Each of the five forms of fitness — flexibility, strength, cardiovascular or aerobic, posture and balance, and speed— combines to create functional fitness. This is the ability to enjoy the tasks of life well into old age and to reap the multiple benefits of good health.

Fitness emerges from physical challenge. If the body and its muscles, bones and ligaments are extended, they adapt to meet the increased load. Muscles grow stronger, longer and thicker, bones lay down more calcium, the heart becomes stronger, more blood vessels grow to all trained muscle (including the heart), and the blood delivers more energy and oxygen to the cells. In turn, the cells become more efficient and effective power generators.

In the background, your immune system, hormones and vital neurotransmitters upgrade and reflect a more youthful and resilient physiology. Consequently, these benefits are experienced in every organ and every function of our lives. Specifically, the performance of the brain and mind get a measurable upgrade. Even in older people where brain atrophy is expected, those who exercise not only maintain brain volume and function but can also improve them.

In moderation, all the benefits of exercise increase as one becomes fitter. We respect age, progressive adaptation, adequate rest, variety and enjoyment. Olympic performances tend to extend well beyond moderation, and are better viewed as an extreme form of work. We are learning how various extreme training techniques used in athletes and elite soldiers are being adapted to deliver real benefits for those of us seeking a fulfilling life.

The benefits of exercise are well studied and documented. They include:

- prevention of heart disease, stroke, obesity, diabetes and depression
- maintenance of your optimal body weight
- reduction of blood pressure and pulse rate
- reduced risk of colon cancer
- increase of the levels of good cholesterol (HDL) in the blood
- reduction of bad cholesterol (LDL) and triglycerides
- improvement and maintenance of muscle strength and flexibility
- reduction of calcium loss from bones (preventing osteoporosis)
- improvement of circulation to the heart, muscles and organs
- reduction in stress, which promotes vitality and improves concentration
- improvement in sleep patterns and quality of sleep
- improvement in joint function and the prevention of arthritis
- living a longer and higher quality life
- improved sex life.

The Mayo Clinic (http://www.mayoclinic.com/health/exercise/HQ01676) summarises these benefits as having seven position results:

1. weight control
2. disease combat
3. improved mood
4. boosted energy
5. promotes sleep
6. sparks sex life
7. can be fun.

Clearly, there is every reason to be and stay active. However, be sensible and cautious. Some people have done little over a number of years and a sudden start is likely to cause injury and unnecessary mental stress. If in doubt, discuss your exercise requirements with your doctor (preferably a fit one) or a qualified consultant.

One third of us are inactive and about one third of us are only mildly active. Step one is to ensure that you start to establish a pattern of activity that protects and maintains your health. Focus on your life. Concentrate on benefits, in particular; you will feel better and enjoy life more.

First, we will concentrate on the different components of exercise so we understand the role and practice of flexibility, strength, aerobic fitness, posture and balance, and speed. Second, we will advise how these can be integrated into your fitness plan from basic to more advanced levels. Everyone should exercise for health and functional fitness. You may like to extend the benefits into adventure or competitive sport, or to achieve your dreams. A healthy and active life beyond age 80 is a goal for all of us.

## 1. Flexibility

Stretching is one of the last subjects to be scrutinised by modern science. It has been neglected, poorly taught and incorrectly practised. Eastern schools of physical training, including yoga, tai chi, kung fu, karate and judo, have developed extensive stretching routines as fundamental to the disciplines. It is becoming part of every form of activity today. The yoga boom suggests that there may be many more benefits enjoyed by practitioners. The main benefits of stretching from a medical perspective are performance enhancement and reduction of injury.

Stretching is something built into the behaviours of most creatures, particularly carnivores. It feels good and the body calls for it when we wake up, or feel stiff or uncomfortable. Part of the success of activities that promote stretching is a process of self-awareness. As we stretch, we feel the body, connect our muscles and extend rhythmic breathing.

The masters of stretching, such as experienced yogis, martial artists or gymnasts, have high self-awareness and confidence in their bodies. What they can do is inspiring. Those who take on a stretching discipline quickly comment on the benefits they experience, which include alertness, readiness for the day, relaxation, reduced aches and pains, and more confidence in their bodies, particularly the spine. A well-stretched body holds a relaxed and upright posture, improving physical presence.

For those who suffer from stress, anxiety and muscle tension, stretching is a reliable tool for relaxing, easing muscle tension, calming breathing and settling high blood pressure. Certain stretches can be used to wake up, prepare for sleep, improve digestion, focus the mind and increase emotional energy.

## Practice

Basic stretching requires five to ten minutes every morning. Selected stretches can be used throughout the day to combat fatigue, ease occupational overuse injury, prepare for exercise and cool down. Correct stretching requires skilled personal coaching and should not be attempted casually.

Some knowledge of the basic muscle groups is useful. This should include names, basic action, angle of stretch and opposing muscles. An understanding of the underlying joints and good joint posture is also helpful. When you stretch, you should:

1. Stand tall and straight before starting.
2. Correct all slouching, hunching and asymmetry.
3. Exhale completely and breathe deep into the diaphragm.
4. Make sure you are warm and start gently.
5. Initiate the stretch slowly with soft, even breathing.
6. Take the muscle to a point of stretch, not pain.
7. Breathe into each stretch for a minimum of 20 seconds; 40 seconds is preferable.
8. Keep the opposing muscle contracted (for example, stretch the hamstring, tighten the quad).
9. Stretch equally on both sides.
10. Don't bounce or overstretch.

Get help to understand the basic stretches and to secure good technique: it's an investment that will have lifelong payback. A simple stretch routine is illustrated and is available on our website: www.resiliencei.com/data/media/documents/Resilience%20Stretches.pdf. Most gyms will have experienced instructors and stretching diagrams available.

Figure 22 on pages 122 and 123 outlines the basic stretch routine advocated by The Resilience Institute.

While yoga is not for everyone, it is a very carefully developed discipline with well-designed exercises that can be fun to learn and improve with practice. Alongside the benefits of stretching in yoga, it is also good for balance, breathing, relaxation and strength.

•••••••••••••••••••••••••••••••••••••••••••••••••••••••••••••••••

## 2. Strength

In the past, strength was necessary to hunt, climb, carry and fight. Today we can get by without really lifting anything. Even holding an upright posture, which is necessary to carry objects, has become too hard for many people. Over time the failure to activate the muscles leads to poor control of joints and thence to back, knee, hip, shoulder and neck problems.

The earlier that children develop basic strength of the core support and moving muscles, the easier it is to maintain this strength. If not developed before age 18, it is difficult to build thereafter. A flood of studies is available showing how simple strengthening exercises have an enormous benefit to the wellbeing and functional independence of older people. The cognitive benefits are especially interesting. Strength training builds willpower.

Strength is derived from the muscle fibre. Technically, it is a measure of the muscles' ability to contract against force. The strength we have is determined by genetics and early development. White fibres give speed and fatigue quickly. Red fibres provide endurance. Each person has a unique basic mix that can be shaped by training. Strength peaks around age 20 and declines from the age of 35. Loss of power is also caused by cardiac weakness, muscle atrophy (from illness or disuse), loss of flexibility and scar tissue. Most will be familiar with how hard athletes work to develop and maintain strength. Older athletes can prolong their careers provided they maintain their strength.

Naturally, some strength is gained from aerobic activity, but the full potential of the muscle requires forceful contraction against a weight that causes fatigue within eight to 12 repetitions. Traditional weight training has focused on working one muscle at a time in this way, but many more options have become available, and more will emerge as interest develops in this area.

## Guide to Stretching

Welcome to a philosophy of body maintenance. Most animals (watch your cat) stretch each morning, skilfully stretching out each muscle. People have forgotten this simple and natural skill which mobilises joints and tendons. We recommend you do the following stretches **every morning for life**. A habit of stretching is safe, and will prevent injury, improve posture, correct muscle balance and soothe arthritic pain.

Figure 22: Basic Stretch Routine

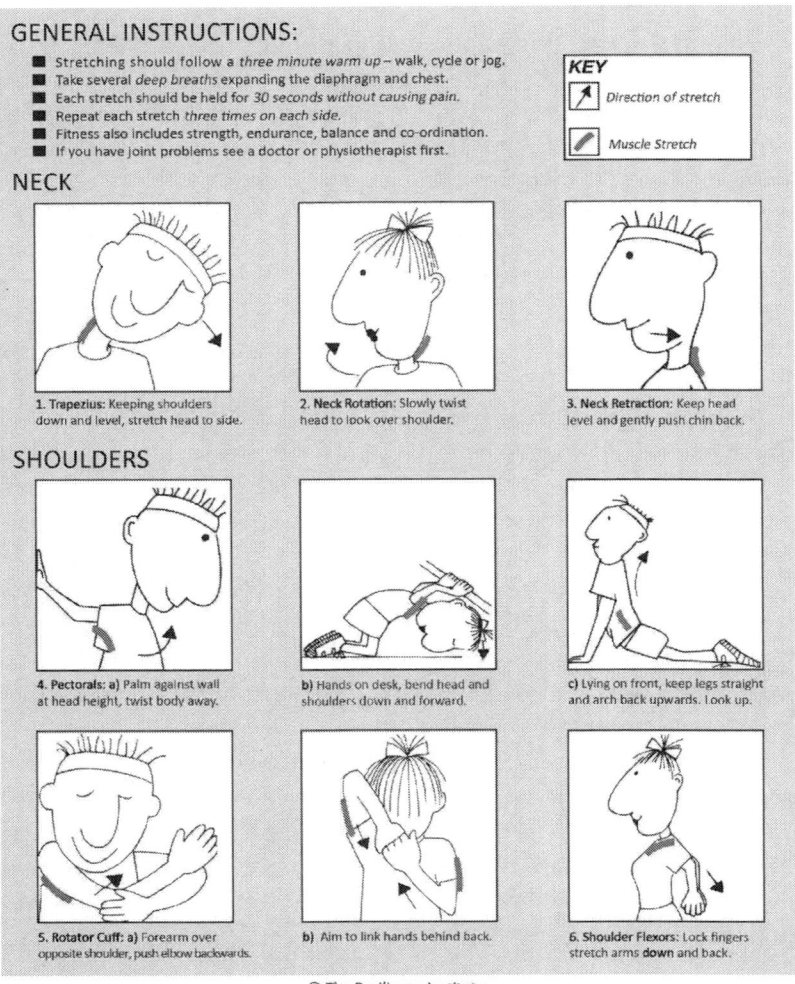

© The Resilience Institute
Website: www.resiliencei.com

## BACK

**7. Side Flexion:** Legs apart, bend sideways sliding hand down thigh.

**8. Rotation: a)** Feet facing away and firmly planted, rotate and touch wall.

**b.** Lying on back, legs bent and together, lower to side.

## HIPS AND LOWER LIMBS

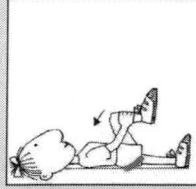 

**9. Gluteals:** Lie on back and bring knee over chest. Add pressure to opposite side.

**10. Ilio-tibal Band:** Sit with foot against opposite thigh. Pull knee to chest and keep back straight.

**11. Hamstring:** Leg raised on bench, straighten leg and then back. Hips square.

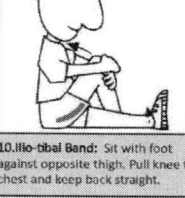   

**12. Iliopsoas:** Push hips forward and down. Keep hips square and stomach tight.

**13. Quadriceps:** Pull foot up behind. Push knee backwards, keep belly sucked in.

**14. Adductors:** Sit with soles of feet together and push knees to floor.

## CALF

**15. Gastrocnemius:** Keep leg straight while leaning hips forward.

**16. Soleus and Achilles Tendon:** Bend knee and push latter down and forward.

## BALANCE

Stand in bare feet on one leg and try to balance with eyes closed for 30 seconds on each foot.

With eyes closed reach slowly up on to toes attempting to "touch the sky". Keep stomach tight and back flat.

© The Resilience Institute
Website: www.resiliencei.com

The Centre for Disease Control (CDC 2011: http://www.cdc.gov) in the US lists the following benefits of strength training.

- Reduction of the impact of diseases and chronic conditions, including arthritis (43% reduction in pain and increased function), diabetes, osteoporosis, obesity, back pain and depression.
- Restoration of balance and reduction of falls with simple strength and balance training.
- Strengthening of bone with reduced fractures has been shown in women over 50.
- Proper weight maintenance. Strength training produces muscle mass, which is active and consumes calories. This can increase metabolic rate by 15%.
- Improved glucose control. Strength training dramatically improves glucose control. One study showed 16 weeks of strength training is as effective as taking diabetes medication. The participants were stronger, gained muscle, lost body fat, experienced less depression and felt more self-confident.
- Healthy state of mind. Strength training provides similar improvements in depression as anti-depressant medications. Self-confidence and self-esteem are better, improving overall quality of life.
- Sleep improvement. The sleep benefits of strength training are comparable to treatment with medication, but without the side effects. People fall asleep more quickly, sleep more deeply, awaken less often and sleep longer.
- Healthy heart tissue. Cardiac patients gained not only strength and flexibility but also aerobic capacity when they did strength training three times a week.
- The American Heart Association recommends strength training to reduce the risk of heart disease and as a therapy for patients in cardiac rehabilitation.

While strength is a natural component of an active life, many of us are actually quite weak and fragile (even young people). As we get older, we should seek qualified assistance. Working in a good quality gym or with a qualified instructor is a smart investment. Good technique will increase the benefit and reduce injury.

There are many options available, including gyms with free weights or high-tech machines, home exercise gyms or weights, body weight systems such as the TRX trainer (a simple strap system, see www.trxtraining.com) and simple sit-ups, push-ups, pull-ups and squats. My own preference is to vary my outdoor exercise to include hills, rapids and waves and to complement these with simple floor routines such as sit-ups, push-ups and core strength. I have recently added the TRX trainer, which is easily packed into a corner of a travel bag.

Remember, any strenuous activity, from hill climbing to lifting and digging, will contribute to strength. Make it easy for your children to do these activities naturally. Tree climbing, digging in sandpits, lifting and throwing stones, jumping and building things are part of the joyful underpinnings of strength.

## Practice

A strength exercise is a short, firm contraction of a muscle group followed by a slower, smooth and controlled extension. For example, one would do a push-up or sit-up quickly, hold for a second, then lower slowly with control before starting again. Ideally, eight to 12 repetitions should exhaust the muscles being used. Holding a half-contracted position such as a squat, biceps lift or sit-up until the muscle fails is another simple option.

Pay attention to your posture by doing the following:

▷ align your feet, knees and hips with a balanced stable stance

▷ use the stomach muscles to support your spine and pelvis

▷ hold your spine upright

▷ keep your shoulders back (shoulder blades pulled towards the mid spine)

▷ hold your head upright with relaxed neck

▷ breathe out on contraction and in on relaxation.

If done correctly and with the correct equipment, one set of exercises with up to 12 repetitions will have a powerful effect. Repeated sets of repetitions should be done with caution. Remember, the muscles need at least a day to repair the damage and reinforce muscle contractility. Therefore, three sessions per week is plenty. Some believe that one session per week will comfortably maintain and slowly build strength.

Keep these principles in mind if you are using more natural strength work such as gardening, heavy manual labour or climbing hills. When walking downhill be particularly careful to control the landing leg. Keep the knees over the middle toes and avoid the 'knock-kneed' look. Take a rest if they do collapse or if you cannot brake smoothly.

A good routine is well articulated by Dr Jeffry Life (www.drlife.com) in his two books *The Life Plan* (2011) and *Mastering the Life Plan* (2013).

·······························································

## 3. Aerobic (Cardiovascular) Fitness

Aerobic fitness is a measure of the body's ability to absorb, carry and burn oxygen to provide energy for muscular activity. It depends on the functioning of the lungs, heart, blood, arteries and muscle cells, and the body's ability to remove waste products. As we move faster in any activity, the muscle cells powering the limbs have to contract and relax at an increased rate. This increases the rate at which ATP (adenosine triphosphate) is used.

ATP is produced in the mitochondria from the combustion of glucose and oxygen. The glucose is broken down from glycogen stored in muscle cells. Glycogen in turn comes from carbohydrate foods via glucose in the blood. Oxygen is extracted by the lungs from inhaled air, attaches to haemoglobin in the blood and is then transferred to a cell. In the muscle cell, aerobic metabolism burns oxygen and glucose to produce energy. When glucose is in short supply, the muscles will also burn fat. Athletes are exploring how to increase the amount of fat oxidation because we have far more energy available as fat than as glucose. This requires a very low carbohydrate diet and the adaptation of the body and brain to burn ketones.

Aerobic activity, from walking to running, swimming, biking and paddling, engages this metabolism gradually, from rest up until about 85% of your maximum power output. Aerobic activity thus stimulates the heart, lungs, arteries, blood, muscles and energy-producing mitochondria. When repeated, the stimulus drives positive adaptations in all of the following systems.

- The heart becomes stronger and more efficient — resting heart rate and blood pressure reduce.
- New arteries grow into heart and muscle.
- The lungs are exercised and the diaphragm becomes more efficient (second wind).
- Exercise can reduce asthma and other respiratory conditions.
- The blood adapts to carry more oxygen and remove carbon dioxide.
- Training on low carbohydrate–high fat diets helps the body adapt to fat burning.
- Trained muscles become larger, stronger and more efficient.
- ATP is produced more efficiently as the mitochondria become more active and numerous.
- The mitochondria learn how to metabolise fat in order to save glucose for longer distance and greater power.
- Aerobic activity increases the mitochondrial numbers in the brain building will, mood and memory.
- Ligaments, tendons and bone are also stimulated and reshape themselves into a stronger and more durable skeleton.
- Aerobic fitness reduces the risk of injury and increases the likelihood of pain-free function in old age.

## Practice

The best proxies are pulse and breathing rates. When you cannot complete a ten-word sentence, you have shifted into high intensity work. Slow down. When you start to think about sex, work or e-mail, speed up!

Those who require a more precise measure can learn to monitor pulse. It is the closest thing we have to a rev. counter, and quickly gives the driver feedback as to the health of the system. Subtract your age from 220 and train at about 75% of this. Push up from this and you will get faster and burn more glucose. Drop back from this and you tend to build endurance and burn fat. This is shown below for a 45-year old with a resting pulse of 60.

| Heart rate | Work Intensity | % Max | Benefits |
|---|---|---|---|
| 170–180 | Maximum speed | 100% | Speed, athletic adaptation, willpower — needs caution |
| 145–155 | Strenuous | 85% | Speed, willpower, strength, sleep |
| 120–140 | Moderate | 75% | Cardiovascular fitness, endurance, relaxation |
| 110–120 | Light | 65% | Health, pleasure, fat burning |
| 60 | Rest for unfit | | Recovery |
| 45 | Rest for fit and trained | | Accelerated recovery |

Taking your pulse at the neck, below the angle of the jaw, or at the wrist, is easy. Simply count the pulse over a period of time and multiply to get a figure of beats per minute. For example, count for six seconds x ten = beats per minute. Pulse monitors are now an affordable alternative and many exercisers will use a Polar or Garmin device.

Include at least one rest day as part of cardiovascular fitness. This gives the body time to replenish fuel reserves within the muscle and also time to heal the muscle damage that occurs as a result of exercise.

If motivation is lacking, grab a training buddy (the dog won't argue!), but most importantly make sure you enjoy what you are doing. Those with a competitive spirit will find it essential to train with friends (or enemies). Exercise for fitness must have a high fun-score and stimulate (rather than reduce) libido and available energy.

Finally, chose an activity that suits you. Seek pleasure, friendship, nature and safety.

| Activity | Aerobic value | Safety |
|---|---|---|
| Running | High | Good feet, knees and shoes |
| Cycling | High | Accidents common |
| Cross-country skiing | Very high | Skill and snow necessary |
| Swimming | High | Need balance, flexible shoulders |
| Paddling: canoe, stand up | High | Good shoulders and hamstrings |
| Walking | Low unless brisk/hills | Stride and use good shoes |

## 4. Posture and Balance

The way we hold and balance our bodies in all situations, from sitting to challenging skill-based sport, determines much of our mental, emotional and physical state. Many of us are clueless as to how to master the basic positions of life and activity. As a consequence, we breathe poorly, damage joints — particularly the spine — and present as disengaged. Correction is relatively easy to achieve. Let us take a look at just a few of the critical roles played by posture:

- ▶ basic protection of spine and joints — sitting, standing and moving
- ▶ holding the head in a balanced position to optimise focus of the senses
- ▶ structural support for full, relaxed diaphragmatic breathing
- ▶ support and proper position of heart, abdominal organs and pelvis
- ▶ health of bladder, bowel, prostate and sexual organs
- ▶ physical presence signals your well-being, confidence and competence — critical for leadership
- ▶ support for tasks of modern life — using computers, prolonged sitting, repetitive work
- ▶ alignment of bones, ligaments, joints, tendons and muscles in all activities
- ▶ basic communication of emotional signals and orchestration of responses
- ▶ awareness of body position reduces falls and injuries, and aids decision-making
- ▶ the support of spiritual practices such as meditation and breath control.

Most Eastern physical and spiritual practices work with posture extensively. Interest and opportunity to correct our slow start in the West is now abundant through yoga, Pilates, gyms and floor exercises.

As a simple experiment, sit upright on a bench with a perfectly vertical spine from coccyx to head. See how long you can maintain this position. Most people ache and collapse within five minutes — thus we slump in chairs for a good eight hours per day. Endemic back, neck, hip, knee and shoulder pain is our reward. As we age, the bladder and bowel leak, the spine collapses and the hips fracture. The longer we live, the more poor postural habits will increasingly compromise life.

Once bad postural habits have set in, they are challenging to correct. We develop a chronic weakness associated with a lengthening or shortening of the postural muscles. They begin to function abnormally and we rely on the muscles of action, ligaments and joints to support us. These structures become worn and abused. By this stage, the brain has learned a range of incorrect firing patterns to get you through a normal day. Pain is a probable, common outcome.

..........................................................................

## Practice

Periodically, pay careful attention to maintaining a good posture. This requires concentration and awareness. Regularly check in with your body. Refresh your sitting posture, balance your stance and focus on how you use your body to lift, carry and bend. Move frequently. Get up and walk about. Stretch in your chair or against a wall. Balance on one foot for a time during daily tasks. If you have chronic pain or are unclear on the instructions, seek help. Physiotherapy, yoga and Pilates are the most common sources of guidance.

### Get a standing desk for work

This is a wonderful solution that is becoming popular. Standing for work can add up to two years of life. Standing engages many more muscles than sitting, and thus burns calories and maintains postural strength. I recommend standing barefoot. It takes some time to get fit for standing. Take regular breaks and move about and sit.

### Holding the head and neck

The head, with 1.5 kg of brain and a large chunk of bone, is a heavy load for our relatively long and thin necks. Correctly aligned, it sits lightly balanced on the top of the spine, causing minimal distress to the deep postural muscles of the neck. In this state the active neck muscles can work lightly and accurately to align vision, hearing, smell and the gestures of facial communication.

A common error is allowing the head to push forward, creating a hump at the base of the neck and a sharp notch of extension at the top. Hanging forward, the head places huge stress on the neck muscles and shoulder support. The strain on these muscles and supporting ligaments results in headaches, fatigue and neck pain that over time refer to the shoulders and upper spine (mid-back).

The correction is to lengthen the back of the neck, lifting the back of the head and tucking the chin in while maintaining space between the chin and chest. If it creates a double chin you are overdoing it. Standing with your back to a wall and using the muscles to pull the lower and upper spine flat against the surface is a safe way to self-correct.

Over time the forward-head position causes chronic shortening and inflammation in the trapezius and levator scapulae muscles. This is felt as painful nodules around the shoulder blades. The entire neck is shortened and normal rotation, extension and side flexion are restricted. Massage can provide temporary relief.

### Open shoulders
When the shoulders slump forward and down, the muscles of the chest shorten and the muscles controlling the shoulder blades weaken. This can lead to a humpback. The mid-back aches and the shoulders are vulnerable to injury. Breathing becomes tight. Round shoulders are often seen in people with asthma and may be a physical sign of depression or low self-esteem.

The key to correcting this posture is to hold the shoulder blades back and down so that the inner edge of the shoulder blade hugs the thoracic spine. The military position is an exaggeration of this, but is still a good exercise. Good shoulder blade control is critical to all upper body activity from work to sport. Seek help if you have problems. Deep tissue massage of the strained muscles can provide relief.

### Lower back function
There are many causes of lower back problems. Most are associated with stiffness and weakness of the lower spine. Poor sitting posture is a primary reason, but it is also often secondary to tight hip flexors and hamstrings or weak lower abdominal and spinal extensor muscles. Among the consequences are pain, stiffness, an inability to bend and a sense of insecurity when moving.

Moving, standing or sitting upright is the primary correction exercise. It should feel as if you are lifting the lower spine out of the pelvis. At the same time, the lower belly muscles that wrap around the lower part of the abdomen need to be lightly contracted. Think about pulling the belly button back towards the spine. Stretching the hamstrings, hip flexors and quadriceps can help. Strengthening spinal extension — such as lying flat on the belly and lifting the legs and shoulders — can be very helpful. For many the combination of strengthening abdominals and spinal extensors will lead to huge improvements.

*Pelvic stability*
Think of the pelvis as a bowl of oysters. You need to keep it stable and balanced. Weakness can lead to a potbelly hanging over the belt. The belt line will angle forward (the oysters are sloshing out the front). In other cases, the butt muscles are flat and weak. The pelvis is a critical link between the spine (and upper body) and the legs. It has to be firm and balanced for standing and all activity. Golf, tennis, running and garden work require a strong, stable and balanced pelvis.

To correct, stand with the knees slightly bent above the line of the second toe. Lightly contract the buttock and abdominal muscles. Good strong abdominals make a big difference. Keep the oysters in the bowl. Remember that the pelvic organs are literally soft and vulnerable, like oysters. They need protection. Get some assistance if you don't understand.

*Pelvic floor stability*
Thin sling muscles run under and support the pelvic organs. These muscles support the bowel, bladder, prostate and sex organs and control of the apertures. Collapsed pelvic floor muscles result in incontinence (stool and urine), haemorrhoids (bowel wall slides out the anus) and reduced sexual satisfaction.

Men can learn to contract and lift the anus and women to contract and lift the vagina. Ideally it is the perineum (just in front of the anus) that should be lifted. Do not be shy of learning through touch. The short- and long-term benefits cannot be underestimated.

*Strong knees*
Weak knees are easily spotted as someone runs towards you. The knees roll inward creating a knock-kneed look. It is the primary cause of most knee problems, from runner's knee (patello-femoral pain) to dislocated kneecaps and major joint disruptions. Commonly, the quadriceps group is tight, the inner knee muscles are weak and the feet roll inwards. Activity of almost any kind with this alignment will cause excess wear, pain and damage under abnormal loads.

Good supportive shoes, knee extensions and controlled knee bends with careful quadricep stretching will ease discomfort and correct the problem. As in all posture issues, this is a lifelong discipline.

### Balance

Attempt to stand on one leg with your eyes closed for 30 seconds. Count the number of times you need to make a correction with the other foot or your hand. One or two corrections every 30 seconds is okay, but more indicates that your proprioception is poor. Proprioception or internal balance is supported by feedback from a rich network of neural signals from skin, ligaments, muscles and tendons. The inner canals of the ear are also critical. When the eyes are closed this reflex should ideally operate automatically, but most of us have to relearn this by consciously using the brain.

Working on proprioception dramatically reduces injury (up to 80% in some large studies). Proprioception training has become embedded in exercise for older people as there is a very strong correlation between proprioception, reduced falls and improved cognitive performance. There is some evidence that decision-making can improve with this practice. As a hunter, we need to know exactly where the body is before making the decision about where to move (think of a cat preparing to pounce). Healthy ageing specialists use this test as a primary marker of neurological age. We should all be able to balance firmly on one foot, with eyes closed, for 30 seconds each side. Do this every day (it's easy with your standing desk).

Posture is challenging. Be sure to get the necessary help if you need it. Yoga is very helpful.

## 5. High Intensity Training

Exercise research and practice is rapidly embracing high intensity training — also referred to as speedwork. The long, slow aerobic run was the basis of fitness research for many years. As we now know this activates the cardiovascular system and slow-twitch red fibres of muscles. When we activate higher levels of intensity we push the cardiovascular system to its limit, challenge anaerobic energy systems and activate the fast-twitch white fibres.

Towards the mid-1980s, athletics coaches started to notice the benefits of intense training sessions that focused on shorter bursts at greater speed or power output. Runners called this a 'fartlek' and cyclists did hill work. Now almost all sports engage high intensity training a couple of days a week to secure better performances all around. Watch how pool swimmers train in short bursts varying from 25 m to 200 m, with short recovery breaks.

More recently, it has been noticed that the general health benefits of high intensity training seem to dwarf the benefits of long, slow aerobic sessions. Stephen Boutcher from the University of New South Wales has produced some interesting research on this. Under the name of High Intensity Intermittent Exercise,[52] he lists the following benefits:

- increased aerobic and anaerobic fitness that is more quickly secured
- increased insulin sensitivity preventing and controlling type 2 diabetes
- accelerated abdominal and subcutaneous fat loss
- increased adrenaline and noradrenaline levels triggering fat release
- increased growth hormone levels — people pay good money for this
- better sleep and better cognition.

Over recent years a flood of studies has reinforced the idea. Protocols vary dramatically and there will be lots more to learn, but the lesson is simple: sprint and recovery routines over about 30 minutes have surprising benefits. If you want quick payback on the time you invest in exercise, this is the answer. You will feel your fitness accelerate within two weeks. You will lose weight much faster, improve your mental state, increase your energy and sleep better. In the background, you will reverse ageing effects and prevent diabetes.

## Practice

Make sure you have basic flexibility, strength, aerobic fitness and posture/balance. Warm up and stretch for at least ten minutes prior to high intensity training to reduce injury and discomfort. During the 'sprint' phase you will be extending your muscles, heart and lungs to between 85% and 95% of your maximum. The bursts can be from eight seconds to five minutes, depending on your fitness. Each burst should be followed by a low intensity recovery period of the same length or more. Studies have recently shown that a one-minute burst of high intensity training per day can secure most of the benefits of exercise.

Make sure you are wide-awake and alert. My preference is to minimise loud music and make sure that you are tuned into your body and your technique. Few have the tenacity to do it alone, so joining a class or group will help.

Work up to about 30 minutes of sprint and recovery work as your body gets used to it. One can start on a stationary cycle with short bursts of eight seconds going fast and a 12-second recovery before the next sprint. If you are a walker, you can add 100 metres of fast walking or running to every 200 metres of normal pace (recovery).

The idea can be applied to almost any activity. My favourites include surfing, tennis and chasing the dog. Aim to increase the effort in each sprint to the maximum you can achieve and then try to relax and recover as deeply as you can in the recovery phase.

••••••••••••••••••••••••••••••••••••••••••••••••••••••••••••

High intensity training reminds the body that you still have to hunt for your food and run from your enemies. This is simply natural activity that you see in the wild in most apes, ungulates, predators and rodents. Speed provides enormous advantages when food and other resources are rare and the environment is uncertain.

It may be that the cognitive effort of repeatedly pushing to maximum effort works as a mental exercise. We will return to attention and willpower in the chapter on Mind.

To optimise your chances of success:
- ▶ select activities and environments that appeal to you
- ▶ find a group of friends or a club to provide social connection
- ▶ set family goals such as a walking or beach holiday
- ▶ find playfulness in your exercise — competition, fun or adventure.

## Recommendation for action
### Novice
- ▶ Ask your doctor for a preventive health check. It may be useful to go to a specialist prevention expert (executive health clinics or a sports doctor) to make sure that you get advice suited to an active life.

- Join a gym, yoga studio, walking club or bootcamp and commit to three sessions per week for a minimum of six weeks. Be very clear that you are a beginner and ask for the support you need to build a basic understanding of what you are getting into.
- Every morning do a couple of stretches, ten push-ups and ten sit-ups followed by a 20-minute brisk walk. Try to do this five days a week, as it will take less time than going to a gym or club.
- Play your favourite sport at least twice a week and add in the stretches, balance exercises, push-ups and sit-ups on days you do not play.

**Goals:** save life, lose weight, have fun, sleep better, reduce pain.

## Aspirant

- You are building on the basics of the novice, so make sure you are practising at the novice level first. It is important to have a basic practice.
- Switch on your mind and get curious. Read some books, get a coach, see a physiotherapist and start to learn a bit more about your body and exercise.
- Consider carefully the benefits you are seeking, as this stage is massively enhanced by having some short- and medium-term goals. Perhaps consider a recreational race (swim, bike, run or mountain climb) or a target body shape.
- Let your gym instructor or coach know you are looking to step up your level of fitness and ask for a structured plan to include all five forms of fitness described above.
- Long-term success will require smart scheduling. Your exercise is now a part of your daily life and must be in your diary. Plan with family, friends and work.
- A little competition will help massively. Join a recreational club and enter some competitions with a group of people whose company you enjoy.

**Goals:** a much better life, looking and feeling good, feeling calm, being productive and happy.

## Expert

- Your basics must be well grounded and your training plan embraces all five components of fitness into your week. You must periodise your year into phases to build capacity, peak for races and rest. Variety is important.

- Your physical life is competing with your work, family, bank account and bad habits. You are addicted but gain huge pleasure, animation and social connection.

- You have become opinionated on how to exercise and non-exercisers may find you tiresome or intimidating. Your training group will talk endlessly about the finer points of specific activities.

- A competitive component — against others or simply self-improvement — is key. Regardless of age, your intention is to improve your times, expertise or challenge. A coach, skills course or complex adventure is really helpful.

- You may well have become a 'self-quantifier', using heart rate monitors, GPS devices, SleepTrackers, brain trainers and relaxation biofeedback.

- You are spending a lot of money on equipment and training support. If you are obsessive, take a month off your primary activity at least once a year.

- Whether competing at 20 or at 70, there is nothing like being in peak physical condition. You can do so much more with your life. It is the best drug you can take — but it's not free at this level.

### Summary

- Exercise improves your life, work and happiness.
- Understand the basic components of fitness.
- Get started on a simple discipline.
- Step it up gradually.
- Lock fitness into your life.

# Chapter 10

# Sleep

## Time, Clock, Quality

Sleep, once such a natural and obvious reality of life, has become a vast subject of study and research. Sleep problems and fatigue are a leading source of frustration, anguish, loss of productivity and health risk. Sleep disruption destroys resilience. At the physical, emotional and cognitive levels, we are seriously compromised if we do not get a good night's sleep on a regular basis.

In building resilience, sleep is often the first priority to secure. In our training, questions about sleep are more numerous than any other topic. It is a very common concern. Studies suggest that about 25–35% of the population have serious sleep disruption. About 70% of our clients are concerned about sleep.

Sleep problems can manifest in different ways, including:

- difficulty falling sleep
- interrupted sleep
- early waking and inability to get back to sleep
- sleep phase delay (fall asleep late, struggle to get up) or advance (asleep early, up early)
- sleep apnoea (blocked breathing while snoring)
- sleep deprivation through reduced hours and rhythm
- breathing difficulty: asthma, heart failure, sinus blocking
- oversleeping (more than eight hours as an adult)

- young children disrupting sleep
- environmental issues: noise, heat, light and electromagnetic radiation.

While we might feel unique, there are consistent patterns and 'rules' that underpin a good night's sleep. Many sleep problems can be solved or at least significantly improved by recognising your pattern and following some simple corrective actions. However, some sleep issues are complex and serious. If these steps don't work, follow up with a sleep expert.

Given our obsession with productivity and 24/7 lifestyles, it is reasonable to ask: why do humans sleep and why do we need so much relative to a dolphin or giraffe? There is reasonable evidence to support eight evolutionary alternatives.

1. No good reason.
2. To avoid nocturnal predators that are much more dangerous to us at night.
3. Energy conservation given limited food supply.
4. Allow the body and brain to rest and recovery.
5. Improve our long-term memory.
6. To resolve complex problems.
7. To gain deeper insight into issues.
8. To help us regulate emotion.

Before you advertise your capacity to survive on five hours' sleep, consider the characteristics of sleep deprivation:

- fatigue, sleepiness and a fall in performance
- concentration decreases
- memory deteriorates
- mood disturbances including irritability, depression and anxiety
- poor decision-making and risk-taking behaviour (especially teens)
- loss of facial expressiveness interferes with social interaction
- cardiovascular disease and diabetes
- increased accidents: 20–30% increase in road accidents
- obesity increases driven by appetite disturbance

- decreased conscious regulation of destructive emotions — anger, fear, sadness
- increased risk of infection; up to three times the risk of contracting a cold virus
- increased anxiety with reduced slow wave sleep.

Your life is seriously diminished without good sleep discipline. The consequences in modern society affect all age groups, health, learning, families, workplaces, road safety and social engagement. If children's learning, social coherence and business productivity is important, a good night's sleep really matters.

> 12 May 2014: Society has become "supremely arrogant" in ignoring the importance of sleep, leading researchers have told the BBC's Day of the Body Clock. Scientists from Oxford, Cambridge, Harvard, Manchester and Surrey universities warn cutting sleep is leading to "serious health problems". They say people and governments need to take the problem seriously. Cancer, heart disease, type-2 diabetes, infections and obesity have all been linked to reduced sleep.[53]

Where performance is critical, such as with pilots, elite soldiers, athletes and air traffic controllers, sleep is very carefully managed. Errors are very expensive and potentially fatal, so there is a stack of research on the importance of sleep. The significant portion of workers doing shiftwork has also been a stimulus to research.

In this section we will try to keep it simple and practical so that parents, students, adults and older people can make better decisions about sleep management.

Imagine you have had a challenging and satisfying day. You are tired in body and mind, and you go to bed at a reasonable time. As your head sinks into the pillow, your body relaxes with a pleasurable exhalation. Just as you savour the feeling of deep relaxation, your mind goes quiet, drifts and drops into an unbroken seven-and-a-half hours of sleep. Next thing you come to consciousness in the dawn light, refreshed and ready to go.

This is the goal.

## The Biology of Sleep

The first step is to understand the basics of human sleep.[54] Three systems govern sleep: sleep requirement (S for sleep need) refers to how much sleep we require, circadian rhythm alignment (C for clock) refers to the timing of sleep, and sleep quality (U for ultradian rhythm) describes the components and timing of optimal sleep.

### Sleep Requirement

The first system (S for sleep need) is our daily requirement for sleep to sustain optimal function. Newborns need between 12 and 18 hours, toddlers about 12 hours and teenagers 9 to 10 hours. Adult requirements are still being debated. Most authorities are suggesting 7 to 8 hours per night. The average adult today sleeps for 7.2 hours. Sleeping too little or too much has health, wellbeing and performance risks. Problems with metabolism, obesity, diabetes, heart disease, or diminished emotional intelligence and brain function are just some risks of sleeping too little or too much.

Quality or sleep continuity is a critical factor in our cognitive performance. There is evidence that at times in the past we have slept in two shifts: one before and one after midnight. This may work for some. Most other recommendations, such as the four-hour cycle, should be restricted to people doing heroic tasks such as sailing around the world.

Estimates are that in our hyper-stimulated society we are sleeping 30–60 minutes less than we used to. Sleep debt can accumulate over time and will increase negative consequences. Some research claims that the average adult misses a full night of sleep per week. Studies in rodents have shown that when deprived of sleep in the way that many humans are today, up to 25% of brain cells simply die (and don't recover). Occasional sleep deprivation is clearly normal through evolution. We can repay sleep debt effectively. Within a couple of days the body will recoup the deep and dreaming sleep that it needs to function well. However, there is evidence of a long-term cost.

For practical purposes, estimate your sleep need based on what works best for you. It is likely to be between 7 and 8 hours. Experiment with shorter and longer sleeps. Explore what happens when you go camping and limit unnatural light and stimulation. Each of us will have an optimal time. The length of time is particularly important for school-age children and teenagers. Too little or too much reduces measures of cognitive performance.

Individually, we grossly underestimate how tired we are and the extent of our compromised performance. Repeated studies have shown that we believe we are much more functional than we are. This is a serious blind spot in a world that is fast moving, complex and uncertain. Humans need their sleep. Be humble and sort this out.

## Circadian Alignment

The second system (C) is linked through our genes to the cycles of day and night. Humans are diurnal creatures. Since primates moved into the trees around 60 million years ago, we have been governed by the circadian clock. During the day we are adapted to living in a colourful, three-dimensional world of light. At night our senses are limited and we are vulnerable to predation and injury. In contrast, many predators have very different clocks. A lion can sleep for 20 hours a day, mostly in daylight, but is a sophisticated, lethal hunter at night.

The circadian cycle is the primary biological rhythm that paces sleep, alertness and the cycles of deep sleep, dream sleep, appetite, digestion, immune function, hormone release and activity. The human cycle is just over 24 hours. In larks (early wakers) it tends to be closer to 24.2 hours, and in owls (late wakers) may be up to 24.9 hours. These differences are largely governed by our clock genes. The extra bit (over 24 hours) allows for adaptation as we migrate and accommodate the daylight changes through summer and winter.

In human evolution, the morning blue light around sunrise resets the clock to 24 hours each day. When we live without light the reset fails and the circadian cycle 'free runs' forward. We wake up about 30 minutes later each day, becoming increasingly desynchronised. The same thing happens when we sleep in on weekends or travel west. On Monday, or travelling back westward, we find ourselves deeply jet lagged.

Figure 23 shows a rough guide to the circadian rhythm. We are warm, active and alert during the day and cool, dark and quiet at night. Temperature drops to its lowest about 4 a.m. when we begin to release cortisol, warm up and elevate blood pressure to prepare for the day. The blue light before dawn is a key signal to reset the circadian clock. Light stimulates melanopsin in the retina, which in turn activates the suprachiasmatic nucleus (SCN) in the brain. The SCN is our central clock. A central clock reset at dawn aligns all the peripheral clocks. Most cells have a clock system.

Figure 23: The Human Circadian Rhythm

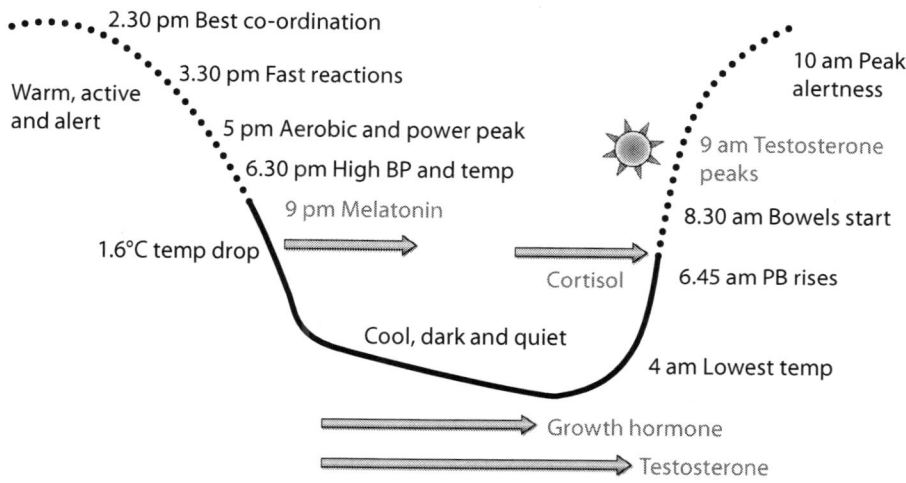

When in synchrony, the circadian system operates efficiently and in tight alignment. Hormones, temperature, digestion, repair, cognition and physical performance are optimised. When we wake up for blue light two hours after lowest body temperature (about 6 a.m.) our circadian cycle is synchronised and human biology is optimised. It is easier to get up and be productive during the day. Our brain waves operate in the higher alertness bands of alpha and beta waves. Life rocks.

Many factors, including physical and cognitive fatigue and the reduced light and temperature of the evening, help us prepare for sleep. Melatonin release helps sleep preparation and the cooling required to fall asleep. Adenosine builds up through the day and appears to signal the need for sleep. Adenosine is removed by sleep.

Finally, sleep and wakefulness operate on a flip-flop mechanism. As we head to sleep a wave of biological and environmental changes secure the 'flop' into sleep. If the system is synchronised, sleep is hard to avoid without radical stimulation. As we approach dawn, another wave of biological and environmental changes 'flip' us to wakefulness.

Human life has been governed by light. Every morning, survival demanded we get up. The blue light of dawn kept the clock honest. After telling a few stories around the fire (yellow light), we got bored and went to sleep somewhere safe. There was plenty of time to sleep (S) and no disruption of circadian rhythm (C).

Enter the 21st century. We have 24/7 light, bright devices, connectivity, competition and unlimited stimulation. This hyper-stimulation would be quite incomprehensible to our ancestors. Imagine your teenager in bed after you fall asleep — he or she is glued to laptop, smartphone or iPad. Bright blue light beams into the eye and the body is soaked in electromagnetic radiation. Messages and updates stream in from different applications and online shopping, porn, violence, gaming and gambling is a touch away.

### Case study: The tragedy of the broken clock

Our heroine is tired and sleep deprived (broken S). She slept in this morning and feels 'very stressed' about an exam/friends/a fingernail. Her biology is desynchronised. Adenosine is high. The fatigue is real. Bright light, loud music and the digital screen beaming images of desirable items and the hyper-competitive chatter of her school friends is one hell of a 'wake signal'. Wake maintenance overdrive kicks in and she is ready to pump through to 1 a.m.

At 1.05 a.m. she is lying in bed, checks her messages one more time and wishes she could fall asleep. She is literally sick with exhaustion. Her body is tense, her breathing is shallow, her heart is pumping, she feels anxious about tomorrow, and worries that she did no homework or preparation. At 2 a.m. she is still wondering if Sally did more homework and might beat her in the exam. Then again, Sally was also on Flappy Birds.

Our heroine fell asleep at 2.40 a.m. Just in time to miss all deep sleep. Mum and Dad burst in at 7 a.m. Bright light, clothes, car, classroom and the exam begins. Both the 'flop' into sleep and the 'flip' into wakefulness have failed.

Against all odds, our heroine makes it to party night on Friday. Caffeine, Red Bull, alcohol and sugar secure the rave. At last, at 4.10 a.m. on Saturday, our heroine really does fall into deep sleep. She wakes at 12 p.m. (broken C). Nearly eight hours in the bag. Saturday is late movie night and on Sunday she wakes at 2 p.m. Another ten hours (S) in the bag (very broken C). Feeling better at last, she resolves to get a good night of sleep on Sunday. But she woke up only six hours ago and her body is not interested in sleep. Toss, turn, check messages, chat, shop and watch a horror movie. Terrible sleep. At 7 a.m. Mum and Dad enter, and the drama starts again …

Sleep medicine understands our heroine. She has sleep phase delay. We can predict that she will be overweight, anxious, subject to cravings and struggling to achieve her potential at school. She might also have slightly raised blood pressure, raised pulse, rapid breathing and vitamin D deficiency. She has pain in her shoulders and back. Her appetite centre is broken, with abnormally high ghrelin (greed) and low leptin (fullness). Her cortisol levels are high in the evening and measures of growth hormone and testosterone are down. Her concentration and test performances are dismal. She is disappointed, Mum is desperate, Dad is angry, and teachers are intimidated and depressed. Adolescence is disrupted and her health is heading in an expensive and painful direction.

Sleep phase delay is endemic today. Mum, Dad, son, teacher and even young children are stuck in variations of sleep phase delay. Pressure, technology and light nudge us towards staying up too late, and consequently waking up too late. Exposure to blue light happens later in the morning (if at all). Melatonin release happens later, sleep signals act later in the evening, and a 'wake maintenance signal' counters the fatigue associated with adenosine. We are desynchronised from the circadian rhythm (broken C). Biology is disrupted. Our natural resilience is undermined at genetic, hormonal, physiological, physical, emotional and cognitive levels.

## Sleep Quality

The third system to understand and master is the ultradian rhythm (U) and its effects on the quality of sleep. Humans run a second biorhythm that cycles every 90 to 110 minutes. During the day this ultradian rhythm cycles us between phases of increased alertness and quieter phases. At night it cycles us between deep (NREM: non-rapid eye movement or slow wave sleep) and dreaming sleep (REM or rapid eye movement sleep). This rhythm is also linked to gene expression, glucose metabolism, temperature, hormone regulation, emotion and cognitive activity. It is another reminder that life is phased.

At night the ultradian cycle gives us the base architecture of sleep.

During the day electroencephalogram (EEG) monitoring would show cycles of beta and alpha waves in the brain. This relates to active consciousness. Beta has been correlated with high alertness, focus and peak performance. It is expensive biologically and will lead to exhaustion. Alpha states are more relaxed and reflective, and can lead to drowsiness.

Figure 24: Sleep Architecture —The Ultradian Rhythm with Deep and Dream Sleep

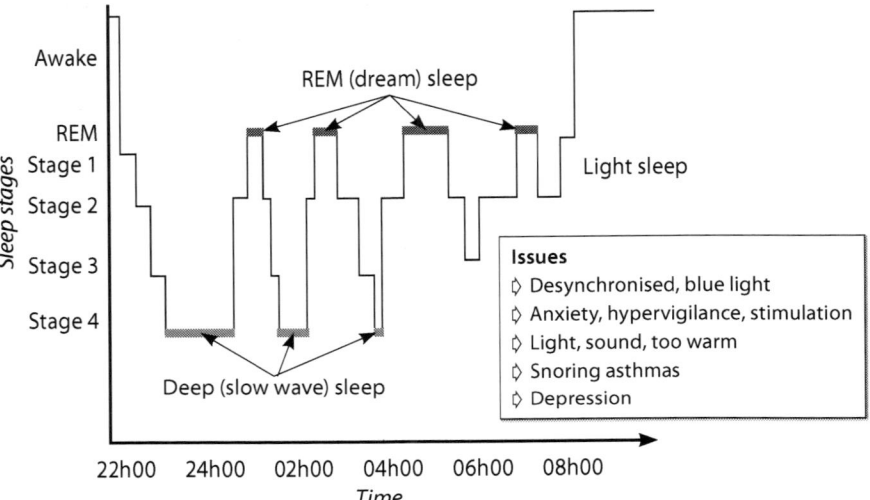

The end of the day for our ancestors was a period of quiet. Light reduced with dusk, temperature dropped and the environment became quieter. The combination of high adenosine and melatonin release, following activity in daylight, lowered temperature and gave us a powerful sleep signal. Around 9 or 10 p.m. they hit the downward drift of the ultradian rhythm, the flop, and sank rapidly down through alpha, theta and into the delta wave of deep sleep.

The first and second cycles of the night are primarily deep sleep (NREM). Deep sleep is a very low metabolic state for body and brain. Repair, hormone release, brain recovery and muscle recovery are assisted. Recent studies show a strong correlation between reduced deep sleep and anxiety. Reduced deep sleep also reduces the night-time drowsiness signal.

The body prioritises deep sleep. When sleep deprived or jet-lagged this is the first sleep the body recaptures.

The second part of the night is dreaming, or rapid eye movement (REM) sleep. There is evidence that dream sleep is important for consolidation of memory into long-term storage and may play a role in emotion regulation. We still do not understand it fully. The balance of deep and dream sleep shown in figure 24 is the only sustainable solution to human wellbeing and performance. When sleep is deprived or disrupted the body seeks to restore sleep architecture.

Let's get back to our heroine (and heroes). Three systems are disrupted: not enough sleep (S), sleep phase delay (C) and sleep architecture (U). Clearly she is missing the first wave (sometimes more) of deep sleep. The rest of the night is spent in shallow, anxious or dream sleep. Flip and flop have failed. Biological integrity is deeply disrupted:

- gene pacing of the cycles is interrupted and gene expression changes
- cortisol rises at night (distress) rather than in the morning (fatigue)
- melatonin releases in the early hours of the morning rather than before sleep (fatigue)
- temperature regulation is disturbed
- appetite regulation is disturbed (high grehlin and low leptin): we crave carbohydrate
- growth hormone, testosterone, insulin and multiple hormone systems are disrupted
- deep sleep is restricted and anxiety increases
- weight gain, obesity and diabetes are triggered
- the immune system is less effective at repair and protection
- emotional expression, regulation and recognition are compromised
- alertness, concentration, memory and test performance are reduced.

Like many of us, our heroine is in a 'sleep deprivation death spiral'. The remedy is simple. The benefits to our resilience — body, heart and mind — are obvious.

........................................................................

### Practice: cycle disruption and repair

1. If you think you may have disrupted cycles (S, C and U), get serious about fixing them.
2. Wake up early enough to get 20 minutes of blue dawn light.
3. Force consistency into your wake-up time until resynchronised — never sleep in.

4. Get out in bright daylight for at least 20 minutes a day, preferably exercising.
5. Shut off all screens, bright lights and electrical devices an hour (ideally two hours) before sleep.
6. Build a cool-down phase into your evening about 90 minutes before bed: read, talk, intimacy.
7. Make your bedroom cool (<18°C), dark and quiet. Use earplugs and eye mask if needed.
8. Watch for the ultradian dip and feelings of tiredness and go straight to bed.
9. Take the time to relax body, heart and mind before sleep.
10. Breathe slowly from the diaphragm to help calm and quiet yourself.

........................................................................

## Hypervigilance: Anxiety and Disturbed Sleep

The next most common sleep concern is sleep that is disturbed, interrupted and shallow. We measure this as sleep continuity. When reduced, both adults and young people suffer cognitive declines. We go to bed exhausted and desperate to sleep, but the mind becomes active. We start to worry about tomorrow. The mind scans, analyses and evaluates possible outcomes and whirls with anxious thoughts. It is hard to get to sleep, we find ourselves tossing and turning, and we wake repeatedly. Predictably we wake frustrated, tired and overwhelmed before the day has even started.

We are overloaded with information, demands, aspirations and concerns in a 24/7 world. The media pummels us with every bad event and risk facing humanity. Expectations of work performance continue to increase. This is the overload factor in our death spiral. It is quite normal to worry about the future. Worry leads to anxiety and fear. Fear compromises our ability to think clearly and blocks sleep onset.

The continual external and internal pressure to worry forces us into a high alertness and high arousal state. We are not sensitive to our biology. The vagal brake is off. The sympathetic system is overactive. Self-awareness switches off to attend to an imminent crisis somewhere. Over time this becomes a chronic state of hypervigilance, just like a soldier with PTSD. Sleep, decision-making, enjoyment and health become seriously compromised.

Going to bed too late, over-stimulated, hot or disturbed reduces deep sleep in the early part of the night. This further activates anxiety. The anxiety further compromises deep sleep. Instead we fall into stage one sleep, or dreaming sleep. This is easily disturbed and can lead to disrupted sleep with multiple wake-ups. It is exhausting to think about it, let alone live it!

Depression can also disturb sleep. Often one falls asleep easily but wakes up in the early hours, unable to go back to sleep.

## Practice: deepening sleep

1. If sleep timing is disrupted, fix this first, as described in the cycle disruption and repair practice.
2. Revisit coherence and build a relaxation practice into every day.
3. Learn to watch for worry and gently remind yourself to come back to the present.
4. Commit to daily exercise with a focus on some strength and high intensity training.
5. Make sure you get some bright light and, preferably, sunshine most days.
6. Learn a mindfulness practice that teaches you to control unhelpful, anxious thoughts.
7. Commit to your cool-down period before bed — relax, read a book, take a gentle walk in the dark.
8. Use your relaxation practice to calm body, heart and mind when you get into bed.
9. If you feel the need to empty your bladder, do so promptly, avoiding lights.
10. If you are disturbed, stay in bed, don't switch on any lights and go back to relaxation.
11. Remember, coffee (half-life of 4.9 hours), alcohol and tobacco interfere with sleep architecture.

## Snoring and Sleep Apnoea

Snoring has become a common problem as obesity levels have increased over the past decades. Particularly in men, fat accumulates around the neck and this can increase the risk of airways blocking as the small muscles of the neck relax. While light, uninterrupted snoring is a nuisance for sleeping partners, it is sleep apnoea that is the real problem. In sleep apnoea the throat closes and blocks breathing, leading to pauses and noisy recovery.

If inhalation is blocked in sleep we activate a distress response that floods the body with adrenaline and wakes us up to get a breath. Often the sufferer is unaware and falls straight into sleep and another blocking episode. In severe cases breathing can stop hundreds of times a night, leading to serious sleep disturbance and chronic distress linked to further weight gain, high blood pressure and cardiovascular risk.

Sleep apnoea is serious and requires professional assessment and correction. While weight loss, breathing exercises and fitness can solve the problem, it is best to have it corrected. Start with lifestyle change, progress to mechanical support of the jaw or tongue, then to breathing masks (continuous positive airway pressure or CPAP devices) and, as a last resort, surgery. Those who find a device that works have a stunning recovery. They feel fantastic within weeks: blood pressure drops, weight falls and hormones improve.

Alcohol and heavy evening meals are absolutely contraindicated in sleep apnoea.

## Sleep Debt

Sleep debt is the accumulated hours of sleep that you are not getting. Many of us build up sleep debt over a week, during busy periods or following overseas travel. Try to discharge this sleep debt as soon as possible. Sleeping in on Saturday or Sunday morning will lead to compromised performance, health risk and accident risk on Monday and Tuesday mornings. Don't even think about it.

The best way to discharge sleep debt is by going to bed — and to sleep — an hour and a half earlier than your normal time. When deprived the brain will recover deep sleep first. If you go to bed early and relaxed you will fall into deep sleep and get up to three cycles before dreaming starts.

Dreaming sleep is recovered next. There is reasonable evidence that 0.5–3 mg of melatonin can help reset the clock and facilitate deep sleep recovery. I have found it helpful, particularly in time-zone changes when travelling.

The second option attracting much attention and research is the powernap, a short, six- to 20-minute sleep, preferably in the dip that follows lunch. From a productivity perspective it is clear that our alertness and performance improve for about two hours following a 15-minute powernap. It is well worth thinking through ways to secure this in your life. Unfortunately many businesses frown on a nap during this day. This is a big mistake as it would significantly improve afternoon productivity and reduce error and accidents if allowed to happen.

Try not to nap for more than 20 minutes as it can lead to a prolonged ultradian dip that might compromise productivity and alertness for the next hour and a half. Additionally, if we nap too long we will reduce our night-time drowsiness signals and disturb the drop into deep sleep at night.

Figure 25: Summary of Key Benefits from Sleeping Well

| Resilience Assets | Sleep inputs |
|---|---|
| Spirit in Action | Critical to team performance<br>Supports ethical behaviour<br>Restores insight and self-awareness<br>Enables self control |
| Train Mind | Restores concentration<br>Increases test performance<br>Facilitates memory formation<br>Removes toxins from brain |
| Engage Emotion | Allows facial recognition and empathy<br>Increases facial expressiveness<br>Improves mood<br>Supports impulse control |
| Energise Body | Optimises hormones for growth and repair<br>Prevents metabolic disease — craving, obesity, diabetes, heart disease.<br>Immune system optimised |
| Master Stress | Enables optimal performance states<br>Reduces anxiety (deep or slow wave sleep)<br>Facilitates calm, focused attention<br>Foundation of bounce back practices |

## Sleep, Children and Family

Sleep is a challenge for many families and children. A study in *The Lancet* in early 2012 showed that sleep disturbance is as much of a concern — and perhaps greater — than the lack of good nutrition and exercise in young children. If a child is not sleeping well there can be multiple destructive effects, including:

- reduced attention span and learning difficulties at school
- interference in emotion regulation and social engagement
- increase in weight gain and disordered glucose metabolism (diabetes)
- reduced resistance to infection
- increased risk of behavioural problems
- raised blood pressure and increased cardiovascular risk
- conflict at home, particularly in getting children up for school
- exhausted, irritable and miserable parents.

Parents can easily fall into the trap of letting their young children fall into disrupted sleep patterns. It is a parental responsibility to help your children establish good sleep habits as soon as possible. Children need between ten hours as toddlers to eight hours in their pre-teens. Sleep phase delay, where you let children stay up too late with electronic stimulation, is the primary culprit, as we have previously explored.

The issue is so serious that one of the mini-health booms is sleep coaching. Parents are hiring coaches to help restore good sleep patterns. Sad!

Many studies show that young children and teenagers should get up around dawn and have time to be exposed to the blue light of that time before heading off to school. Practically, this means getting your kids up around 6 a.m. and ideally getting them outside and active. It also means time for a quality breakfast. To achieve adequate sleep they need to be relaxed and in bed around 8 p.m. to be asleep by 9 p.m.

All electronic gadgets should be removed from a child's bedroom. Consider turning off the family wireless device. The bedroom must be strongly associated with relaxation and sleep. Again, a dark, quiet and cool (under 18° C) bedroom is better. Teaching your children simple relaxation exercises such as breathing and the habit of reading before sleep (not on a device) will help.

In the teenage years, sleep disturbance will have a disruptive effect on the hormonal transitions to adulthood. Melatonin release occurs about an hour later in the teenage years, so you are up against 'wake maintenance'. Evolution sets up the teenage years for courting and fertility, so it is quite natural. A good first step is to recognise the entry to teenage years with a little more evening time and the odd party.

However, this teenage shift can rapidly get out of control, as we explored with our heroine in our case study.

Letting your teenagers fall into this pattern is a parental nightmare and is dangerous for their healthy development. Hormone regulation is disturbed, glucose metabolism is disrupted, behaviour is more difficult than it should be and the young adult is exposed to all the risks of late nights: online sex and violence, motor vehicle accidents, alcohol and drugs. It is a challenging time.

Strong but empathic guidance is needed over this time. Teenagers need to go out and socialise, but parents and caregivers have a responsibility to keep it healthy and safe. Let them go out on occasion; don't let them sleep in. Teach them to powernap after lunch and, after a late night, to go to bed early. Every now and then you will have to hold the line and impose discipline.

Sleep awareness makes great sense.

Sleep discipline is a non-negotiable.

## Summary

- ☀ Know your sleep systems: S, C and U.
- ☀ Get the basics right.
- ☀ Deepen your quality of sleep.
- ☀ Learn to nap and discharge sleep debt.
- ☀ Get your family into good sleep habits.

# Chapter 11

# Nourish

## You Are What You Eat

The human digestive system can make do with almost anything. Nutrition gets a lot of media attention and conversational coverage. Despite an endless flood of books, articles and scientific recommendations, confusion reigns. Unhappily, despite all of the information available, about one-third of the world is eating itself to death, one-third are starved of good food, and the rest muddle through.

Today, the way we eat is driven by money. As we have seen, a multi-trillion dollar food industry wants your money and is openly willing to put your health at risk. In fact, they invest a fortune urging us to stuff ourselves with their most profitable lines. In general, health messages such as 'low fat', 'low cholesterol' and 'high fibre' are simply gimmicks to secure volume and profit.

Government-subsidised farmers pump out genetically modified and industrialised grains, cereals and oils. We have industrialised food processing and distribution to suck in the produce and engineer a convenient food that keeps forever and hits the bliss point in your mouth. A mass of heavily processed, low fibre, high carbohydrate-, vegetable oil- and salt-laden food in bright, promising packages is distributed with wicked effectiveness to every corner of the planet.

The design of supermarkets helps to undermine your will and encourages you to buy what you do not need. Think of check-out areas, laden with toxic sugars and carbohydrates. After a long day, with many shopping decisions and irritable kids, we fall for the bright array of toxic sugars. Most suburban blocks will have a couple of fast food outlets promoting industrialised glop along with the obligatory bottle shop and corner cafe.

Supposedly good science has been bought by the food industry. Heart Foundation ticks abound on processed cereals and grains. Doctors have long pushed the low fat and high carbohydrate diet despite the lack of evidence to support it. The agriculture and food industries sponsored their organisations. Sports medicine advocated pushing hydration through sports drinks for 20 years, after it was clearly shown that over-hydration (hypoatraemia) was killing and hospitalising athletes. Gatorade sponsored the American College of Sport Medicine. Between them, Michael Bloomberg and Michelle Obama could not reduce the size of sugared drink servings in New York.

A massive supplement industry urges you to secure your wellbeing, treat your symptoms and improve your sex life despite no good evidence that they provide any benefit whatsoever. Floods of books advocate protein (Atkins), carbohydrate (Ornish), vegetarianism (Esselstyn) and, more recently, fats (Phinney, Volek and Noakes). Imagine the power behind the fast food industry, sugared drinks and snacks. No wonder we are fat, confused and frustrated.

The focus of this chapter is to find ways to enjoy food, secure sound nutrition for body, heart and mind, and consider the planet. Success is tricky. The key concepts are described and referenced in the first chapter of this section, Prevent and Heal. Here, we cover simple principles and practical suggestions.

As a son of a professor of paediatrics and nutrition, I was denied access to butter, cream and sugar and survived on a sliver of meat and one egg a week. It was painful. Unfortunately, at the time the current scourge of processed carbohydrate was considered good for you. As active kids we gulped carbohydrates. We followed the science of the time and we know now that we massively increased our risk of diabetes and other inflammatory diseases.

My next lesson was in special forces, where I discovered how little one could survive on. Sometimes we had no food for days, and less than a litre of water a day, yet we patrolled upwards of 40 km per day in hostile territory carrying heavy packs and weapons in 30+°C temperatures. Clearly the body could perform on almost no carbohydrate and little water. Medical training was the polar opposite. We were absolutely focused on disease and cure and barely had a lecture on nutrition or wellbeing.

In sports medicine there was no option but to learn about food and performance. At the time we followed beliefs about carbohydrate and hydration loading. However, my practice helped me understand the importance of vegetables and fruit, low glycaemic foods, and fit to performance requirements. While triathletes can eat loads of food, most athletes have to watch their energy intake very carefully. The mind is as important as the body.

Entering executive medicine in the 1990s was a shock. At least 50% of business people were, simply, fat. They had little idea of what or how to eat. Two things worked for those willing to take the journey to better health: low glycaemic, high vegetable diets, and exercise. PERIOD. More recently the metabolic cost of sleep disorders has become obvious. I have read hundreds of books and thousands of scientific papers. Over the years one statement has stuck with me.

## Eat Food, Mostly Plants and Not Too Much.

Thank you, Michael Pollan. Brilliance in a nutshell.

Pollan's 'Eat food' includes core nutrient groups of proteins, carbohydrates, fats, vitamins and minerals. Source these as close as possible to the natural form to which our body has adapted over millions of years. Reduce the amount of interference between nature and your mouth.

'Mostly plants' reminds us that plant-based food provides the essential nutrition that protects our health, energises our lives, and fights disease and ageing. 'Mostly' refers to the fact that humans are omnivores — we have learned to nourish ourselves from many sources including meats, eggs, fish and poultry. Although there are benefits, vegetarianism is not for everyone.

'Not too much' may be the key in our toxic food environment. Humans are adapted to scarce food supply. To survive, our craving to find and secure food sources has to be strong. In a world of abundance and skilfully manipulated convenience food it is easy to eat too much. Six principles are safe and well supported.

### Principle 1: Enjoyment

We are heading towards the creative element of emotion and mind. Food goes far beyond physical survival and nutrition. Eating is a social and emotional reward in life — perhaps a creative passion. It is a cornerstone of good relationships and a nurturing family. In fact, eating dinner as a family without electronic distraction is the most important habit for your children's development.[55] There is too much angst, craving and despair in our modern attitude to food. Obsessive concern with what we eat misses the point.

If you eat with fierce self-restraint, unfettered greed or calorie-counting conscientiousness, you are missing the joy, connection and relaxation of a shared meal.

There is a trap. The short-term bliss delivered by convenient, processed foods is not true joy. It is a scientifically delivered experience to trap your senses with a combination of chemicals (they are rarely food) including simple carbohydrate (sugars), polyunsaturated short-chain fats, salt and AGEs. They taste great on the tongue but once they enter the stomach there is only regret, discomfort and shame. These foods will trigger a desire to consume more than you need. The spike in glucose is followed by craving.

Good nutrition begins with a structured approach to how you eat. Take time to choose your foods, prepare them with loved ones and celebrate the meal together. As much as possible, engage all of your senses to enrich colours, aromas, sounds of preparation, texture and taste. This is conscious nutrition.

·····································

### Practice

Build consciousness around food. Don't outsource your shopping and food preparation completely. Prepare at least a couple of meals at home with friends and family. Eat together with a commitment to put all devices aside for the meal. Explore the food chain by visiting farms and farmers' markets, and trialling different forms of vegetables and fruit. An attitude of gratitude and appreciation of those around the table creates a physiological state optimised for digestion and nutrition.

·····································

## Principle 2: Vegetables and fruit

In terms of nutritional science and wisdom, increasing vegetable intake to nine servings (what fits in the palm of your hand) a day and fruits to three servings per day is the first priority in your food. This is the gatherer part of our hunter-gatherer past. Make this your key priority and once achieved, keep working at it.

Vegetables ensure that you are getting adequate micronutrients (including antioxidants) and plenty of fluid and fibres. The combination is protective and optimises your longevity and performance. Vegetables link us to nature in a peaceful way. Their colours and flavours are rich and preparation has much creative potential. Chewing is great for teeth and jaws. Thanks to the fibre, energy is released slowly and over time. Fibre also stimulates peristalsis (synchronised bowel contractions) and is well linked to more healthy digestion and reduced digestive disease.

The preventive impact of vegetables on heart disease, stroke, obesity and dementia, and their contribution to general wellbeing, are well proven.

Start introducing your children early, with a colourful fruit bowl kept full on the kitchen counter. Make carrots, celery, baby tomatoes and avocado easily available. Sneak onion, garlic, tomato, courgettes and mushrooms into pasta and cooked meats. Cover broccoli and cauliflower with cheese. Allow kids to lean towards fruit and gently persist on vegetables. Most teenagers will adapt. Never surrender.

Grow a couple of vegetables in your garden. There are many creative ways to connect nature and food — all pretty simple, very safe and a wise investment in yourself and your family.

## Practice

1. Do your own research as it is you who needs to be convinced.
2. Pause when you enter the supermarket and fill your basket with veggies.
3. Avoid the inside aisles where processed food pounces.
4. Grow a few vegetables at home and involve your children.
5. Eat fresh veggies, from local sources where possible.
6. Ideally, learn how to prepare vegetables simply at home, using herbs and spices.
7. Frozen vegetables are a reasonable, convenient option. Tinned veggies are okay.
8. Go easy on high glycaemic veggies and fruit (for example, potatoes and tropical fruit).

9. Enjoy berries, bright colours and variety.
10. Prepare extra vegetables or salad in the evening to take to school or work the next day.

## Principle 3: Squeeze out processed carbohydrate

First, veggies and fruit provide most of the carbohydrate we need. Second, food processing interferes with the food chain, softening, sweetening and dehydrating food. The glycaemic index increases as fibre is removed, and sugars, oils and salts are added. The combination is a pleasurable but high-calorie drama for your wellbeing.

Third, be cautious of the vast amount of processed grain in convenience foods. Wheat-based cereals and snack foods provide cheap but nasty fuel. Some people feel dramatically better when they cut out wheat and the associated gluten protein. It is worth experimenting with removing processed carbohydrate to evaluate the impact. While it is difficult to adapt and maintain, the impact is marked.

### Case study: Executive rejuvenation

I recently caught up with a CEO of a bank with whom I have worked. One of his take-outs was to restrict processed carbohydrate. He, like many who have become champions of this approach, took it very seriously. He had been working at it for a year. When I saw him, it was a real double take. My instant response was: 'Wow, you are looking young!' He told me how he had lost 20 kg. On further questioning, he had also maintained his exercise. Reducing weight by 20 kg and looking vastly better is a huge win. His family is actively involved and they shared how testing it was to secure the change. Totally worth it.

Fourth, grains found in cereals and breads provide a significant source of fuel and fullness for many people. If we are to restrict them, we need to find a replacement. Beans and legumes supplemented with mashed cauliflower and grated courgettes are best if you want to be strict. Oat porridge and basmati or long-grain rice are the next if you are more relaxed.

Fifth, a current wave of research and opinion is showing that fats may, at worst, not be bad. At best, most of the fats now appear to be a smart way to replace the energy gap created when we dump the processed carbohydrates. Many of my athlete and executive clients are shifting towards increasing good fats and saturated fats.

## Practice

1. Remove sweets and sugar, biscuits, muffins, white breads and breakfast cereals from home, school and office.
2. Work hard to remove bread. If desperate, treat yourself to a slice of whole-grain bread.
3. If you use pasta or rice, go for low glycaemic versions (whole grain, basmati rice).
4. Use vegetables such as mushrooms, courgettes, pumpkin, cauliflower and broccoli to bulk out a meal.
5. Add fats (see principle 4) to your meals to provide flavour, fullness and added calories.

### Principle 4: Balance food groups

Be cautious of diets that have excessive bias towards any one food group. Humans need protein, carbohydrate (vegetable and fruit) and fat. Our success as a species rests on our omnivorous flexibility. We use all sources effectively and interchangeably.

We need protein to build our structure, but can use only 1.5 grams of protein per kilogram of body weight. This is one serving of meat, chicken, fish or eggs. It can be achieved with a large serving of beans and nuts as well. All extra protein is shunted into gluconeogenesis. The liver turns protein into glucose at some cost to the body. This ineffective conversion to energy is how the high-protein diet supports weight loss. While the high-protein and low-carbohydrate diets have merit for weight loss, they are not optimal for health and take great willpower to sustain.

Grass-fed meats, organic chicken, fish and eggs are good sources of protein. Adding these to your meal reduces glycaemic spiking and helps you feel full. Vegetarians have a more challenging job and will have to use legumes, nuts, avocado and dairy.

A 40-year fear of fat nurtured the 'low fat–high carbohydrate' diet. It is now well recognised that fats and oils have an essential role in the body and are not as bad as has been widely advocated. Many successful nutritional approaches are increasing fat into the diet and finding ways to help the body use fat constructively.[56]

In short, the only risk is excess consumption of the Omega 6 or polyunsaturated vegetable oils. These oils, mostly soy but also sunflower, corn, safflower and sesame, have invaded our diets. Physiologically they should form less than 1% of our daily energy needs. We consume much more. The consequence is increased inflammation and for many, a feeling of nausea.

Monounsaturated fatty acids (MUFA) found in olive oil, avocado, nuts and canola oil are an integral part of the Mediterranean diet. These are definitely good fats for both health and taste. We can increase our use of them with a clear conscience and joy.

Omega 3 fatty acids are primarily found in fish. Small amounts are converted in the body from flaxseed oil, canola oil and nuts, but it is not efficient. Good sources are salmon, tuna, sardines, herring, blue cod and snapper. Vegetarians might like to consider a supplement. Most athletic and longevity programmes take a daily supplement of Omega 3 with EPA and DHA. Choose good quality products such as Nordic, Life Extension or the Zone.

Consumption of saturated fats is now known to have NO association with cardiovascular disease. While we must be aware of the calories they hold, most of us can now drop all guilt from enjoying the fat in meat or chicken skin. The low carbohydrate–high fat diets actually reduce glucose, the dangerous triglyceride, and atherogenic LDL cholesterols.[57]

There is strong evidence that many physically active people can consume increased fat with very low carbohydrate diets and improve physical and cognitive performance. To achieve the benefits one needs to adapt to burning fat for fuel — keto-adaptation. This approach challenges the high-carbohydrate approach to performance and demonstrates that fat is a far better fuel for endurance sport, performance, exercise recovery and prevention of fatigue. Keep in mind that per serving size fat has double the calories of carbohydrate. Add fat in small amounts.

Processed carbohydrate undermines fat use as fuel and reverses keto-adaptation.

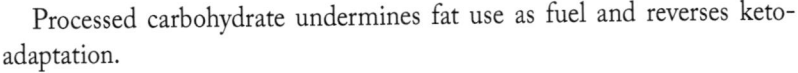

## Practice

1. Build a balance of food groups into each meal and aim for quality, freshness and minimal processing.
2. Always have vegetables, and if vegetarian seek nuts, legumes (beans) and mushrooms.
3. Be liberal with olive oil, avocado, nuts and fish.
4. If meat is your choice make sure it is grass fed and preferable not mass-farmed with antibiotics and hormones.

## Principle 5: Big breakfast, small dinner

In a busy life, good nutrition must be easy. For some, preparing food is a joy. For most, it is a chore. Success is simple if the right food is ready in your fridge, cupboard, office, car or sports bag. A little planning can go a long way.

Shopping for fresh foods should be done every couple of days to make sure your vegetables, fruits and meats are fresh and in good shape. This optimises the nutrient value and taste. Frozen vegetables or fruit, tinned beans, tomatoes, oats and nuts, all store well. Eggs, cheese, smoked salmon, yoghurt and root vegetables are intermediate.

Breakfast is the most important meal. Creating space and intelligence to serve your body and brain needs your attention. There are many good and healthy options that are worth trying until you find what works best. Carbohydrates, proteins and, most recently, fats are all on the table.

The best options include oat porridge or an oat-based muesli, made at home so you can control the amount of sugar. Add a bit of fruit with blueberries or strawberries at the top of your list. Milk, nuts or yoghurt reduce glycaemic index. My current favourite is homemade nut muesli: crushed or sliced nuts fried in three tablespoons of coconut oil, cinnamon, nutmeg and ginger. I mix this in with a whole-fat yoghurt and a good helping of blueberries.

Eggs are a good breakfast food. An egg is a good source of protein and cholesterol. Omega 3 eggs can add healthy DHA and EPA. Eggs do not cause cholesterol or heart disease. Six to eight eggs per week are fine. For a low-carbohydrate breakfast add avocado, salmon, spinach, bacon, mushrooms and tomato. If you are comfortable with a wholegrain toast (with lots of seeds and fibre), this is still a good breakfast. Removing bread does help weight loss.

Introducing berries, bananas, kiwifruit and other lower glycaemic fruits is always a good option for antioxidant protection. Enjoy a cup of tea or coffee with breakfast, if your body tolerates it. Both are excellent sources of antioxidants and the health benefits of a couple of cups of coffee in the morning are well established.

For those remaining coffee sceptics, please take some time to adjust. There are now thousands of studies showing a wide range of health benefits from drinking coffee on a regular basis. For sure, some people are sensitive and should leave it alone. The upside of coffee includes reduced mortality, less bowel and prostate cancer, reduced Parkinson's and Alzheimer's, diabetes protection, better liver function, improved mood, and mental performance — just to name a few. For a short summary see www.huffingtonpost.com/2013/10/17/coffee-health-benefits_n_4102133.html. The only caution on coffee is caffeine's long half life — the time taken to metabolise 50%. In a normal adult this is 4.9 hours. In pregnancy or on contraception it can be double. Coffee is a morning luxury best avoided after lunch.

Lunch is a good time to seek out salads and vegetables alongside chicken, fish or lean meats. Limit your processed carbohydrates at lunch and add fats such as olive oil, avocado and even saturated fats.

Dinner in an ideal world would be your lightest meal. Stay away from too much protein as it can act as a stimulant and interfere with quality sleep. The bulk of dinner should be vegetables, alongside small amounts of protein and fat.

For those seeking optimal physical and cognitive performance, smart snacking is a natural next step. This takes a little discipline and planning. Nuts, fruit, cold salads, whole-fat yoghurt and sushi are all good options.

## Principle 6: Smart fasting, weight loss and performance

One of the current debates in performance literature is the value of keto-adaptation. In short, a range of studies are accumulating evidence to support a switch from carbohydrate-based fuel to fat-based fuel. The improvement in blood-test measures, hormones, weight loss, diabetes reversal and prevention and mental alertness is consistent. We have much to learn and it is a good time to trial this and see how it works for you.

Remember, when we have easily available carbohydrates the body will use these first. High carbohydrate intake will stimulate insulin release and fat storage. Some of us tolerate carbohydrate and can use it effectively as fuel, but many people are oversensitive to carbohydrate. They become insulin resistant and the body stops burning fat as fuel. Weight gain, diabetes risk and reduced energy and alertness are common. These people get huge benefits from keto-adaptation.

Lurching to masses of meat and saturated fat is the wrong message. All of the above principles hold true.

## Practice

There are three suggested ways to achieve and benefit from keto-adaption.

1. Fiercely reduce carbohydrate to 50 g per day (two slices of bread or two cups of vegetables) and stay active. This approach is well supported today. Keep the 50 g vegetable based and supplement your energy needs with increased fats (as described in principle 4). Many athletes and business professionals who cannot afford to fast find this the best way to keto-adapt. Remaining active on a daily basis will help your body burn fats preferentially. Carbohydrate resources are protected for the brain. Most people will lose weight and feel great on this approach. It can take six weeks to adapt, so be patient. *The Real Meal Revolution* by Noakes and his team is a very helpful guide, with great recipes that include heaps of vegetables.

2. Eat your food between 7 a.m. and 3 p.m. and then fast until breakfast. This approach allows you to be a little more relaxed with what you eat between 7 a.m. and 3 p.m., but it is quite challenging to drop the evening meal and the associated social and family time. If working a normal job or being a family with kids at school, this is unlikely to work. Novak Djokovic has found this to work for his tennis career.[58] Because your liver stores glucose/glycogen for only 12 hours, this overnight fast forces your body to learn to burn fat (keto-adapt).

3. Intermittent fasting is another approach that has evolved from longevity medicine and caloric restriction. Animal studies show that reducing calories might slow the ageing process and may have a healthy impact on cellular health. It appears to promote 'cell clean-up', reduce oxidative damage and counter inflammation. Human studies show that fasting both forces keto-adaptation and increases the hormones of youth and vitality (growth hormone, insulin-like growth factor, DHEA). A popular approach[59] is aggressively to restrict what you eat on two days per week to 150 calories. This is an egg, a piece of fruit and a bowl of soup. This takes some willpower, but many friends, colleagues and clients swear by its effectiveness. It supports sustainable weight loss.

.........................................................................

Alcohol has a low to negligent glycaemic index but is basically carbohydrate. If you are serious about optimising your health, a glass of red wine a few times per week is the answer. Alcohol will interfere with keto-adaptation, healthy hormone levels, sleep, emotion control and cognition.

.........................................................................

## Summary

- ✸ Know your basic nutrition.
- ✸ Enjoy eating.
- ✸ Get your veggies.
- ✸ Squeeze out processed carbohydrate.
- ✸ Stay balanced.
- ✸ Sort out simple meal plans.
- ✸ Trial keto-adaptation.

.........................................................................

## Part Four

# Creativity

| | | |
|---|---|---|
| 12 | Emotion | **169** |
| 13 | Mind | **190** |
| 14 | Mastery | **205** |
| 15 | Flow | **217** |

Chapter 12

# Emotion

## The Hidden Power of Emotion

Working with your emotions is for me the most interesting, surprising and satisfying element of resilience. Emotion expert Paul Ekman has suggested that humans are not designed to be conscious of emotion. This makes sense. Our emotional systems are primarily physical and started as strong, genetically loaded dispositions to act in response to environmental stimulus.

For example, if challenged by a dangerous animal we have three choices — freeze, flight or fight. These very physical reactions could be easily observed and trigger three very different responses. The many dangerous situations we faced in our evolution required fast and definitive action to survive. It was risky to weigh up the costs and benefits of each before acting. Essentially, an emotional response drove us towards definitive action. Strong reactions were likely to be successful — such as a fast retreat or quick attack — and thus have been selected through evolution.

Emotion is deeply etched into the genetics, brain and body. Emotions are the same in all humans — no exceptions. We feel the same emotions, show them in the same ways and describe them in similar words. Charles Darwin described the emotions in one of his key books, *The Expression of the Emotions in Man and Animals*.[60] This book is a deeply insightful and clearly articulated expression of emotions. Then, science practically forgot about the observations for over a hundred years. Professor Paul Ekman brought them back into the spotlight while working on facial expressions and the Facial Action Coding System (FACS).[61]

Over the past 20 years authors such as Daniel Goleman (*Emotional Intelligence*), Martin Seligman (*Positive Psychology*), Richard Davidson (*Affective Neurobiology*) and Barbara Fredrikson (*Positivity*) have brought emotions into common language. The field is flourishing and transforming our understanding of what being a good human being involves. It will continue to be a lively field of study and practice.

While the topic deepens and matures, we can already conclude that emotion is a key factor in determining wellbeing or disease, good decisions versus bad, selected behaviours, and creative success or personal failure. Remember the Performance Supply Chain?

First, we will show how emotion is grounded in the body, influences how we think and drives how we act, thus determining our performance in situations. Second, we will go deeply into the territory of the emotions, discovering their richness and variety. Third, we will learn how to master destructive emotions and, fourth, we will learn how to cultivate and express the positive and creative emotions in our lives.

From a biological point of view, we have already explored how the basic emotions of collapse, fear and anger can be activated. Emotional predispositions are deeply embedded in our brain, neurology and physiology. These mature and can hardwire into our behaviour. For example, if a baby primate or human sees an adult showing fear on the appearance of a snake, the baby shows fear and displays this fear each time a snake appears. Let's explore the chain of events, all of which happen in sub-second speed. Generally, these reactions unfold within 0.3 seconds.

## Flight and Fear

**Appraisal** The image of the snake is presented to the thalamus in the centre of the brain by the eyes. The thalamus acts as a central server. Highly coded images such as a snake or attacking predator are quickly detected in the amygdala, two almond-shaped bodies inside the temporal lobes. If the image fits a fear scenario then the amygdala fire up the hypothalamic axis, triggering the fear response.

**Activation** The sympathetic part of the autonomic nervous system is activated, adrenaline is released and a well-codified series of physical changes take place. Blood shifts from brain, skin and bowel to the muscles of the legs. Hair stands on end or gives a prickling sensation for us less hairy folk. Heart rate and blood pressure are raised.

**Response**  At the same time, we see the face change. Eyebrows fly upwards in a straight line, the eyes open wide and the mouth pulls horizontally, showing the classic 'pulling away' face of fear that is commonly recognised across primates. The body tenses, jumps back and prepares to run. All of this occurs before we have time to think. It is only later that we become conscious of the feeling of fear. Who would think one emotion could be so rich and powerful?

## Freeze, Collapse and Tears

The freeze reaction is a variation of fear. The old vagus nerve fires, bowels and bladder void, and the body collapses with a drop in heart rate and blood pressure. Sometimes playing dead can save us. The common variant today is when we burst into tears or stonewall and become sulky.

## Fight and Anger

In anger the body activates a very different critical chain. The hypothalamus, sympathetic nerves and adrenaline force blood pressure and heart rate upwards. Blood pours into the chest, arms and jaw, with a tightening of these muscles and a bunching of fists. The eyebrows draw down and inwards, the lower lids tighten and the lips purse into a straight, hard line. As we move into attack, the jaw juts forwards and the mouth opens to show the teeth in a snarl. Once again the entire cascade can drive a physical or verbal attack before we know it.

If we step back for a moment, we notice that the entire display of these common emotions is very visible. It is an objective change that we can observe and measure, and from which we can predict behaviour and even thinking. Emotions can be seen, photographed and measured. They are objective facts. They happen in the body. Yes, the brain mediates the process, but even that can be seen objectively in a brain scanner. This is an important fact.

Emotion is an objective physical reaction that takes place in the body. Emotional reactions are partly processed in the brain but are only sometimes conscious. In animals, we believe that emotions are not conscious but they most certainly direct the brain, and then the body, to take action. Think of a dog salivating over a bone or bristling before an attack. In humans we have a broader scope of consciousness. We can become aware of a feeling as the body takes on an emotion. This is the brain mapping the body state into the brain as an image. Now we are able to define and think about the feeling we have experienced.

We also know that putting our body into an emotion can trigger a deeper emotional state, feeling and associated thoughts. This is why we are reminded to keep smiling or to do laughter yoga. Faking the body actions of emotion will create a feeling consistent with that emotion. You can practise this by putting on a big smile with crinkly eyes. Or by bunching your fists, tightening your shoulders, pursing your lips and drawing your eyebrows down and inward, you will feel the anger. Squeezing a pen between your lips increases your tendency to anger and irritation.

Emotions will change how we think, which is why understanding emotions is so important. The way we think when angry is very different to when we are grateful. Further, the action that follows is very different. In this way we can begin to recognise how life flows up and down the Performance Supply Chain — body, feeling, thinking, action and back.

Figure 26 shows how we can explore the signatures of different emotional states. It shows how over time emotion affects the body and therefore health. It also shows what kind of thinking and mental state follows each of the emotions and, finally, the likely behavioural response to each signature.

Take some time to study and reflect on these patterns. Can you identify a pattern in yourself right now? What about the last conflict? Or can you recall a recent success? This powerful concept has wide and exciting implications. If we focus on happiness we improve health, thinking, connection and work effectiveness. But equally, it is clear that some people are trapped in destructive patterns such as fear and anger from early on in their lives. There is a life's work in the idea.

Positive emotions are associated with approach and behavioural activation. These positive emotions, such as joy, enthusiasm, compassion, contentment and gratitude, locate and are activated in the left prefrontal cortex (PFC). The more active the left PFC on functional magnetic resonance imaging (fMRI), the more we experience positive states, the more healthy we become and the faster we bounce from setbacks.

Figure 26: Physical, Emotional, Cognitive and Behavioural Scripts

| Body | Heart | Mind | Action |
|---|---|---|---|
| Adrenaline and cortisol<br>Restricted breathing<br>Poor immune function<br>Cardiovascular disease | Anger<br>Frustration<br>Hostility<br>Rage | Restricted focus<br>Loss of choice and impulsivity<br>Poor risk assessment<br>Escalating rumination | Tense and stiff<br>Clenched fists<br>Aggressive outbursts<br>Offend and repel others |
| Adrenaline and cortisol<br>Multiple stress symptoms<br>Hyperventilation<br>Digestive problems | Fear<br>Worry<br>Anxiety<br>Terror | Narrow, exaggerated focus<br>Future-based rumination<br>Loss of creativity<br>Mind blank | Insomnia<br>Fatigue<br>Avoidance<br>Freeze/fright reactions |
| Fatigue<br>Digestive and sleep<br>  disturbance | Sadness<br>Disappointment<br>Grief | Slow, dull, repetitive<br>Personalisation (my fault)<br>Rumination on past<br>Poor decision-making | Low energy<br>Withdrawal<br>Insomnia<br>Drag others down |
| Energised<br>Longevity and health<br>Improved immunity | Happy<br>Joy<br>Love | Fast, idea-rich, hopeful<br>Generous world<br>Think about others | High energy<br>Risk tolerant<br>Reach out to others |
| Relaxation<br>Recovery<br>Improved sleep | Gratitude<br>Appreciation | Efficient thinking<br>Steadiness<br>Responsive | Relaxed and contented<br>Fewer cravings<br>Relaxed readiness |

On the other side, negative emotions are associated with withdrawal and behavioural inhibition. These states can be seen in the fMRI as activation of the right PFC and amygdala. Davidson (in *The Emotional Life of your Brain*)[62] has measured a 30% variation across left and right PFC in individuals. Some individuals can have 3000% more activity than others in the left PFC. This shows clearly that we can up-regulate the activity in the left PFC — we can train joy.

## Emotional Intelligence

Daniel Goleman popularised the concept of Emotional Intelligence (EQ) in 1995 in his book, *Emotional Intelligence*.[63] He ushered in an era in which emotional awareness and skill was shown to be significantly more important to leadership and influence than intelligence (IQ) and technical skill. A number of studies suggest that when we look at star performance in leadership, 85% was based on EQ rather than IQ. When looking at star performance across all jobs, EQ was considered to be twice as important as IQ. This was a reality check to those of us who worship and seek intellect.

Intuitively, we recognise that successful people in leadership or influencing roles display emotional skill. On the flip side, sometimes those who are very smart at school fail to live up to expectations in the real world of working with others. Given the rapid rise in autism diagnoses — where people have difficulty dealing with emotions and social situations — it is clear that to some degree it is a failure of EQ. Simon Baron-Cohen has written extensively on the impact of autism and low empathy on our lives.[64] Autism is linked to low empathy, whereas cruelty is linked to psychopathy, narcissism and borderline personality disorder. In the latter, the low empathy is associated with hurtful behaviour.

Today we understand, as demonstrated in figure 26, that emotion is inextricably linked to physiology, health, mind and even spirit. Most of us have moved on from EQ as an all embracing model, but it still has considerable value in our inside-out journey.

## Waking Up to Emotions — Emotional Awareness

Before we can apply emotion skilfully in our lives, we need a basic understanding of the emotions. For more detail about the raw material of emotion, Paul Ekman's *Emotions Revealed* is the benchmark. For now all you need is a little time and a mirror, and you can build a basic understanding of the raw material of emotion. Seriously, do this.

## Happy

Close your eyes and think of the most delicious experience you can imagine. Put yourself right in the experience (laughing, being massaged, surfing, sipping champagne). Engage all of your senses: see, taste, smell, feel and hear the experience. What can you feel in your body? Notice your skin, muscles, face, gut and chest. Can you feel the glow?

What can you see in your face? Look at the mouth and examine your eyes. As you do this, think about your loved ones, your greatest success or a private pleasurable fantasy. When happy, both corners of the mouth curve upwards and as enjoyment increases the teeth may become more exposed. This can be faked. Try it! Now examine the eyes and notice when you feel genuine pleasure that the outer corner of the eyes crinkles and the lower lid tightens. This is hard to fake — only 10% of people succeed.

By examining the outer corner of the eyes we can differentiate a genuine (Duchenne) smile from a fake. There are apparently 19 variations of the smile. Ekman lists 16 enjoyable emotions, including the five sensory pleasures, amusement, contentment, excitement, relief, wonderment, ecstasy, fiero (passion), naches (pride), elevation, gratitude and gloating. Try them.

Smiling is a very strong predictor of better life outcomes. If you smile, research shows that fortune smiles on you — health, happiness, friends, longevity and success. Even practising the smile as you have just done will increase your wellbeing. If you need help, shove a pen between the back of your teeth, stretching the lips into a smile. While it is preferable to have spontaneous happiness, by exercising 'happy drills' you will experience more genuine happiness.

Happy emotions move us up the resilience spiral, creating energy, optimism, creativity, quick thinking and decisiveness. Make time for them regularly.

## Sad

Now, close your eyes again and imagine great loss. Perhaps imagine losing your family, a favourite pet or a time of deep disappointment. Again, tune into all the senses: feel your body, face and breath. Notice your thoughts and your energy levels.

Now open your eyes and examine your face. Repeat the exercise with your eyes open, watching your forehead, eyes, lips and chin. When sad, the eyes divert downwards with a heaviness of the upper eyelid. The inner corners of the eyebrows move up and inwards, even to the point of creating an inverted horseshoe above and between the eyebrows. This is the retriever puppy look. Try to emphasise this movement. Then pull the corners of your lips downward while pouting your lower lip. You can deepen the expression by lifting the cheeks and opening the mouth.

Find a picture of someone in grief — for example, a suffering child. Newspapers are good for this. You will notice that it is easy to empathise with deep suffering.

Sadness is the dominant emotion in depression. Sadness causes us to withdraw, and to seek shelter and support. This gives us time to grieve and recover. Sadness slows our thinking, reduces creativity, causes fatigue and dampens motivation. Unresolved sadness becomes depression. Sadness is valuable in recovering from loss, but needs resolution to move forward in life.

A variation on sadness is compassion. When we connect to someone with interest and care, seeking to feel their internal state, the eyebrows will tilt inwards and upwards. When others see this movement they feel cared about. It builds resonance with the other person. Watching a parent engage with a child will show this clearly. It is well understood that counsellors, coaches, doctors and actors will use this expression to connect deeply with clients or audiences. Again, genuine heartfelt concern and care for another is the authentic answer. Make sure you do not frown with concentration when seeking to connect. It looks like anger.

### Fear

Now close your eyes and imagine the most fearsome threat you can. Feel your vulnerability, the invasion of your safety, the looming pain and damage. You may like to think of a bus bearing down on you, a dog attack or falling off a cliff onto the rocks below. Brace for impact and then open your eyes.

In fear, the eyes widen, leaving a white ring around the iris. The eyebrows fly upwards and pull inwards so that they are raised and straight. The jaw tightens and draws the mouth wide, baring the teeth and tightening the lips. Exaggerate this face and notice the bodily changes. Heart rate increases, blood shunts to the legs, skin pales and hands may become sweaty. In fear the brain may shift into freeze or flight. If fear persists we develop a state of anxiety — a background style associated with excess worry, poor sleep and distress symptoms. Remember that disrupted deep, slow wave sleep increases fear.

Fear can quickly activate the low-road amygdala response and we may subjugate our thinking to reptilian responses. This is very rarely helpful and can become debilitating, such as in the phobias (fear of heights, close spaces, spiders). Others prefer to engage anger to retaliate against the vulnerability of fear. If we can be aware of fear it can alert us to danger and risk and help us attenuate impulse behaviour. This is neatly demonstrated in gamblers who adjust their play to signals of distress long before they are consciously aware of their behaviour change.

Ultimately, building resilience allows fear to drop away. Fear is inhibiting and can seriously undermine love, productivity, health and happiness. The only thing to fear is fear itself.

## Surprise

True surprise is hard to fake, but while looking in the mirror imagine a sudden surprise. Watch the eyebrows fly upwards. In surprise they are curved, while in fear they are flatter. The eyes widen much like fear, and the mouth drops open with slack lips and mouth. Milder use of the eyebrows punctuates interest in our conversations.

Surprise is fleeting. It may be positive or negative, but usually leads to another emotion such as joy, fear, anger or amusement.

## Disgust

As you look into the mirror, imagine you have just stood in dog droppings. Notice how the centre of the face wrinkles, the upper lip is drawn up and the nostrils flare. The eyebrows draw downwards and inwards. Disgust signals can vary between people and cultures — and ages (watch a child being served broccoli). Disgust is commonly shown towards bodily excretions (blood, urine, faeces), food, and toxic smells, but can be shown towards other people or their behaviours.

Interestingly, once our bodily excretions leave our body they become fascinating but quickly disgusting. Swallow some saliva. Now spit the same saliva into a glass of water and see if you can drink it. There you have disgust.

## Anger

Anger is the most dangerous emotion. Anger causes harm to you and others. Close your eyes and recall a time someone has really offended you. Think of people who have committed shameful crimes against innocent or vulnerable people. Notice what you feel in your face or body. Notice how your muscles change and see if you can feel any changes in your chest, neck, jaw, eyes and hands.

Now, in the mirror tighten your lower lip and push your jaw out a little. Lift your upper eyelids into a stare and pull your eyebrows down and inwards in the middle. Purse your lips into a straight line. Finally, tighten your lower eyelids. Clench your fists, tighten your chest and draw back your lips. As you do this you may feel heat in your face and hands, along with tightness in your chest. If you have been successful your pulse and blood pressure have increased. Your immune system is compromised. Prolonged anger or the hostile style is strongly associated with poor health outcomes, in particular, significantly increasing your risk of heart disease.

Anger focuses and narrows our attention on the offending person or object. The mind deletes information that may contradict your anger and you are loaded towards verbal or physical violence. Anger creates severe distortions in thinking, problem solving and impulse control. Experts consider the opening of the lips in anger (it looks like a snarl with teeth showing) as a sign that someone is likely to strike out and do damage. This signals attack and the need for defence.

## Contempt

In contempt, one side of the mouth lifts and we look down on the object of contempt. Contempt signals superiority. It can be satisfying. It is closely related to disgust and can flare into anger. It is a very destructive facial expression in social environments.

Simon Baron-Cohen and his team at Cambridge University have completed a learning tool for 412 semantically discrete human emotions in 24 groups (Mind Reading). Emotion is the universal means of human communication. Some read these emotions quickly and accurately and others miss them entirely. Baron-Cohen's research suggests that women are better empathisers and men better systematisers.

Regardless of our setting on the empathy spectrum, emotional awareness is a learnable skill. Once we become aware, we open the door to mastering emotion. This is a tipping point for development in many lives.

### Practice

1. Watch the faces of people you interact with and name the expressions.
2. Practise privately in front of your mirror to make sure you can express at least ten emotions.
3. Visit www.paulekman.com; you can practise and join a training course for a small fee.
4. Take a few minutes at the end of each day to reflect on and journal your feelings of the day.
5. When you suspect an emotion in others, be respectfully curious and ask, 'How do you feel?'

## Impulse Control

The next step in emotional skill is to understand how emotions can drive behaviours and responses that are ultimately destructive. Which of the following situations do you recognise?

1. You are driving to work and running late. As you push to make a traffic light, an old car slows down and blocks you. You yell and shake your fist. You are gripping the wheel, leaning forward and hunched, your jaw tightens and your fists are bunched. You beep your horn. Your boss looks back from the car in front and gives you the finger.
2. You have made a serious error in a client proposal and lose the bid. A colleague starts screaming at you and blaming you for costing the firm $150,000. You burst into tears in front of the team.
3. You are walking on the beach and a dog rushes up to you. As a child you were bitten by a dog. You scream, freeze and fall over clumsily. Lying on the ground, hands over your head in terror, the friendly dog licks your face. Children are doubled up laughing.
4. It has been a good day. As you open your mail you find a letter from Inland Revenue. Your gut tightens as you imagine a massive tax bill. It is a refund but you feel charged and restless.

5. You come home looking forward to a relaxing evening. Your husband/wife is watching TV and the kitchen counter is covered with dirty dishes. You yell at him/her and get into an argument. The evening is ruined and everyone is upset. Or, you look at him/her with contempt and bitterly start to clean up. The evening is ruined. Later, you discover that he/she has been laid off work.

In each case, there has been a rapid and largely involuntary reaction. The first two situations could compromise your livelihood, the third is humorous and the fourth is disturbing but purely internal. The last might ruin your marriage. Not one adds value to your life. You have been hijacked by destructive emotion. In order: anger, sadness, fear, fear, and anger or contempt. In retrospect it is highly likely that you will feel regret and wish you had been a little more restrained and skilful.

We call these destructive reactions 'amygdala hijacks'. There is a common pattern:

1. **A trigger event**   Violation of rights, guilt or threat.
2. **An instantaneous reaction**   Fight, freeze or flight.
3. **Strong emotion**   Anger, sadness or fear.
4. **A feeling of regret**   You know it was not your best move.

Somewhere far back in evolution, emotion was a subconscious reaction to an event that mobilised your resources. It must have worked well millions of years ago because the mechanisms are still carefully embedded in central parts of our brain. We are able to watch the amygdala, the two almond-shaped bodies in the middle of the temporal lobes (about earlobe level), trigger and drive the reaction.

In a hijack, the amygdala gets a fast, rough impression of the trigger. If the impression matches a codified threat it reacts with a flood of adrenaline and muscular action. For example, while walking in the grass you pass a coiled rope, but the amygdala 'sees' a snake. The amygdala reacts within 0.3 seconds, which means we have no time to reflect and adjust. You are in the air and screaming — fear is all over your face and your legs are rigid.

The amygdala hijack is a thoughtless and unhelpful way to deal with life today. It is low-road emotional processing. We have retained this part of our brain and it can wreck your life. When we are sleep deprived, distressed or have faced a major threat such as a natural disaster, the amygdala is charged and super-vigilant. The smallest disturbance can provoke an extreme reaction. This is what happens after an earthquake or in Post-Traumatic Stress Disorder (PTSD). At our worst, the amygdala asserts itself and at our best it is quiet.

Be humble. The thinking brain is shut down in a hijack. You may have no conscious memory of a hijack event or at best you'll have a rudimentary recollection. This is a complicating factor in crimes of passion. Those captured by the destructive emotions frequently do not remember the evidence. It is easy to notice other people being hijacked and remain quite unaware of our own hijacks. A reality check from your family and work colleagues can be helpful to see yourself from another view.

Assuming you are well and functional, an amygdala hijack is never a good thing.

Worse, when we get hijacked in the presence of others, they never forget. This can wreck relationships with children or work colleagues. Step two in EQ is to learn to beat your amygdala. We call this impulse control.

## Mastering impulse control

To master the amygdala hijack we must change how the brain works. We still have the reptilian wiring but we also have a second, high-road, emotional processing centre. This part of the brain is located in the PFC, just behind the forehead. Closely associated with the executive attention network in the centre of the PFC, we have the emotional awareness (medial) and emotional restraint centres (dorso-lateral). When we get hijacked, the amygdala glow on a brain scan and the PFC is quiet — or hijacked. The neurobiological training required is to quieten the amygdala and activate the PFC.

The amygdala is unconscious, at least initially, and the PFC allows conscious emotional awareness, restraint and redirection towards more useful decisions and responses. Each of the steps below will help you to train your brain to use the high road in preference to the low road. At one extreme we have practised meditators who have very quiet amygdalae and up to 30 times more activity in the left PFC as described by Davidson. Amygdala hijack is rare. At the other extreme, we have highly distressed people — PTSD being an example — who have highly active and reactive amygdala on brain scans. These poor folk will have outbursts of anger, tears and extreme fear provoked by the smallest of triggers — minor frustrations, disappointments and sounds.

The goal is to be able to master situations in life that normally trigger you by activating the high-road emotional system. When someone in a brain scanner names a destructive emotion the PFC lights up and the amygdala quietens. From this we know that insight trains the brain to process emotion in the PFC rather than in the amygdala. We also know that mastering a situation trains a set of fibres that run from the PFC to the amygdala. The more we practise impulse control the more capable the brain becomes. The PFC is bigger and more active and the amygdala is smaller and less active. We are becoming an aware and effective human being. Children can learn impulse control. Mastery leads to far better life outcomes in terms of jobs, income, marriage, friendships and performance.

The same benefits are abundantly obvious in parenting, teenagers, sports, combat and leadership. Leaders who practise good impulse control are seven times more likely to get the CEO position. Helping people master impulse control is perhaps the most powerful lever for a healthy family, a successful business and a prosperous society. Prisons, hospitals, casinos and bars are full of people who let amygdala hijacks run their lives.

Impulse control starts with recognition, and leads to restraint, calming skills in conflict, skilful resolution and a powerful person.

............................................................

## Practice

Step one is recognition post event. Take time once you have cooled down to reflect on the trigger, your reaction, the emotion and consequences. Honest reflection becomes a strong motivator for change. Pick one situation at a time for mastery.

Step two is to create a clear picture of how you would prefer to respond to the target situation. This image of your desired response is critical to effective planning and practice. The response evolves as we become more competent and confident. The pathway of development is clear:

1. Learn to practise restraint. Sometimes we are better to do nothing. Leave the room. Zip it!
2. When entering the situation or sensing your hijack, breathe out and relax — try tactical breathing.

3. Stay calmly engaged and honestly express your feelings. Repression is not the answer.
4. Seek to maintain a calm and positive state regardless of the situation

Step three is to rehearse in your mind and to practise in safe and less challenging situations. Talk to people around you about what you are trying to achieve. Recognise and apologise for times you have been hijacked and ask people for their support. You may simply ask, 'When you see me tense up, please remind me to breathe out.'

Step four is to pick a situation that usually gets you hijacked and practise. Stay alert and very connected to your emotions. If you can notice and name an emotion (for example, I am getting angry), you are winning.

Step five is to review the experience. A coach can be very helpful if you are dealing with difficult people or children. Evaluate your competence by asking how far down the list you reached. In this case you may like to invite someone to join you as a mediator to have the level three conversation that is needed. A brilliant book on this is *Fierce Conversations* by Susan Scott.[65]

......................................................................

Mastering impulse control is satisfying and grows EQ. When calm and conscious of emotion, you expand your ability to be effective in all manner of situations. Remember that you must take care of the physiological risks. Bounce from adversity, practise relaxation, get a good night's sleep, eat and be fit as they all help to keep the amygdala and its reptilian behaviour at bay.

## Purposeful Positivity

At the heart of modern psychology — often called positive psychology — is a very convincing and powerful message:

> **Positive emotions are much better for us than negative emotions. Cultivate the positive.**

Naturally, the idea triggers cynical reactions — reactions driven by the negative emotions that make life short, brutish and miserable. It is entirely reasonable to be cautious. The past century has been a grim experience for many. Medicine and psychiatry have an unhealthy absorption with the

184  PART FOUR: CREATIVITY

destructive emotions. In 2000, Martin Seligman[66] and Chris Petersen brought to our attention that research on negative emotion overwhelmed research on positive emotion. This catalysed what is now a rich and deeply respected science on how we can use positive emotion to improve our lives and organisations.[67] The works of Seligman and Barbara Fredrickson are recommended.

Let's pause and reflect on our journey. You have had a taste of the basics of an inside-out approach to resilience. When we spiral downwards, we can take definitive, practical action to bounce back. Mastering calm and the practices of relaxation, breath control and coherence create a calm,

Figure 27: The Resilience Diagnostic Model — Insight, Mastery, Empathy and Influence

alert presence. Physical health comes from prevention, exercise, sleep and nutrition. Now we have gone deeper inside, into the much less tangible domain of emotion. Mind and spirit are ahead of us.

Once out of the death spiral, calm and energised, we have the opportunity to be creative with emotion. Up until this stage insight into emotions is limited and ability to manage hijacks is patchy at best. As emotional awareness and impulse control mature, we enter a biological state enabling the power of emotion. Positive emotions move us up the spiral. Neurobiology shows that we can measure, train and secure growth in the PFC. This PFC activity — particularly the left PFC — has been correlated with positive emotion, coherence (and vagal tone), better health, more happiness, improved attention, creativity and social engagement. Fredrickson describes this as the broaden and build theory.

As we build insight and mastery we discover the power of calm, energy, constructive emotion and effective mind. At a community level, we engage all of these and build our empathy and influence to help others up the spiral. It's inside-out. Master self as the key to skilfully help others.

The work of purposeful positivity begins with taking stock. This is difficult. Few of us are trained to notice and describe our emotions. It does not feel natural and, as Ekman says, we are not designed for emotional awareness. This is emotional literacy. An athlete learns to understand and master the muscles to perform a sport — kinaesthetic, or movement literacy. We can learn to understand and master our emotions. Positive emotion, in general, allows the mind to work at its best.

Purposeful positivity is not just happiness. Hundreds of books and conferences urge us to happiness. It is a start, but a simplistic and misleading solution. There is a much better way. Emotional literacy (insight) opens the door to purposeful positivity. Let's start with a simple example.

•••••••••••••••••••••••••••••••••••••••••••••••••••••••••••••••

## Case study: The upside of anger

John is described as an irritable man, prone to frustration and angry outbursts. John has a very clear idea of how things should be. One morning his car breaks down on the way to work. He is late and he is mad. Two hours later he loses a deal. People notice his stern, frowning face and his hunched shoulders. He perseveres and digs in. During a midday meeting a colleague spills her tea over his folder. He leaps up and explodes. His colleague is distraught and bursts into tears. Everyone is upset. It is not the first time.

Through the lens of emotional literacy we can see irritation, frustration, impatience and explosive rage. These are all variations on the primary emotion of anger. It is obvious to all who work with John, but he does not label it as anger. He feels tense and under huge pressure. He has a headache, raised blood pressure and sleeps poorly. He accepts it as 'life'. However, his mind is very active with a stream of, 'they are just so stupid … what's wrong with … how dare they … what a useless … this is the final straw … I am the only one who cares …' Where possible, people avoid John.

Step one is for John to recognise and name his anger and frustration. His challenge is to see the cause of the drama — not just before the explosion (impulse control) but in the hours preceding that moment. Step two is for him to recognise the implications of the anger — the danger to his health, his relationships and his work. Step three is to find the courage to explore a different emotional response to testing situations. The answer is compassion — love, to be blunt.[68]

Compassion is built step by step, starting with respect and acceptance of self, others and events. Out of respect and acceptance emerges kindness. Kindness is the altruistic impulse for self and others not to suffer. We may go further and dedicate ourselves to the desire and action to bring peace, joy and success to self and others. As we accept others and intend kindness our anger dissolves. It is a relief!

John's challenge is to understand and master the emotional muscle of altruism. Just as the athlete must train physical muscle, so John must train his emotional muscle. As the altruistic muscles strengthen, John will become calm, open, gentle and patient — not least with himself. This is serious transformation to a healthier, happier, smarter and socially skilled person.

•••••••••••••••••••••••••••••••••••••••••••••••••••••••••••••••••••••••

Purposeful positivity is emotional gymnastics. We learn to understand the forces of emotion and to apply the right emotional action for a situation. Nothing new here. Love thy neighbour! Be still! Go in peace! Spiritual traditions have long advocated a more loving, courageous, calm and passionate life. Modern science has caught up. Let's explore the basic emotional muscles.

Figure 28: Emotional Combat — Cultivating Constructive Emotions

| Default Trap | Counter | Stage 1: Open | Stage 2: Grow | Stage 3: Radiate |
|---|---|---|---|---|
| Anger/frustration | Accept | Respect | Kindness | Compassion |
| Sadness | Acknowledge | Curious | Appreciation | Joy |
| Fatigue/boredom | Own it | Engage | Excitement | Passion |
| Craving | Laugh | Detach | Contentment | Gratitude |
| Fear/anxiety | Breathe out | Relax | Embrace present | Equanimity |

On the left we start with a set of the common emotional traps. These defaults are wired into our being and will pop up under challenge. First we must name them and activate a counter. Second, we start to investigate a more resourceful way forward — we open ourselves to a different position. Finally, we begin to develop the constructive emotional muscles. As we become competent we may even begin to radiate higher forms.

A few guidelines to be aware of:

▶ The emotional world is complex and much is below consciousness. Keep it simple.
▶ Accept and describe the default or destructive emotion and feeling.
▶ Rejection, repression and denial will block your progress.
▶ Pick your desired level of constructive emotion — we are not all saints.
▶ Identify the default emotion causing suffering and tackle that first.
▶ Use your experiences, loved ones and activities to guide your progress.
▶ Accept your human frailty and keep working in the right direction.

••••••••••••••••••••••••••••••••••••••••••••••••••••••••••

### Case study: The downside of wine

Jane loves a couple of glasses of wine in the evening. In fact she's never had an alcohol-free day, unless sick. She finds herself looking forward to a drink before lunch. After all, life is crazy and she deserves a treat. As she drives home she is excited and the first thing she does is pour a drink. Heaven! And then another …

Jane is captured by craving. For others it may be a cigarette, checking the smartphone, online titillation, TV, work or food. Modern life provides an abundant supply of short-term pleasures that erode long-term wellbeing and families. A simple audit of your spending, thought pre-occupation, lifestyle, sleep impacts, and the effect on others might indicate that all is not well. Craving begets more craving and slowly hollows out your life. Craving is the feeling of emptiness.

Jane's first step might be to learn to laugh out loud (or smile) when the first impulse arises. Laughter is liberating and expands perspective when all you can see is yellow liquid in a pretty glass. Then she actively detaches from the glass by asking what else is going on. This space allows her to tune into what she cares about — home, children and rest. She feels more content. She has everything she needs to be perfect right here and now. Gratitude is the extension. She feels grateful for all she has right now. Gratitude is fullness. Emptiness is gone. You are replete.

You can still have a glass of wine but make sure you generate the gratitude before you pour the wine.

..........................................................................

The benefits of competence and confidence in generating these constructive emotions has a massive upside for you personally. It will take you up the Spiral. The hard evidence demonstrating the positive impacts physically, emotionally and cognitively is clear. In our roles as parents, leaders and friends, you will be more able to connect with and influence those around you. It is the best example you can be. Nudging yourself up the scale of purposeful positivity is demanding but wonderfully liberating work.

..........................................................................

## Practice

1. Visit www.positivityratio.com and complete the questionnaire to get your positivity ratio.
2. Where do you see the idea of positive emotion in your spiritual heritage?
3. Take ten minutes per day to describe situations that have triggered default responses.
    ▷ Describe what you might have done to counter with a positive shift.
    ▷ Visualise yourself taking action at the next opportunity.
4. Think about practical ways to catalyse and drive the shift toward constructive emotion.

- ▷ A good night's sleep and daily exercise set your base.
- ▷ Learn and practise a form of mindfulness or relaxation.
- ▷ Book times for your favourite activities, hobbies and people.
- ▷ Hold good posture — upright spine and open shoulders.
- ▷ Smile and hold a pen between your teeth if needed.
- ▷ Take time to appreciate — birdsong, sunrise, moon, silence, laughter, children.

5. Practise the growth and radiate positive emotions on a regular basis — show others.
   - ▷ In your morning practice, see if you can generate each of the stage 3 emotions (see page 187).
   - ▷ Choose a focus such as a parent, favourite activity or wonderful place.
   - ▷ Encourage the feeling to radiate throughout your body.
6. Be authentic, don't repress and firmly communicate what you feel.
   - ▷ There are times that we need to be fierce and honest.
7. In crowded places, mumble 'peace, love and joy' to each person around you.
8. Say something complementary or appreciative to those you care about.
9. Watch funny movies when you can.
10. Do good things — help, pick up litter, contribute to a meaningful cause, check on those you care for.

••••••••••••••••••••••••••••••••••••••••••••••••••••••••••••••

••••••••••••••••••••••••••••••••••••••••••••••••••••••••••••••

## Summary

- ✳ Study up the biology of emotion.
- ✳ Wake up to emotion in your life.
- ✳ Master destructive emotions.
- ✳ Aim for purposeful positivity.

••••••••••••••••••••••••••••••••••••••••••••••••••••••••••••••

## Chapter 13

# Mind

### The Mind Revealed

René Descartes was a genius philosopher of the early 17th century. Famous for his phrase, 'Cogito ergo sum' (I think therefore I am), Descartes divided mind and body. He viewed the body as machine-like and the mind as non-material and freed from nature. He located the soul in the pineal gland. Ever since, we have wrestled with the mind–body problem. It has taken four centuries to restore an integrated view of how the mind works. Medicine, psychology and religion still retain a split view of mind and body. This opinion has done much damage to a practical and integral view of human consciousness.

Descartes honoured thought as something separate from the body. He was wrong. In this chapter we investigate a modern, evidence-based view that reconnects mind with body and emotion in very practical ways. We are beginning to understand how consciousness comes to be in humans. It is not that different from what ancient spiritual traditions (the Perennial Philosophy) found to be true some two millennia ago. A rich understanding of mind will guide us, ultimately liberating the power within.

First, Descartes was right about us being thinking beings. Researchers believe we have 50–70,000 thoughts per day. This is nearly one thought per second — more if we subtract deep sleep. This is monkey mind. How many of yesterday's thoughts were of value to you? Most are a repetitive drivel of distraction, desire, judgements, fears and worry. This chattering clusters under some often arbitrary beliefs. These include, 'the world is dangerous …

people should ... if only I ... I should ... be careful ... look at me ... I am a failure .... how am I doing?' and so on.

We deal with as much information in a day as our hunter-gatherer ancestors dealt with in a lifetime. Clearly, we have very busy minds. Often this busy thinking interferes with our ability to be present. Harvard psychologists estimate that 46.9% of the time we are thinking about something other than what we are doing.[69] We are distracted, complaining, worrying and day-dreaming. Life, connection and opportunities pass us by. Our minds are a mess!

Second, thinking is a process of neural activity measured in the physical substrate of the brain. The physical brain processes thought in about 0.6 seconds. The process is simple. Inputs come from our senses (sight, sound, taste, feel, smell), our emotions and our memories. The mind brings our attention to these inputs and we become conscious of x, y or z. Then the brain will connect related inputs. The output is generally a judgement about the input being expected or unexpected, and whether it is good and desirable or bad and to be avoided.

Third, a few patterns describe most of this activity. Worry is the recycling of anxious concerns or fears about the future. The monkeys have escaped into the future. Round and round we go, thinking about something in the future that has not happened and probably never will. Worry is largely unrelated to reality and compromises your ability to function in the present. Closely related is desire, or craving, for something we think we should have.

••••••••••••••••••••••••••••••••••••••••••••••••••••••••••••••

## Case study: Worry

It was a tough day. Sue checks her e-mail and there is a note from her son's teacher that she needs to talk to her. 'Oh my gosh, what has he done? Here we go again. Why does he keep getting into trouble? What have I done wrong as a mother? Has he bullied someone?' After upsetting her husband and a long talk about the difficulties her son has had, she tries to go to sleep but the thoughts don't stop. Two hours pass. The floods of worry escalate as fatigue and anxiety build. Sue is tense, feels her heart beat and tosses about. Eventually she collapses into a fitful, disturbed sleep. At 2 a.m. she wakes with the thought, 'Has he molested someone? Will this involve the police? Will we be on the news? How will we ever recover?' Overnight, Sue has exhausted 50,000 thoughts. She starts the day distraught, exhausted and in despair. She hurries to school with her son to face the calamity. The teacher is delighted with her son's progress.

The mind is a mess!

•••••••••••••••••••••••••••••••••••••••••••••••••••••••••••••

Processing of past events tends to diverge into blaming of others or self. These monkeys escape into the past. Blaming is a recycling of judgement about why something should not have happened, whose fault it was, how your rights were violated, how unfair it was, how typical it is, and that it is the final straw. If the target of blame is someone else, you will find yourself angry and resentful. If the target is you, you will find yourself sad and disappointed.

•••••••••••••••••••••••••••••••••••••••••••••••••••••••••••••

### Case study: Anger

Someone drives their car recklessly and causes you to fall off your bike. You could have been killed. They didn't even apologise. You discover your insurance has lapsed. 'I can't believe it, what an idiot. What can you expect from xxx drivers? They are all the same. Probably drank too much. Not like us. They should be in jail. I knew I should have voted for (the right wing). This is the final straw. I am going to get my own back. I will go to the media, my MP, the police. I will get revenge!' The day is spent raging to everyone who will listen. Angry blaming invades every quiet moment. Your head and muscles ache. You think it must be the fall. The doctor tells you it is 'stress'. Three days later you come down with a nasty cold. Again, the mind is a mess!

•••••••••••••••••••••••••••••••••••••••••••••••••••••••••••••

Fourth, mind, emotion and body are intimately linked — not separate as Descartes believed. As we journey from inside-out, we know how distress and the death spiral undermine thinking and concentration. We know that breathing regulates how the mind works. Coherence nourishes a calm mind, sharper focus, creativity and the ability to use the empathy circuits in the brain. We have seen how critical are physical fitness, good sleep and nutrition for brain function and mental ability. We have explored how emotions can set the brain for certain predictable patterns of thinking. Anger drives blame, fear drives worry, while happiness opens the mind to broader perspectives and creativity.

It is equally true that the thoughts we have affect our emotions and drive down into the body. If I remember a difficult test coming up, I consider the risk of failure and become anxious (fear). As the worry loops run, adrenaline rises, followed by cortisol. My heart beats faster, coherence declines, blood departs my skin and bowels, inflammation flares and I am less able to learn, think and perform my test.

Even the most noble thought is only possible with the inputs of our physical and emotional biology. Neurobiologist Antonio Damasio has shown how the body is the base for our interaction with life and the substrate for autobiographical thought.[70] He describes the origins of thought as biological dispositions based on survival needs, including the drive for food, shelter, sex and acquisition.

Figure 29 is a conception from Damasio's view on how consciousness is an extension of the body and emotional relationship with life. Animals share the proto-self and core self, but humans are uniquely able to reflect on the process. We scan the future and the past and can tell our story — the autobiographical self. The column on the right of the diagram is an example of brain activity when we connect with others. Oscillators connect the

Figure 29: How Consciousness and Connection Are Built from the Body Up
(From Damasio, 2010)

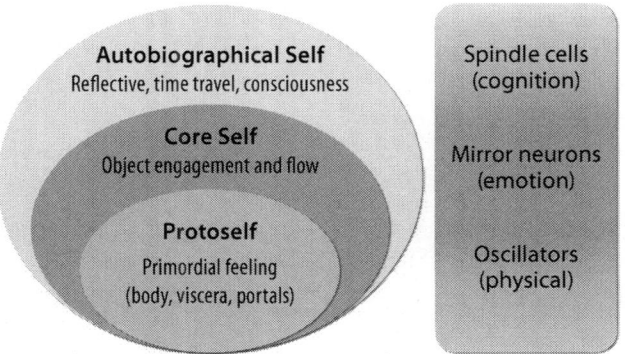

*The self comes to mind in the form of images, relentlessly telling a story of such engagements*

physical level (dancing), mirror neurons the emotion (laughter or tears), and spindle cells help us understand other's perspectives. Spindle cells begin to show in whales, elephants and primates, but reach vast numbers only in humans.[71]

The truth is, 'I am, therefore I think.' For the purposes of cultivating your mind, the foundation is good soil — coherence, wellbeing and emotional literacy. If this is not achieved, thought is chaotic, repetitive and a risk rather than an asset. The monkeys are mad. The mind is a mess.

Fifth, the brain, mind and consciousness are devilishly complex. Much of the 'neuro-babble' currently promoted is unhelpful. People devote entire careers to studying a tiny location, process or chemical within the vast system. We have much to learn and will need to select carefully what is useful to our lives.

Let's define brain, mind and consciousness.

As part of our physical body, the **brain** is made up of cells and vibrant biochemical chatter. Hundreds of billions of cells collaborate over trillions of connections to process and regulate our lives. Most activity never enters the conscious mind, including breathing, hormone production, sleep control, temperature and maintenance. Like emotion, this is objective and can be observed and measured. Brain activity gives rise to mind.

The **mind** is able to perceive, understand, reason, judge and choose. We are subjectively aware of information presenting to the senses, emotions or from memory. I smell bacon, recognise that it comes from the cafe, connect that to my hunger and decide to sit down for breakfast. In effect, we are able to look at the activity of the brain and direct it to take action. For most animals, and sometimes for people, the process of noticing food and securing a meal is automatic. This is a biological disposition (brain activity) and there is limited consciousness.

**Consciousness** is a uniquely human capacity to tune into the workings of brain and mind. We can eat the bacon in many ways:

▶ gulp it down with no awareness and no memory of having eaten it — a disposition

▶ munch away in the bliss of burnt meat, fat and salt while we read the paper — a distraction

▶ notice the flavours, tastes, combinations, mouth feel and gratitude for the nutrition — mindful.

Consciousness is the practice of being more tuned into (or mindful) of the situation we are experiencing. Being mindful of everything happening around us is impossible. Consciousness is selective attention. Of course, there are many levels of depth, as in the case of the bacon. The trick is to choose when and where you want to be tuned in and attentive. This is the level at which we can train the mind. The term 'mindfulness' is used at a broad level to describe the journey.

Enough theory. Let's examine the practical aspects of training our minds. There are five keys:

1. time mastery
2. attention control
3. meditation
4. empathy
5. situation mastery.

We will examine the core idea behind each key, with some practices to try. The main focus will be to show you how to begin the challenging and exciting work of training the mind. Remember, these practices interact and build on the practical work completed so far — specifically coherence, wellbeing, emotional awareness and positivity.

## 1. Practice — Time Mastery

The first step in taking charge of your monkeys, sorry, mind, is to master time. As previously described, half of your 50,000-plus thoughts per day are not about the life being lived in that moment. Thoughts can reflect on the big bang 15 billion years ago through to the end of the universe in another few billion years. Some of us devote our lives to the distant past or imagined future. The worried fret about the future, while the angry and sad ruminate on the past. The hopeful Pollyanna optimist fantasises about winning lotto or fame. The nostalgist remembers the past with gratitude.

This creates a map of where we place our mind in time.

| Upside nostalgia | Unfolding now, | Upside hope |
|---|---|---|
| Downside anger or sadness | the present | Downside worry |

The first distinction is between considered thought and rumination. If you consciously choose to reflect on the past or plan for the future, fine. You are directing your attention to focus on better understanding or preparation. We are present to our mind. For example, there are good reasons to take time to reflect on an experience to extract learnings. There is also value in sitting down to think through — and maybe even visualise — an upcoming event.

The problem is rumination, where the mind wanders off into repetitive and unhelpful worry about the future and pondering on the past. This rumination in almost every case leads to distress in the forms of anxiety or fear (future) and anger or sadness (past). As we have seen, we can devote thousands of thoughts to this useless, painful activity. We are disengaged. The monkeys have bolted. We lose touch with the moment. Suffering follows. If we take time to watch, we recognise how easy it is to drift into mindless daydreaming.

The challenge is to invest more of our thinking in the present moment. When we are consciously tuned into the present, distress fades away and we become fully open to the flow of life as it unfolds. The mind is calm, alert and engaged. When fully present to the moment, everything is more vibrant and you are connected to relationship between self, others and environment. It is in these moments that we are most content, effective and connected. Inside has merged with outside.

### BE     HERE     NOW!

Unbelievably simple but very, very difficult to sustain. Remember the judges and their parole granting decisions in chapter 5, The Death Spiral? Where did their minds go when not considering parole?

Time mastery is the trainable ability to direct your mind into the present moment and to hold it there when it matters. For example, take the reconnection we have with loved ones at the end of the day. You have had a busy day but your loved ones long for real connection. Here is how you might work through time mastery (Q for question, A for answer):

Q: Where is my mind?

A: My mind is leaping through the events of the day and what I still have to do.

Q: Is this an important moment?

A: Being present to my children now is the most important thing in my life.

Q: Where is the centre of this moment?

A: With love, direct attention to the eyes, voice and expressions of my child.

It is much easier to let the tired mind drift. This is low energy, easy thinking, or Kahneman's Type 1.[72] Stopping to reflect and focus with intention on what really matters is much more demanding. It takes effort. The effort is needed to activate blood flow to the prefrontal cortex (PFC), stimulate neurons and sharpen attention, memory and awareness, the activation of which opens the doorway to Kahneman's Type 2 thinking. The simplest practice to begin this work is finding your cognitive switch. Work on four steps:

1. **Awake**  Ask yourself where your mind is right now.
2. **Attend**  Bring your attention to what is actually happening.
3. **Love**  Direct positive emotion such as curiosity, love, appreciation into your attention.
4. **Laugh**  Keep your sense of humour, stay light, smile and laugh.

Being present to the moment takes effort. The monkeys are skilled escapees. Just when you feel the connection with a loved one, that meeting jumps into your mind and you are lost to the preparation you still need to do. The monkeys took off into the future. Ever wonder what your child thinks when they see the anxiety in your face? Or how the dark cloud of anger crosses your face when a memory of conflict pushes into an intimate moment?

Being more present is simple and practical and requires no esoteric practices. The work of Eckhart Tolle[73] is recommended to help you in this journey.

### Practice

1. Watch for moments when you tune out and feel anxiety, frustration or disappointment.
2. Use your cognitive switch (awake, attend, love, laugh).
3. Pick a few key times or events in the day where you really want to be fully engaged.
4. Use a long, slow exhalation to bring yourself back into the moment.
5. Bring your attention to your posture, feelings and senses.
6. Hold your attention on the expressions, voices and presence of those you are with.
7. Be patient with the monkeys and keep your sense of humour when they escape.
8. Take regular breaks to allow your mind to rest and refresh.
9. Calm your mind and attention into relaxed, even breathing at night.

## 2. Practice — Attention Control

Attention is the basic muscle of the mind. Being present is an excellent base for attention. Attention is like a beam of light. It has intensity or brightness, direction, and focus or steadiness. Holding on the light of attention takes energy. This is type 2 thinking, or the willpower of self-control.[74] It is an expensive resource that consumes glucose and oxygen, so the battery can run out very fast. Attention has directional focus. We choose where to place the beam of attention. Imagine the beam of light. Is it directed at the object of attention or does it lurch around like an unsteady flashlight? How bright is the beam? How sharp is the resolution?

To get a feel for this, find a leaf or flower. Get up close and direct your full attention to the object. Screen out all surrounding distractions and direct 100% of your mental energy on exploring the object — colours, contours, surfaces, smell, feel, taste and the sound of its movement. Notice how much information is available. See how long you can stay absorbed. This is one end of the attention spectrum — narrow, detailed, focused and intense. The beam of light is very narrow and directed. Everything else fades to darkness.

At the other end is open presence. Step back and take in everything around you — room, floor, ceiling, furniture, temperature, light, sky and so on. How much of what is present to your senses can you stretch your awareness over? Now the light beam is broad and diffuse. While there is much more to see, the detail fades from awareness.

Attention is a focus of the work of Richard Davidson. He has shown how attention is primarily sourced in the PFC behind the forehead. It is supported by the dopamine system of the nucleus accumbens. Davidson suggests that we all range on a spectrum from high focus to distracted attention. At one extreme is the super-focus of a target shooter and at the other is someone with Attention Deficit and Hyperactivity Disorder (ADHD). There are advantages to both if they are not too extreme. Those who are more focused in attention can study deeply and execute complex plans, while those less focused may be more creative and exciting.

In an information-dense world, the ability to focus attention when required on what matters can be an enormous advantage. Davidson and Baumeister have shown that we can build attention, self-control and willpower. Attention responds to training within weeks. There are many pathways. You might start with getting fit, mastering a new sport or hobby, learning yoga, taking a meditation class, or taking a challenging course of study or reading.

As you practise your ability to pay attention, the battery source becomes stronger and more durable. Your ability to switch the beam from narrow and directed to broad and diffuse will improve. You will need to rest well between practice sessions. Be reassured that this is not esoteric or spiritual. This is simply training your mind to be more effective and powerful. One could call this being mindful. When the word mindfulness is used it is primarily in this context of paying attention to your attention. This is a meta-awareness.

A number of biofeedback devices are now available (see Practice, next page) that record brainwaves and allow you to see the process of directing and strengthening your mind unfolding on a screen as real, objective data.

## Practice

1. Sleep well, stay fit and eat breakfast.
2. Take regular recovery breaks.
3. Pay attention to your posture — stay light and tall.
4. Pick a meaningful focus to work on — a skill, an idea, meditation, a book or communication.
5. Take a little time each day to direct your full attention to focus.
6. Start with bursts of five minutes and work up to 30 minutes.
7. Biofeedback devices you might consider are:
   - Emwave (Heartmath) — tracks heart rate variability (HRV) and vagal tone. Visual and effective.
   - Mindwave (Neurosky) — with a simple EEG headband, this device tracks brainwaves. Great for attention training.
   - Muse (InteraXon) — a new and more complex EEG headband.

## 3. Practice — Meditation

Meditation techniques have a 2000-year-old history. They are integral to many cultures, spiritual practices, artists and healers. Over the past century these practices have merged into mainstream Western secular thinking and practice. Millions of people have learned and now practise meditation in its different forms. Practitioners claim valued personal benefits. Science has been sceptical, but is accepting the hard evidence of measurability and benefit.

In the last two decades meditation has captured modern medicine, psychiatry, psychology and brain sciences. There is a community of highly respected professionals including Jon Kabat-Zinn, Daniel Siegel, Paul Ekman, Martin Seligman, Barbara Fredrickson, Daniel Goleman, and Richard Davidson who have been involved in research, practice and teaching. The scientific case for practising meditation is clear. Practice leads to calmer physiology, better health, positive emotions and better thinking.

Examining brain scans of experienced meditators, one is left in no doubt that this is a powerful practice with extensive objective benefits. Meditation could and should stand shoulder-to-shoulder with exercise in terms of value to modern life.

It is a difficult skill to master when most of our lives fidget about in overload, busyness and confusion. A confident teacher, respected school or the support of fellow students can make a real difference. My experience is that yoga, Buddhist meditation, Vipasanna meditation and the teaching of Jon Kabat-Zinn[75] are some of the most accessible ways to progress.

Good meditation requires deep relaxation of the body, calming of the emotions, and discipline of the mind. The combination makes successful practice demanding. If you think building your biceps in the gym is hard, just wait to discover how hard it is to build biceps in the brain. Ask carefully if it is the right thing for you. Check it out with people you know who meditate. Read the works by the authors listed above. Start slowly and with support.

Your objective is to learn how to hold your mind calm, stable, alert and very clear. Most teachers encourage 20–30 minutes twice a day. However, there is some evidence to suggest that regular short practices of a minute[76] can be effective. The first challenge is finding a quiet, secluded time in your busy day to 'do the work'. If you are too excited or too sleepy, your practice will be frustrating. It has to be a priority and requires preparation.

The calm and focused mental state depends on feeling physically good. Get a good night's sleep, eat with intelligence and stay fit. Progress also requires a positive, relaxed emotional state. Therefore a priority is to increase emotional awareness and the capacity for maintaining constructive emotions such as calm, appreciation, joy, passion and kindness.

## How to practise meditation

For those who would like to develop their own practice, the following instructions will help you to make a start.

### Preparation
▷ Select your time of day, location and dress, and get family support.
▷ Toilet, have something to drink and keep lights low.
▷ Spend a few minutes stretching all muscle groups.

**Sitting position**
- Sit in an upright chair or on a cushion — keep it comfortable.
- Ensure your spine is vertical, light and long from coccyx to head.
- Keep your chest open and your arms and legs relaxed.

**Diaphragmatic breath**
- Start with observing the breath, noting the rising and falling feeling.
- Lengthen the exhalation, smooth the flow and keep the belly/chest soft.
- To help focus, repeat to yourself: 'rising' as you inhale (three seconds) and 'falling' as you exhale (five seconds).

**Engaging the heart**
- Take your attention to the area of your heart and notice any feelings.
- On the next exhalation, nurture a feeling of calm contentedness.
- On the inhalation, nurture feelings of appreciation and gratitude.
- Move towards a feeling of joy on the inhalation and kindness on the exhalation.

**Choosing a focus**
- You can continue to maintain focus on the breath or a feeling, or focus on a part of the body (forehead, umbilicus) or a word.
- Narrow your focus to a point and strengthen the beam of attention.

**Training the mind**
- The mind will wander, thoughts interfere and it is easy to be distracted — this is normal.
- Notice 'thinking', release the thought and gently refocus with an exhalation.
- Bring the focus and beam strength of attention back to the focus point.
- Practise lengthening the time you can hold the mind intensely focused.
- Reflect again on the meaning of a stable, calm, alert and clear mind.

**Witness reality, self and integration**
- In time the mind becomes strong, stable and focused.
- You will become increasingly aware of the quality of your attention.
- Look into this awareness, seeking the source of self and reality.

▷ There is space, connection, and expansion in this 'big mind' state.

▷ This 'witness' or 'open presence' awareness brings everything together seamlessly.

▷ It is surprisingly delightful when it eventually reveals itself.

**Completion**

▷ When you are done, reverse out of the deep concentration.

▷ Notice your feelings, your breath, your body and the room.

▷ Lengthen your breath, stretch your fingers and shoulders.

▷ Connect back to your day with peace, love and joy.

·····································

Despite the difficulty of mastering meditation — and every caution is justified — the rewards are wonderful. The experience can be uplifting and enriching. Even in the short duration of five minutes, there are measurable physiological, emotional and psychological changes that leave you feeling refreshed, uplifted and sometimes even blissful.

Short-term payback is felt as greater energy through the day, a sense of calm clarity, and a reduction in reactive behaviour. The changes in hormones, oxygen efficiency, blood pressure and brain patterns are clearly measurable over a couple of weeks.

Longer-term benefits include better health outcomes. There are profound changes in the brain. Among others, the PFC is more active. This serves to maintain a higher level of consciousness as the drama of life unfolds. We are more able to be aware and skilfully responsive rather than impulsive and reactive. Richard Davidson and others have shown that the minds of practised meditators are profoundly more effective than non-meditators.

Explore, learn, develop your skills and enjoy the journey. Your willpower will be tested and strengthened.

## 4. Practice — Empathy

We have worked through the basic emotions in the last chapter. This is the base for empathy. As we understand more about the emotions and how to read them in ourselves and others, we can begin to ask the question: 'How does this person feel?' Empathy begins with interest in others. We can suspend our own self-interest to pay attention to the world of others. Cognitive empathy is the ability to read others accurately. Emotional empathy is the ability to feel what others are feeling.

Empathy circuits in the brain are trainable. Again, we range across a wide spectrum from tuned out (sometimes part of autism) to sensitive to every nuance in others. Both have their risks and benefits. Those high on the empathy scale are great at making connection, counselling and coaching. Those at the other end may be better in creative or technological tasks.

We will explore empathy in more detail in part five, Connection.

## Summary

- ✳ Develop a workable understanding of your mind.
- ✳ Practise being present with time mastery.
- ✳ Train your capacity for attention.
- ✳ Trial and practise some forms of meditation.

## Chapter 14

# Mastery

### Reframing Body, Heart and Mind

Mastery is an integrating competence. It engages all the practical elements of the work we have covered so far in a dynamic assessment and mastery process. It is complex at first, but well worth working through. Situation mastery is the purpose of inside-out in the real world of action. Mastery is primarily a brain training competence. It is a process of becoming aware of the default reaction to a situation and the actions we take as habit. As we notice this we are able to evaluate the appropriateness and effectiveness of our responses to a situation. If we want to change and grow, mastery gives us the method to explore, develop and practise novel ways to do better.

First we look at the awareness needed to master situations with skill. This is the foundation of leadership, competitive sport, creative work, relationships and an effective life. We will work through this concept in three steps: situation assessment, visioning a solution, and securing mastery. These three steps train the mind and engage our body and emotions in the process. All aspects of the inside-out journey can be embraced as you build competence in mastery.

Situation assessment is a distinct, trainable ability. We are all familiar with those who can quickly tune into their environment — social, sport or discipline. They quickly understand a situation by reading multiple cues and making an accurate assessment of what is going on. Imagine a skilful doctor in the emergency room. Others might find themselves in a similar situation but they will be awkward and ineffective.

Performance Supply Chain

**INSIGHT**
**PRACTICE**
**MASTERY**

We can better understand the assessment phase by remembering our performance supply chain (above).

Post-Traumatic Stress Disorder (PTSD) is an extreme example, where simple daily challenges can overwhelm a person's ability to comprehend and cope. Using the diagram above, we can imagine a soldier coming back from a gruesome war zone with PTSD. Let's say he is walking down the road at home and a plank clatters on to the pavement. The soldier freezes as his heart rate accelerates and he is flooded with adrenaline (body). Fear surges through his body, shunting blood from brain, organs and skin to legs. The mind believes it is a mortar (mind) and the soldier crashes to the ground in a panic (action). The response is neither appropriate nor effective.

Daily events become catastrophic as the panic and fear reactions pepper every unexpected event. He struggles with change, surprise, relationships or conflict. We know that in the brain of this soldier with PTSD the amygdala is overactive to fear and the hippocampus is diminished. The hippocampus is a curved body in the brain, well correlated with our ability to assess a situation.

When the amygdala is calm (coherence, vagal tone and impulse control) we are much better able to pause long enough to assess an event accurately. Likewise, those with a strong, active hippocampus are quickly able to map a situation accurately as it evolves. This person hears the clatter of the plank, swiftly checks auditory and visual input, and maps the situation accurately. The situation is assessed as surprising but not dangerous. Heart rate stays slow, coherence is strong and the person can act appropriately and effectively to avoid injury or help others.

Thinking back to the last chapter, the soldier's mind has gone back to the war zone and is focusing on totally inappropriate and potentially harmful activity. There is little mindfulness and unlikely to be any empathy. The effective response stays in the present and focuses on appropriate, skilful activity — mindful and empathic. We can also see that if the physical and emotional systems are disturbed or out of control, it is very hard to get access to the mind.

Mastery allows us to take situations with undesirable outcomes and rebuild our response to be more appropriate and effective. A simple example of sleep was introduced in part one, chapter 2: Altitude. Please take one or two situations that you would like to work on and follow the process. Situations that are relatively simple will help you develop the mental skills to develop new responses. As one becomes more competent, it is easier to tackle more complex situations. Below is a list of mastery challenges people find helpful, listed from simple to more complex.

- ▶ Securing a better quality night of sleep.
- ▶ Establishing a regular exercise habit.
- ▶ Changing cravings for junk food, alcohol, cigarettes …
- ▶ Removing anger and frustration from your daily commute.
- ▶ Transforming procrastination into results.
- ▶ Learning a new sporting skill or playing in a different emotional state.
- ▶ Shifting from high anxiety to relaxed in a performance/interview.
- ▶ Taking a proactive leadership role in your team.
- ▶ Improving the quality of an intimate relationship.

The first step is to select a situation to assess and map carefully. What happened at the physical, emotional, cognitive and action levels? Learn to describe this in rich language that captures the situation and your inner dynamics at all levels and to see how they interrelate. This is insight. For example, if I hold my breath I stiffen and become apprehensive. Then I doubt my ability.

A simple framework to complete appears on page 208. Think about a situation in your recent past that did not work out. Take time to reflect on the situation and to note all you can remember during the experience. It can be helpful to have someone who was there to review and contribute to your mapping of the situation. This is where the power of good coaching emanates. A video recording is humbling and valuable.

PART FOUR: CREATIVITY

Figure 30: Situation Mastery Worksheet: — Assessment of Current State

**Action**

**1. Behaviours**
What would we see on video?
What was the intention?
What was the impact — human and technical?

**Mind**

**2. Cognitive**
Describe mental dialogue.
Is there a clear thought?
What are the main ideas?
Is there a deeper belief?

**Heart**

**3. Emotional**
Name the emotions.
Describe feelings.
Where do you feel it?
How did they affect you?

**Body**

**4. Physical**
What was your body like?
Energy levels?
Breathing pattern?
Muscular tension?
Discomfort?

As we define our experience of sub-optimal situations, we exercise the brain through a reflective and analytic loop. We are exercising the hippocampus and memory systems to create a rich picture of something that can happen quite fast and with little awareness. We begin to wake up to ourselves in these situations. Athletes and their coaches carefully analyse footage of competition to understand fully how a situation unfolded and where the opportunities for adjustment exist. In exactly the same way, situation assessment allows you to see how the situation unfolded in a new light. You are able to see the key triggers and reactions. You can map the links between body, emotion, mind and outcome in the situation.

This practice is self-awareness in context. We see ourselves in stark profile. We can see what we want to keep, what to stop and what to do more of. It is also a form of motivation. The practice of reflection opens the door to change, growth and transformation. There may be small adjustments such as breathing out or significant changes such as exploring a new perspective on the situation. This is a deliberate, structured and daily practice of high performers in sport, combat and business. We can take advantage of the mastery process by then building an alternative response to the situation.

As we shift from assessment to mastery, a key step is to define how we would prefer to 'see' the targeted situation evolving. This is what you aspire to. You may have an example of someone else to help you visualise the mastery you are targeting. An example relating to exercise appears on page 210.

In the early days it can be helpful to use a paint-by-numbers approach, following the steps described above to create a clear picture of current versus desired state. Some coaches use the words 'old way' versus 'new way' to help create a clear distinction between the past and the future. It is essential to describe the new way so that you can visualise it happening in the actual situation when it next presents. Experts routinely create time to articulate clearly and then visualise this new way. Multiple studies show visualisation is as effective as actual physical practice in developing both structure and function of the brain — and therefore a desired outcome.

Remember that visualisation is most effective if we are relaxed, confident in its impact and consistent in practice. So if success in mastery is important, be sure to allocate enough time and the right conditions to practise visualising the desired outcome. Choose a quiet and relaxing environment, preferably early in the day when your cognitive resources are fully charged.

Figure 31: Mapping and Visualising the Mastery State with Exercise as an Example

| | Body | Heart | Mind | Action |
|---|---|---|---|---|
| **Resilient** | 8. What is required of your body? | 7. What feelings support you? | 6. What thoughts will drive this? | 2. Describe desired outcome. |
| | Energised, resolute, and strong. | Satisfied, confident, proud. Feel engaged and good. | I love exercise. Walking is a highlight of my day. It makes such a difference. | Scheduled into my day. Booked with a coach. On my way to work. |
| **Vulnerable** | 5. What is the effect on your body? | 4. What feelings do you have? | 3. What are you thinking? | 1. Describe situation to change. |
| | Low energy, dull and depleted. | Sad, fearful, ashamed. Feelings of withdrawal and avoidance. | Exercise is hard. I will never get this right. How could I put on shorts? I hate exercise. | Never get started. Just too busy. In terrible shape. When I try I get injured. |

MASTERY     PRACTICE     INSIGHT

As you take yourself into the imagined future situation, create a simple process to follow each time. For example:

1. Relax the body and steady your breath, aiming to create the vagal-brake effect described in coherence.
2. Put yourself into the situation and map the environment and participants.
3. Tune your senses to the expected visual map, sounds, smells, taste and feel.
4. Visualise your body coming to life in this environment in exactly the right state.
5. Create the emotions that you want to be able to sustain in the mastery state.
6. Rehearse the thoughts and beliefs you want to be able to sustain as challenge increases.
7. Remember the dynamic element of a situation and the need to adapt body, emotion and mind.
8. Consider using biofeedback to review and secure the optimal physiological state: emWave can be used to secure coherence and Mindwave can be used to monitor brain waves.

The final stage of mastery is to develop the skills required to lock success in place. Visualisation creates a strong base and begins to train the brain and neurology for the practice. Some studies show that visualisation can even develop muscular strength and skill. However, reality is where the rubber hits the road and it is critical to practise in real situations. Just as an athlete practises for an event thousands of times before executing on a world stage, so we might consider practising for the key situations we want to master in our lives. Here we can bring the practices we have covered so far into play.

So just as a pianist must practise the finger strengthening, postural support, breathing, emotional state, mindfulness and complex movements, so we can practise the components that will make up the mastery of our life situations. Let's go back to the exercise example to explore how we might put the components together. See figure 32 on page 212.

To transform ourselves from the old way to achieve the visualised new way, we have to add practice. Practices here can be longer-term

212    PART FOUR: CREATIVITY

Figure 32: Situation Mastery and Supporting Practices (the situation in this case is exercise)

| | Body | Heart | Mind | Action |
|---|---|---|---|---|
| **Resilient** | 8. What is required of your body?<br><br>Energised, resolute, and strong. | 7. What feelings support you?<br><br>Satisfied, confident, proud. Feel engaged and good. | 6. What thoughts will drive this?<br><br>I love exercise. Walking is a highlight of my day. It makes such a difference. | 2. Describe desired outcome.<br><br>Scheduled into my day. Booked with a coach. On my way to work. |
| | Sleep<br>Move<br>Nourish | Impulse control<br>Emotion regulation | Mindfulness<br>Optimism | Ritualise<br>Commitment |
| **Vulnerable** | 5. What is the effect on your body?<br><br>Low energy, dull and depleted. | 4. What feelings do you have?<br><br>Sad, fearful, ashamed. Feelings of withdrawal and avoidance. | 3. What are you thinking?<br><br>Exercise is hard. I will never get this right. How could I put on shorts? I hate exercise. | 1. Describe situation to change.<br><br>Never get started. Just too busy. In terrible shape. When I try I get injured. |

MASTERY   PRACTICE   INSIGHT

development investments such as a good sleep routine, or they might be very immediate and practical actions such as meeting with your coach. In the example above, eight key practices were selected to work on. This person has established that getting a good night's sleep, staying active and eating well are physical foundations. Impulse control and positive emotions enable emotion. Mindfulness and optimism support the mind. Creating a habit and committing to a coach establish the action.

Success in securing mastery of exercise as a long-term habit will require repetition, refinement and resourcefulness. Repetition establishes habit and efficiency. We move from overwhelming drama to a daily routine. Refinement helps to make the small adjustments that make it achievable and effective for you. Resourcefulness will be needed to overcome the inevitable tests of illness, injury, travel and family responsibility.

The upside in this case is huge. We recognise the stark contrast between a period of our lives when we are inactive and unfit versus when we are engaged in activity we love and achieve a high level of fitness. As we build up a routine, it is helpful to be present to the enjoyment and wellbeing that comes from mastery. Savour it, share it and explore new ways to bring positive associations into play. I recently had my first paddle of the season. My body was strained, but celebrating the glorious sunrise on the water created an experience infused with 'I want more'. Savouring the good in mastery creates a virtuous circle of improvement.

On page 214 there is one more example of how to work this in sport. Athletes get to do a lot of this work. Figure 34 on page 215 is a template for you to use so you can work on a situation that is meaningful for you.

I encourage you to seek out a coach. Coaching is an ancient profession sourced in parenting, mystics and gurus, apprenticeships and court advisors. As stated in the first sentence of this book, humans have taken a long time to get operational. In our complex society, success is based on learning skills that do not 'come naturally'. Instinct can actually get us into a lot of trouble. You can't just spear someone who disagrees. We have to learn how to listen, reflect, understand, explain and influence. This growth is basic mastery. It is developed by watching experts, being disciplined, and through encouragement.

Working with a small group of super-successful entrepreneurs some years ago was when I first seriously understood this concept. In a casual conversation about what exercise each person did, I realised that every single

Figure 33: Situation Assessment and Mastery in Sport

| | Body | Heart | Mind | Action |
|---|---|---|---|---|
| **Resilient** (MASTERY) | 8. What is required of your body?<br><br>*Relaxed body posture, soft grip, breathe out. fast.* | 7. What feelings support you?<br><br>*Equanimity, self compassion, curiosity, and intensity.* | 6. What thoughts will drive this?<br><br>*OK, fair effort. What can I learn? Making progress. I am learning* | 2. Describe desired outcome.<br><br>*Completely relaxed about poor shots, no visible or auditory evidence of reaction.* |
| (PRACTICE) | Breath out<br>Relax | Impulse control<br>Emotion regulation<br>Empathy | Mindfulness<br>Optimism | Commitment<br>Challenge-skill match (Flow) |
| **Vulnerable** (INSIGHT) | 5. What is the effect on your body?<br><br>*Tense, stiff and disconnected from ball.* | 4. What feelings do you have?<br><br>*Sad, fearful, shame, avoidance and fatigue.* | 3. What are you thinking?<br><br>*What a fool! Can't I get anything right? What must they be thinking about me?* | 1. Describe situation to change.<br><br>*Missing easy shots. Showing frustration. Angry face. Vocal outbursts.* |

MASTERY 215

Figure 34: Situation Mastery Worksheet

|  | *Body* | *Heart* | *Mind* | *Action* |
|---|---|---|---|---|
| MASTERY | **Resilient**<br>8. What is required of your body? | 7. What feelings support you? | 6. What thoughts will drive this? | 2. Describe desired outcome. |
| PRACTICE | **Breath out**<br>Relax<br>Move, sleep<br>Nourish | Impulse control<br>Emotion regulation<br>Empathy | Mindfulness<br>Attention control<br>Optimism | Ritualise<br>Purpose (Spirit in Action)<br>Commitment<br>Challenge-skill match (Flow) |
| INSIGHT | **Vulnerable**<br>5. What is the effect on your body? | 4. What feelings do you have? | 3. What are you thinking? | 1. Describe situation to change. |

one of them was using at least one coach. Several had three contracted coaches to help them in different sports. Being of the view that one should just 'toughen up and push through', this was enlightening. With years of experience of working in sports medicine, I knew perfectly well that no athlete or team gets to succeed over time without comprehensive coaching and support. Most athletes have a whole team of coaches and experts nudging them to higher mastery levels — nutrition, flexibility, strength, speed, technique, mental skills, media skills, and so on.

It was shocking to recognise that despite my experience and the abundant evidence for the value of coaching, I had never bothered to apply it to myself as a professional. I set about correcting the error and have since engaged coaches in tennis, surf skiing, swimming and business. It does not always work well and sometimes the fit is not right. However, I have seldom failed to learn something useful and acquire new levels of mastery. When you discover a coach with whom you work well, mastery becomes a part of your life. It is very rewarding and enjoyable. Change, growth and transformation follows in other areas of your life.

## Summary

- ✸ We can all change, grow and transform ourselves and our lives.
- ✸ Target situations that create positive change.
- ✸ Understand the situation as it is — body, heart, mind and action.
- ✸ Map and visualise the situation when you have achieved the optimal outcome.
- ✸ Put in the practice — repeat, reinforce and adapt — and get a coach.

## Chapter 15

# Flow

### The Portal into Creative Excellence

Mihaly Csikszentmihalyi coined the word 'flow' to describe the state in which we are fully engaged and effective in what we do. I had the pleasure of doing a workshop with Mihaly in 2014. He has published on the concept of flow since 1975, and ranks as one of the great psychologists of all time. Originally, flow was described as the optimal psychological state — primarily cognitive. Over the years the concept has been proven profoundly useful to people in sport, business, professions, creativity and play.

Flow is action based. It is a state that emerges or can be created by matching skill with challenge. We are doing something difficult and we have the necessary skills to master the challenge. When we secure flow in our lives we increase our health, happiness and effectiveness. The state of flow is closely linked to success, peak experiences, creativity, joy and world-class performance. Mihalyi estimates that 20% of people enjoy flow on a regular basis. The rest do not.

We can build flow into work, play and life. We can secure more flow with the right training and support. Flow is the portal into our most creative states. If we can find flow in our lives, we open a portal into the very best that we can be. This is the goal of this chapter.

Mihalyi and others have defined criteria that describe the flow state.

▶ The challenge is matched by appropriate skill.
▶ There is a clear goal.
▶ We get immediate feedback.

- ▶ We are focused on the task.
- ▶ There is a sense of control.
- ▶ We are deeply engaged — action and awareness merge.
- ▶ The mind is quiet — even silent — the PFC is quiet (hypofrontality).
- ▶ There is rhythm and pace— time dilates or contracts.
- ▶ It feels right (autotelic) — the activity is meaningful.

····································································

## Practice

Reflecting on these criteria alone can help you understand what this state of engagement feels like for you. Most of us can remember a time when some of these criteria were active. This is the key to discovering flow.

Wherever we are in our life's journey, this remembering and reconstructing times when you achieved a state of flow is a powerful exercise. I encourage you to start this practice today. Use a journal. Even better, engage those you love, play and work with to explore these times. The following questions might help you define the memory more clearly:

- ▷ What were you doing?
- ▷ What were the challenges or situations you faced?
- ▷ What skills did you use?
- ▷ How were you feeling at the time?
- ▷ How did you feel at the end?
- ▷ How were your relationships?
- ▷ What were you thinking?
- ▷ What was your health like?
- ▷ Was your lifestyle remarkable in any way at the time?
- ▷ Are there any common themes across your stories?

····································································

Ideally, this might become a daily reflection. Take a few minutes to scan your day for times in which you approached the flow state. Occasionally, these will be true peak experiences. Mostly they will be degrees of fit between challenge and skill. A reasonable level of difficulty matched to reasonable skill can still evoke the flow state. We do not need to save the world or become millionaires every day.

The next step is to fit the goal of achieving flow in your own life — sport, hobby, work, play or creativity. Sometimes we completely miss flow. There are two basic dimensions to master. The first is the level of challenge. It may be way too difficult or so dull it is barely stimulating. The second is the level of skill available. At times we have plenty of skill and the situation is relaxing, while at other times we cannot muster the skill and find ourselves really anxious or overwhelmed.

Let's take a quick practical overview of the states in which we might find ourselves in any given task, situation or day. We start with flow and see what happens as we master the challenge and our skills exceed demand.

**Flow** is defined by nine characteristics. Some will be more important to you than others. Yoga, dance, creativity, rock climbing and music can all score high on this dimension. It is important to recognise that flow can be edgy. Few seek to dangle off thousand-foot rock faces or win Olympic gold. This is the far top right — macro-flow. The flow that most of us seek approximates the oval space where we have a little margin. Even then, flow is very demanding. We cannot be in high flow all day. We must pace ourselves or we will exhaust our reserves and make errors. An hour of flow

**Figure 35: Flow and the Performance States on Challenge Versus Skill Axes**
(Adapted from Csikzentmihalyi, 1990)

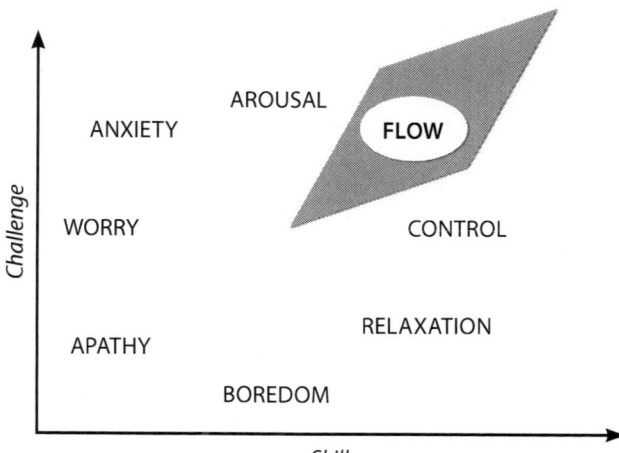

may need two hours of recovery. Microflow — where we have moderate challenge matched by moderate skill — is more sustainable.

**Control** occurs when the challenge is not excessive and you have skill in reserve. You feel confident and assured. This is an engaged and productive state — doing your routine jobs well, driving, working at your job or a hobby. Control is more sustainable. Error is less likely. It is highly desirable in any profession. You would prefer a surgeon to work on you in Control and reserve flow for a crisis or critical phase.

**Relaxation** follows when there is abundant skill and the challenge is easy for you. You are relaxed in an activity and probably in a state of calm enjoyment. Relaxation can be productive and many good leaders use this state to engage and encourage others. Reflecting, reading, dinner conversation, walking or listening to music are good examples. More relaxation in the average work day is highly desirable. Professor Leslie Perlow has shown in multiple studies[77] how structured time off increases productivity, satisfaction and team performance.

**Boredom** can slip in when the challenge appears low or non-existent and you are not paying much attention. This is dangerous as you are not engaged and become exposed to error, injury, self-doubt, worry and frustration. Managers should be careful of this in their teams. Every individual should strive to negotiate out of boredom. No child should be bored.

**Apathy** is a depleted state of low challenge and skill. We are neither stimulated nor resourceful. This is similar to the withdrawal, vulnerability, distress and depression described in the death spiral. Alone, drunk and channel surfing the TV. Or tapping away at your smartphone. Apathy is dangerous. Limit your time here.

On the other side, let's understand what happens when the challenge rises and our skills fail to meet the demand.

**Arousal** is a common state in modern life. We face large, multiple challenges and doubt our resources (perhaps time more than skill) to cope with the overload. It is an activated state and can be found in high excitement, major challenges and in new learning. Provided we can stay focused and marshal our resources to the challenge, it can be productive and lead us into flow.

**Anxiety** is triggered when the challenge looms large and immediate and we seriously doubt our resources to cope. This triggers an acute stress reaction and fear. The state of anxiety can be useful for a minute or two to focus one's attention, trigger the release of adrenaline and prepare for battle. If anxiety is sustained it will destroy our resources by flooding us with cortisol.

**Worry** is a destructive state where small challenge is experienced as overwhelming. We fret and ruminate on how things may turn out badly. Often this happens in the early hours of the morning, or when we fret about things that may go wrong in the future. It is dangerous, pointless and undermines your ability to face a challenge when it does arrive.

## The Biology of Flow

A recent book on flow sheds new light and research on the application of flow. I would like to share the key ideas and recommend to all who aspire to greatness to read Steven Kotler's book, *The Rise of Superman*.[78] Kotler has gathered and integrated current research on flow and applied it through the story of adventure or extreme sport. The lessons are practical and valuable for every pursuit of optimal performance. It is creative, joyous and healthily addictive.

Most of us have heard about the different brain waves. It is one way to help understand what happens in flow. Following is a quick and simple summary.

- 1–3.9 Hertz: delta waves found in deep sleep and deep meditation.
- 4–7.9 Hertz: theta waves found as we fall into sleep and in some creative states.
- 8–13.9 Hertz: alpha waves found in relaxed and alert states.
- 14–30 Hertz: beta waves found in active (type 2) thinking and high arousal.
- >30 Hertz: gamma waves found in highly connected and flow states.

Studies on high performers (experts) show a different combination of brain waves when they enter highly productive states. When we engage with an activity our brain responds along a well-defined process of six stages:

1. baseline

2. analysis and problem solving
3. pre-action readiness
4. execution of action
5. post-action evaluation
6. baseline.

There are two distinct ways in which we can engage our skills into a challenge. The first is explicit learning, where the prefrontal cortex is activated and we follow a logical pathway. Often a coach will yell out explicit instructions. Expensive processing uses beta waves predominantly, but allows us to test a skill and explore its depth and effectiveness. This is what one does when learning how to execute a basic manoeuvre that might be part of a performance.

Explicit learning lays a foundation but is a slower way to process the six stages above. Examples include learning the forehand stroke in tennis, developing a good putt in golf, acquiring the finger skills for a piece of music, or solving a component of an equation. The learner will be able to describe exactly what he or she did.

The second is implicit learning, where we learn by doing and feeling our way into the skill. Rather than analysing and planning, we commit to the practice with faith and curiosity. The planning part of the brain goes quiet. The response is more instinctive or intuitive. It is felt. The prefrontal cortex deactivates (called hypofrontality) and energy is diverted to circuits of awareness and action in the moment.

Many studies show this to be a superior way to learn. The brain is measured in low alpha and high theta. The processing in the brain becomes very fast and efficient. This is the 'Federer forehand', a master putt, a musical maestro, or the insight into relativity that Einstein might have experienced. The learner may not be able to describe how they did it.

People who master flow can enter this implicit state more easily and faster than others. Their ability to run the process through analysis, problem solving, pre-action readiness, execution and post-action evaluation is fast, fluid and efficient. Part of the reason is an ability to activate low alpha and high theta waves with ease. They are able to burrow into the flow state on demand. As a consequence, their performance is vastly superior to the average person. We are able to measure gamma activity in their brains that suggests a very high level of connection and co-ordination across the entire brain. The activity measured is similar to that of an experienced meditator.

Don't forget that the exponentially enhanced performance from intrinsic and deep flow is developed through years of explicit learning. Even extreme adventure athletes always analyse, plan and practise their manoeuvres in great detail, ensuring that they can match the situation to their skills. This part is explicit. Then, when they commit, they transition into the intrinsic state and the front of the brain switches off. We can train to make this transition. Failure to make this transition in an extreme activity can be fatal as success is not possible using explicit processing.

Going just a bit deeper, when we enter flow we dramatically increase decision-making and creative problem solving. This happens in all creative insights or breath-through activities. On the EEG we see a spike of gamma activity 30 milliseconds prior to the 'aha'. There are three preconditions.

First, we have to be able to enter a calm, alpha state as we approach the challenging situation. This is measured pulsing out of the right side of the brain. Anxiety, tension and beta waves close the door. Second, we have to trigger theta waves, which are part of the information processing required in novelty. Third, theta allows the gamma spike that connects the brain. Now accelerated creative decision-making that makes the impossible possible can operate.

## The Voice of Creativity

When we are deep in flow activities, experience is very different to normal life. The judging, chattering mind disappears and we connect deeply with intuition. Even as critical moments for action flash past, there is a deep sense of confidence and control. Some athletes and researchers call it the voice. They claim it saves their lives and it would be fatal not to listen. This is the deep engagement and action-awareness merging described in flow.

Neurobiology is mapping this. As we enter the flow state, the brain changes its function markedly. The dorsolateral PFC deactivates, as discussed above. First, this saves a heap of blood flow and oxygen more usefully applied elsewhere. Second, it silences the noisy critical and anxious mind. Some studies show the medial PFC, where elements of self-expression and emotional awareness reside, becomes more active.

As a consequence, we enter a very pure and trusting state of self-expression. Self-limiting doubt has gone. We know what we must do. The brain stops tracking time in order to free up resources for attention and awareness. Flow can also deactivate an area called the orientation association area in the parietal lobe. This area draws boundaries between self and not-self. Thus, as it quietens, we feel as if we have become one with a situation. Athletes describe being one with the river or the rock.

When the brain tunes out from our normal tracking of self, time and space, we discover a wonderful clarity on what is right and needed. We feel it deeply and we act immediately. This is the voice. When we find a way to tune into it we are the very best expression of who we can be. The brain is in a super-powerful mode of operation and our biological resources are shunted efficiently to where they are most needed — awareness, attention, decision-making, problem solving, creativity, or physical action. When expert observers, spectators or brain scientists watch the performance, there is no doubt that what is happening is exceptional.

## Burrowing into Flow

Flow is available to everyone. Extreme activities are good for study, but it is not where most of us live. However, would anyone choose not to have more joy, wellbeing and performance? Let's look at how we can get more flow into our lives.

We can secure it in dance, music, sport, meditation, business, medicine, art, technology — anything where we can find an intrinsically motivating activity. A creative life begins when we discover a challenge that gives us a buzz. It begins in small awakenings as a child. Those lucky enough to find a match between the challenge and developing skills get a double buzz. Not only do they feel wonderful after the activity, but their entire being is charged and motivated for the next effort.

A great failure of modern childhood and education is the compression of time and expectations of parents. We drive our youth down pretty boring subjects and fill their spare time with dull, repetitive gadgets. The purpose of childhood is to explore, experiment, fail, be surprised, take risks and learn what skills can be applied to master the risk. Finding the right activity requires experimentation. In this view, it is essential to give children the opportunity to work away at many different sports, activities, problem solving and applied learning, increasing the probability that they find something to nourish the creative spirit of flow.

Inside-out has introduced you to a wide range of the explicit practices that build wellbeing, resilience and life performance. Flow brings all of this good work together in a creative expression of our lives. The door to flow is always there. The process, methods and learning mindset are clear. We do not have to be extreme athletes. We can find flow in many activities. In all cases the key criteria listed at the beginning of this chapter will help us on the quest. Three of these external triggers are critical to explore and master.

First, we need to define and focus on clear goals. We need an overarching goal, such as completing a project by a certain date. We need to break this goal into small, sharp goals along the timeline. At the finest level we must immerse ourselves in momentary goals. This is where we are in the flow state. The intrinsic state is operational and we are deeply immersed. Success ultimately requires that we be fully tuned into these momentary goals. The mind is quiet, and you are in the action-awareness state. You feel what is required and the voice is clear. Rapid, creative decision-making switches on. We move from one small adjustment to the next with confidence and clarity.

Second, we need immediate feedback. The more quickly we get an accurate measure of post-action evaluation, the easier it becomes to stay in the flow channel. The difference between an annual performance review and action-based coaching is dramatic. Adventure sport is extremely rapid and its rapidity is one reason those who do it get so much flow. This requires attention; to really increase your flow you will need coaching. Activities that drive quick feedback loops keep you alert to the quality of your decisions and actions. Improvement follows fast.

Third, we need to match challenge and skill. It appears that the best way to enter flow is to set the challenge 4% beyond current skills. Many of us simply do what we know we can achieve comfortably. Flow requires an upwards nudge — a tiny upwards nudge that is repeated over and over again. By nudging upwards we increase alertness, attention, complexity, risk and novelty. This is the door to the sweet-spot of flow. Every single person can learn to nudge upwards. The brain changes towards the intrinsic system and you are flooded with pleasurable dopamine.

It will be obvious to most that this is quite hard work. A fourth requirement is the wisdom to rest. Periods of flow demand maximum function from brain, emotion and body. Deep rest is an absolutely essential step to allow for rejuvenation.

Putting the material we have covered together within the flow model provides a wonderfully clear and structured resource for increasing productivity, creativity, success and joy. We can build the inside-out journey into the flow model as shown below.

Briefly, let's follow what happens as we test and learn how to find more flow with our work so far. Once we define a meaningful challenge and commit to taking it on, we accept risk. Whether this is base jumping or saying hello to someone new, taking a risk means we can fail or be embarrassed. This triggers anxiety (acute fear). This surge of anxiety can derail the process and probably does in most situations we face. We turn away from the challenge. So the skill here is learning to calm anxiety and to use it to identify opportunities for flow. We can only advance into anxiety with coherence, so if you want flow you should be bulletproof in your breathing, relaxing and coherence practices.

The next step is to dive into a rich, complex environment where you have good skills but 4% less than you need to proceed with confidence or control.

Figure 36: Embedding the Inside-Out Practices of Resilience with Flow

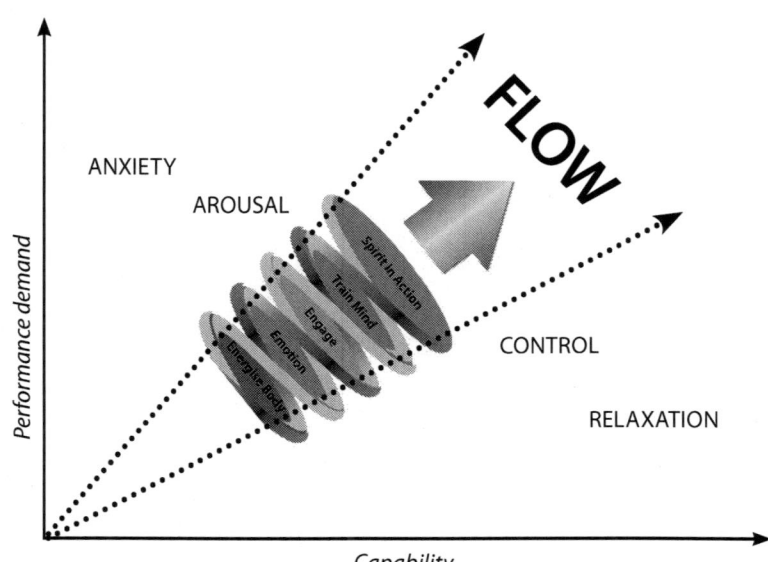

This triggers arousal. We awaken the intrinsic system and, if we can trust the process, we enter flow. Here we need a good night's sleep, nutrition and the physical fitness to immerse ourselves in a demanding biological state.

Then we need to become engaged, immersed or embodied in the activity. While this is clearly physical- and sense-based, the challenge here is to allow the super-fast emotional systems to guide us. Emotional awareness and positivity become essential. We are well fuelled with the associated dopamine, noradrenaline, endorphins and anandamide (cannabis-like). This creates a natural high many would pay for. No wonder the brain works a little differently. We are deep in the experience of flow.

All the work on the mind — being present, attention, and meditative states — is deeply relevant if we want to be able to hold flow more in our lives. It is the key to holding the intrinsic system in play and making space for the theta and gamma of deep creativity. This is Spirit in Action. All parts of you are fully engaged, applying your skills to a meaningful challenge.

As we come out of the flow experience we come back to control, where we can bring the extrinsic (type 2) systems back up and analyse the experience, the learnings and options to improve next time. We are on a serotonin high (ecstasy) at this point.

Then we need deep relaxation. Celebrate, enjoy the high, sleep, stretch and rejuvenate. Consider taking the next day off and savour the feel-good factor. Remember that a little flow each day nudges you into a virtuous spiral towards more.

## Summary

- ☀ Understand how flow fits into your life.
- ☀ Use the biology as needed.
- ☀ Burrow into flow: calm, embody, engage, merge.
- ☀ Listen for the creative voice.
- ☀ Aim for flow in your resilience practices.

# Part Five

# Connection

| | |
|---|---|
| 16　Work | 231 |
| 17　Love | 241 |
| 18　Pray | 254 |
| 19　Discipline | 262 |

## Chapter 16

# Work

### Find Your Calling

Martin Seligman[79] suggests three levels of engagement in life.

- ▶ A happy life in which we seek the maximum moments of pleasure and avoid pain.
- ▶ A good life in which we discover and apply our skills in our roles and work.
- ▶ A meaningful life in which we engage those skills in personally meaningful work.

There are lucky souls who are abundantly engaged and creative in their lives. They radiate confidence, passion, joy and energy. They have a calling in life, be it a profession, a craft, art, entrepreneurship, sport or parenting. Their doubts and hard times are rapidly overcome. When challenged they are able to reach deep and seek solutions. Excitement fuels them into the day and gratitude settles them into sleep — mostly.

Our purpose in this chapter is to help you discover more of this. This is our life's work. We all need to discover — and rediscover — what we are good at and what work is challenging and meaningful to pursue. The alternative is boredom or anxiety. We know this and have all experienced boredom or anxiety at times in our work. Passive acceptance of these states leaves us flirting with the death spiral and wasting the precious moments of our lives.

We must be realistic and accept that we cannot always be at the top of our game. There will always be mismatches. In the current world of work, jobs change frequently. The skills required to master jobs keep changing, as do the challenges we face. Our goal is to master a process for negotiating the world of work.

What are the opportunities out there that match your skills, talents or experience? Which options are exciting, important and meaningful to you? How do we develop our skills and match them to these opportunities? When roles change or jobs dissolve, or we simply outgrow a job, how do we refresh and rebuild meaningful work?

In the last chapter we explored the concept of flow. In this section we will extend this idea into building fulfilling work, a great career, and perhaps even a calling. Remember the criteria for flow and apply this to your current work, and reacquaint yourself with Csikszentmihalyi's flow graph in the previous chapter (figure 35, page 219).

- ▶ The challenge is matched by appropriate skill.
- ▶ There is a clear goal.
- ▶ We get immediate feedback.
- ▶ We are focused on the task.
- ▶ There is a sense of control.
- ▶ We are deeply engaged.
- ▶ The mind is quiet — even silent.
- ▶ There is rhythm and pace — time slips away.
- ▶ It feels right (autotelic) — the activity is meaningful.

······································

## Practice

To refresh and apply the flow chapter, take a moment to review your past week. If needed, pick a week that is about average. Using your diary and your memory, create a table of the week, allocating the amount of time you have been in each of the states. For clarity, include only work-related activity. If you lay awake worrying about a presentation, include it. For simplicity, select a percentage of each day spent in each state.

As we build and develop our careers, they must be periodically reviewed. Where we accumulate flow, we are clearly on the right track. Consider increasing the challenge a fraction. Remember the 4%? When you are in arousal and anxiety,

|  | Mon | Tue | Wed | Thu | Fri | Sat/Sun | Total |
|---|---|---|---|---|---|---|---|
| Flow | | | | | | | |
| Arousal | | | | | | | |
| Anxiety | | | | | | | |
| Worry | | | | | | | |
| Apathy | | | | | | | |
| Boredom | | | | | | | |
| Relaxation | | | | | | | |
| Control | | | | | | | |

you need to ask yourself two questions. First, can I increase my skill development to shift to flow? Second, is this a task that is best done by someone else?

Time spent in control and relaxation is a good investment. Keep it up. If you are finding yourself in worry, apathy or boredom, your work is not well designed for your abilities or aspirations. Perhaps there are elements of your work you can minimise or delegate. Sometimes we need a new challenge.

The goal, in my experience, is to aim for roughly 30% of your day to be spent in each of flow, control and relaxation. Put the other 10% wherever you prefer.

### Case study: Driven by flow

A CEO I work with designs his diary to the flow concept and engages his PA in making sure the structure is upheld. When doing critical work he walls himself away from disruption and allocates 100% of his energy into the task for up to two hours. E-mails and phones are off. Prior to an important meeting he has ten minutes of relaxation booked to sit back and prepare. His meetings are seldom longer than 20 minutes. They are very intense and focused meetings. He checks e-mail only three times a day. Exercise and family time are clearly scheduled into every day. Holidays are booked well in advance.

The productivity and impact of his leadership is beyond question. The discipline is intimidating. I know few people as intensely and meaningfully engaged in life and work. It sets an inspiring example. While many of us do not have such control over our work, every one of us could be a much more effective and fulfilled with a little of this discipline.

## Practice

1. Using the flow concept and the states described above, be sure to review your days against these states. This is a very powerful form of reflection. One starts to see the day in a whole new light. You may be surprised to discover how much time is disappearing into your TV or devices. You may also be shocked to discover that large parts of your day might be spent in anxiety and worry. There is no right or wrong. However, reflecting on your days — particularly at work — will help you define where you want to create change. Look for patterns.

2. Think about what an optimal mix for your day might be. How much flow do you want? Are you willing to tolerate anxiety, worry or apathy? What would it look like if you had more relaxation and it was productive? Define your mix and imagine how you might schedule this into your diary. Remember 30% in each of flow, control and relaxation.

3. Plan your diary to match, as closely as possible, your optimal mix of states. Make sure you plan time for activities that will give you flow, control and relaxation. Space them wisely. If you have a demanding challenge, precede it with a relaxing walk or coffee, and then create undisturbed time to engage in flow. Neurobiology suggests that flow is more likely in the morning. Perhaps schedule relaxing meetings, reading and e-mail for the end of the day. Make sure you have time to bounce and re-energise between events. Many wade through seven successive one-hour meetings.

4. There are times when a situation is testing or boring and you cannot change this. Change yourself. You now have the skills. If testing, remember coherence and see if you can reframe your state to be calm and relaxed. Counter the default urge to anxiety. Breathe out and relax your face. If boring, savour the relaxation but maintain a level of curiosity and playfulness. Stretch, sit upright, tune into the perspectives of others. Stay engaged by adding interest (challenge) or meaning (kindness).

Flow is a great start to creating a fulfilling calling or role in life. It is flexible and can be applied to many different ways of working, competing, parenting or self-completion.

## Skill and Talent

Debate rages about how much talent is inherited versus how much it is acquired. The cultivation of skill during human life defines success. We will use the term 'talent' for attributes we inherit and acquire in early life. These are truly inside.

Talent includes the long arm-to-height ratio of great basketball players, the long, thin legs of distance runners, the visual power of elite tennis or baseball players, the mathematical ability of an Einstein, or the empathy of a saint.[80] It is widely acknowledged that talent, described thus, is sourced in our essence. It is rare for a short, muscular person to win a marathon.

We will use 'skill' to describe the development of abilities through learning, practice, mastery and flow. No matter how perfect her physique, the elite long distance runner must put in the hours of training and develop her race tactics. Likewise, the most mathematical of minds needs thousands of hours' practice to solve string theory or relativity. Again, while it is tempting to believe we can buy skills through weekend courses, they are actually developed through persistent, focused effort from inside-out.

Skills that build on talent will develop fast. It makes good sense to understand where your talent lies and to focus your efforts on extending this natural ability into finely tuned skill. On the other hand, if we try to build skills where we have limited natural talent, life can be an uphill battle. These are critical lessons ideally addressed early in our careers, sports and relationships.

As we have learned in the previous chapters, we can develop better skills in taking care of our physiology, health, emotions and mind. These are general skills that we all need to thrive in life. They are truly inside us. Then there are activity-related skills, where the inside reaches outside to secure an outcome. As an example, imagine a top tennis player facing a break point at the end of a match. They would be working hard on the inner skills of relaxation and breathing (physiological control), maintaining a strong physical presence, down-regulating anxiety, up-regulating passion and calming the mind. This strong inner base allows them to track the ball, move fast, relax into the forehand stroke and deliver a winning point. The latter are all outer skills. Their execution depends on sound inner skills. Even deeper are the core resilience skills of securing sleep, nutrition, specific training and mental preparation before the match. For more insight I recommend Novak Djokovic's book, *Serve to Win*.[81]

## Practice

When we seek to develop skills aligned with our natural talent, it makes good sense to reflect on where our natural talent lies. Howard Gardner's work[82] in this area is a fabulous source of more depth and inspiration. The core talent areas we recommend considering include the following.

| Talent | Explanation (examples) | Your level | | |
|---|---|---|---|---|
| Physical | Body and movement, sport, dance, yoga, martial arts (athlete, coach) | Low | Mod | High |
| Interpersonal | Relationship, connection, communication, empathy (counsellor, team leader) | Low | Mod | High |
| Logical/mathematical | Mathematics, calculation, linear problem solving (accountant, engineer) | Low | Mod | High |
| Musical/linguistic | Expressive connection, sound, timing, tone (musician, entertainer) | Low | Mod | High |
| Visual/spatial | Space, pattern, colour, light, design (painter, architect, strategist) | Low | Mod | High |
| Biological | Physiology, ecology, farming, medicine (doctor, farmer, ecologist) | Low | Mod | High |
| Intrapersonal | Thinking, reflection, imagination (writer, mystic, philosopher) | Low | Mod | High |
| Entrepreneurial | Sales, business process, profit, trade (entrepreneur, manager) | Low | Mod | High |

We all need the basic abilities that education offers, but rarely does school help people define and progress their core talent. We often discover it by accident. Even worse, we might head down a career path for which we are poorly matched. Some creative options in life are found where two combine into one role. Walter Isaacson[83] describes Steve Jobs as the ideal balance of logical and artistic — developing products that work well and look great. Bingo! A money machine.

Stay alert to weaknesses. Jobs often failed at the interpersonal. We all have strengths and weaknesses. Most experts in the field recommend that you define and improve your strengths, partnering with others who can complement your weaknesses.

Talent is then sharpened into our skill base through practice. Howard Gardner researched some of the great creatives of our time and showed how all of them worked with mentors over at least a decade to refine and consolidate their talent into world-class skill. So if you want to be a great biologist, seek out the best people in the field with whom to visit, work and study. If you want to win a Grand Slam, choose a great coach and perfect the elements of play that consolidate your natural movement and visual skills into outstanding technique and a class game.

When it comes to applying yourself to a job, pay more attention to who you will be working for and with, rather than the salary and benefits. The latter will come later. These are job-related skills. The personal skills of inside-out become the fuel and the lubricant for making sure that you can stay the path. An expert in a panic is more dangerous than a calm fool. A depressed doctor will compromise his healing skill. An angry parent can damage talented children.

To summarise, the skill axis of flow can be developed and refined through a three-stage iterative process. Recognise your natural talent, seek out experts and great coaches to work with, and do the inner work of mastering body, emotion and mind. When all three come together you are ready to reach greatness. But what exactly to do?

## Challenge and Passion

The vertical axis of flow — challenge — is the outside calling on our skills. It asks us the question: what do I do with my talent and skill? When your skills are still developing, take it easy. As your skills mature, stretch yourself.

The easy part of challenge is difficulty. As we get better, we can look for more testing opportunities. More searching is needed to find challenges that match your passions. What is it that you really care about? When it really matters to us, the effort required to match skill to challenge is meaningful and joyous. Far too many lives are boring and lack inspiration. The reason may be that we don't care about what we do.

In the short run it may well be necessary to make ends meet and stay out of trouble. Over the long run we don't want to reflect on our life as boring and meaningless. We would not want this for our children. A good life becomes a meaningful life when we find a calling that resonates deeply with our passions and ethics.

## Practice

Finding the passion to seek out worthy challenges is a very personal journey. Parents and those who inspire us lay down the foundations of what is right and good. Then experience provides us with a raft of feedback mechanisms that signal whether what we did was good and satisfying or not. Positive psychology has invested deeply in this concept through the VIA Signature Strengths initiative. The VIA Institute has a questionnaire you can complete online to benchmark yourself against others (see www.viacharacter.org). A biological perspective has been advocated by Nohria and Lawrence from Harvard University.[84]

Below is a very simple perspective on some of the key themes that might ignite passion or drive us.

| Strength/Drive | Explanation (examples) | Your level | | |
|---|---|---|---|---|
| Wisdom Learning | Knowledge, facts, learning, novelty, rich perspectives and deep understanding (academic, philosopher) | Low | Mod | High |
| Courage Acquire | Power, growth, competition, leadership, vision, ambition and tenacity (entrepreneur, investor, military leader) | Low | Mod | High |
| Love Bond | Connection and care for others, desire to feel wanted and appreciated (counsellor, parent, nurse) | Low | Mod | High |
| Justice Defend | Focus on right, wrong and fairness; judgemental, protective and socially aware (law, politics, police) | Low | Mod | High |
| Transcend Spirit | Finds meaning beyond the material world and seeks to liberate spirit of others (minister, leader, guru) | Low | Mod | High |

To build more flow into your life, sport or career, explore where the matches between skill and challenge lie. These are your sweet spots, where you are likely to find success. If you are a talented biologist and love learning, academic medicine probably suits you well. If you are a skilled communicator and love defending those who need help, you may make a great politician or lawyer.

If you have a passion but lack some talent or skill, ask if you can develop them or find a way to team with people who do have the skill. If you have talent and skill but cannot find passion, it is time to try something else. See what matches you can discover. See if you can match your top three talent/skill zones with your top two passions/drives.

| Passion/ Drive | | | | |
|---|---|---|---|---|
| e.g. Wisdom | | | Read, study, learn and communicate, teach or facilitate (consultant) | |
| | | | | |
| | | | e.g. Linguistic | Talent/skill |

There are also times in our lives when work is unfulfilling. You might have a PhD and find yourself making coffee or you might have been a businesswoman who has chosen to be with her young children. The challenge-skill mix is simply wrong for your talents and skills. Sometimes we have to accept the reality and make the best of it. Here we must work more deeply on our emotional, cognitive and social skills.

Could I make a coffee while connecting enjoyably with a fun customer? As I change my fourth nappy of the day, can I do it with love, gentleness and calm? While it might be hard to work on the outer triggers for flow in work, one can always apply the internal triggers with coherence, vitality, positivity and mindfulness. At the very least, you can always strive for relaxation, even if it is not stretching your skills. Be patient, complete the phase you have chosen, but begin to think about how you might introduce flow outside of your current work. This might be study, sport, community work or part-time contracting.

In conclusion, the matching of your talent and skills to a meaningful challenge is an evolving process. Jobs change, we change and the realities of life can be rude or delightful. This is a very helpful approach to keep in mind and periodically to review. This loops back to assessing your day on the flow model. Where have you spent your day and does it agree with you? When you find yourself swinging over towards anxiety it is time to slow down and refocus on skill. When you find things a bit too dull, it is time to look for a more demanding challenge that calls on your skills.

This is how to build a good and meaningful life. That is where real happiness comes from.

### Summary

- ☀ Discern between happy, good and meaningful.
- ☀ Work out your flow zones.
- ☀ Track and plan for flow.
- ☀ Define your talent and skill.
- ☀ Apply talent/skill to your passions.

## Chapter 17

# Love

### Love Is Work

The work of love is the hardest of all. Love can be physical, emotional, cognitive and spiritual. These are often confused. Love starts on the inside with tender care for each of your cells and the body they make up. Love stretches out through family, friends and community to the planet and universe. This is a lot of territory — from cell to universe. We have to be realistic about how much love we have, and where and how we want to direct it.

Love is effortful work. Truly to love is demanding and hard to sustain — even for one's life partner. Popular culture likes to focus on romantic love, where one falls in love accompanied by an explosion of hormones and everlasting bliss. Really? Some even wait for love to come to them. It can be a long wait. Much better to accept that love is an effortful investment over time. This investment can deliver truly awesome returns for you, those you love and the situations in which you live, work and play.

How might we explore the elements of love and secure more of the benefits? Yes, love is natural, but as humans we have many alternatives open to us. That means there are many ways to get it wrong. Be patient and see if there is space to connect in better ways.

Why love?

Great question, and an important one to answer in each of our lives. The foundation for love's existence in higher creatures, primates and specifically in humans is that it feels really good when we get it right. Think of those intimate moments with your chosen partner, family or really close friends. A delightful surprise connection with someone miles from home or a team project/game that goes really well can be positive moments of love. On the flip side, when love is absent we hurt and withdraw from those closest to us. Further out we may seek to undermine, exploit or terrorise other groups in the community.

The impulse to connect with love is the motivator separating:

- resilient and fragile people
- consensual love-making and murder
- thriving and crime-ridden community
- disaster relief and terrorist attacks
- sustainability initiatives and wanton exploitation of our planet.

The impulse to love and the skilful expression of that love in our lives is, could be and should be the primary goal of our species. Love is something worthy of understanding and development. It is a transformative force for good in skilled hands, or can wreak havoc when poorly directed and applied.

Let's begin by trying to answer two questions. How might we make sense of LOVE? And, what exactly are the benefits to us and what we care about?

**Physical love (eros)** — a warm hug or great sex — is so desirable and pleasurable some cannot stop thinking about it. The evolutionary roots are pretty obvious in the reproductive drive that secures survival and gives comfort when we are vulnerable. Some take it a little too far. This love is a basic disposition in lower regions of consciousness supported by a flood of feel-good hormones including testosterone, oxytocin, vassopressin and chemicals such as dopamine, serotonin and phenylethylamine. Desirable, addictive and satisfying! At its most basic: object to object.

**Emotional love (eros)** — feeling closely aligned, understanding, tender and caring — is also deeply rewarding and helps bond couples for the decades of parenting. Emotional love holds family and tribe together. It can inspire us to heroic and creative work. It is the glue of lifelong friendship and successful communities.

Emotional love operates from the higher regions of the brain and requires the empathy circuits to function. We see more than an object of desire. Others become human, sensitive and worthy of respect. We hate to see others suffering. The mirror neurons mimic others' pain in our own consciousness. Emotional love motivates us to console and help others. We share this with primates and many social species. The emotional empathy that underpins this form of love is a stable feature of evolution. Humans, as we will see, have enormous capacity to expand empathy and love.

**Cognitive love (philia)** is the thoughtful construction of commitment to others that we may see in the commitment of parents to children, between friends, within a sports team or in a business unit. This is love based on our values and decisions. Cognitive love draws on yet higher levels of consciousness to direct behaviour. We choose the path of respect, support and commitment to another even when the impulse is to fight or abandon. Culture is the commonly held set of values, beliefs and associated behaviours that form the glue of modern human society.

When we guide emotional love with consciousness we have a skilled and powerful force for good. Emotional love can drive action — but often without skill. Think of a panicked mother with an injured child in her arms. The emotional love evokes a powerful response, but it is not necessarily helpful. Mind allows us to calm the impulse (amygdala), carefully consider the situation and select an appropriate and targeted response. We share this capacity with higher apes, whales, dolphins and elephants.[85]

This is the power of modern medicine. When a genuine desire to heal the sick is combined with the resources and knowledge of medicine we have awesome power. Cognitive love is also the inspiration and power of compassion or loving kindness. Empathy for suffering without wisdom causes extreme distress in the brain and physiology. Wisdom allows us to make sense of the situation, fully appreciate the predicament of others and still take care of ourselves.

**Spiritual love (agape)** — the awe of a glorious sunrise, the bliss of wonder in life, or love of God — is once again a higher level of consciousness. Spiritual love is expressed through the mind. It is described as we mature and evolve. This spiritual love appears to invoke a similar physiological response to that of physical love. The vagal nerve is activated and the brain lights up in areas involving emotional and cognitive love. It is good for us, as research confirms repeatedly.

In the messy construct of human life and love, several levels may co-exist. In a good marriage, we may enjoy the physical and enhance it with emotional, cognitive and perhaps even spiritual love. A great friendship will certainly enjoy appropriate physical, emotional and cognitive elements. Casual sex may be quite basic and purely physical. This does not necessarily make it bad. It can produce children. Those children are more likely to thrive if emotional and cognitive love are present. The love for a parent, mentor or spiritual figure will certainly have a mix of emotional, cognitive and even spiritual elements. The physical elements that infect some families and spiritual communities are a gross violation of love.

Neurobiological studies suggest that we can also create a top-down effect. If we approach an ugly situation, where physical and emotional love collapse, with the open, compassionate presence of loving kindness, then we create the possibility of more love and caring. The image of Mother Teresa or a mission doctor give us a sense of how spiritual — and perhaps cognitive — love can open the door of empathy to engage physical and emotional love.

## The Multilevel Benefits of Love

Take a moment to review where love is active in your life. Create a rich picture and image of each of your love connections — physical, emotional, cognitive and spiritual. As you experience the memory it is practically certain that you will feel good. Both receiving love and giving love soak us in a glow of wellbeing — body, heart and mind. Barbara Fredrickson's work, *Love 2.0*, is a current and powerful case for the benefits of love.[86]

On the contrary, when love is absent we suffer. At the personal level the absence of love is a significant risk factor for our health. We feel lonely. The immune system is weakened. Connection is broken. At a societal level the absence of love allows for selfish and destructive behaviours. We take without considering how others are compromised. We fight and injure, claiming that our cause is right. Those around us suffer. Collaboration breaks down; conflict and war fill the space. If we lose our love of nature and other sentient beings, we put our planet and our future at risk.

Figure 37 summarises the benefits of love in the Resilience Diagnostic and Development model. It's always better to love.

## How to Love?

Learning to love is our most important challenge. Simply hoping that love will come along and work out rarely delivers. Skilfully targeted love will take us so much further. To work skilfully with love is the purpose of this

Figure 37: The Multilevel Benefits of Love to Our Resilience and Lives

| Resilience Assets | Love Benefits |
|---|---|
| Spirit in Action | Infuses work with meaning<br>Strengthens collaborative effort<br>Increases happiness and contentment<br>Stimulates action to improve situations |
| Train Mind | Opens insight into perspectives of others<br>Activates left prefrontal cortex<br>Cools the amygdala<br>Enhances cognitive performance |
| Engage Emotion | Opens the empathy portal<br>Triggers emotional flexibility<br>Improves mood<br>Supports impulse control |
| Energise Body | Stimulates immune system — less illness<br>Reduces cardiovascular risk<br>Leads to longevity in nuns and marriage<br>Appears to optimise hormones of health |
| Master Stress | Calming and reassuring effect<br>Enhances vagal tone and recovery<br>Counters dangers of anger<br>Physical attunement with others |

section. First, we must understand the process — the biology — of love. Second, we have to focus on how to direct and practise love. The creative scope is enormous. Get started and see how this can unfold.

You will, occasionally, fall suddenly and deeply in love. Perhaps with a lover, a friend, a spiritual mentor, a place, work or recreation. This spontaneous falling in love is glorious. The biological signals that cultivate a feeling of connection are important. They can direct you towards love that will work. Enjoy it and make the most of it. What follows may help you make it a lasting connection that brings great joy to all parties. We can work at love. In fact, we dig deep inside to nurture the strength and discipline to focus our resources on building connection. Again, inside-out.

Three stages secure success.

The first is to activate the vagal brake and coherence as described in part two, chapter 7, Coherence. One can think of this as the relaxation phase. When we activate the vagal brake, breathing slows, heart rate variability (HRV) becomes even and we grow calm, focused and connected. Think of this as creating the physical conditions for love to take root. This is truly inside.

The second stage is empathy. Empathy is the emotional competence required to reach from inside to outside. Empathy is a hot topic in neurobiology and psychology. It is established as a stable trait in primates and is rapidly accelerating in modern society.[87] Along with the increase in empathy is a consistent reduction in violence towards each other. Human culture, in the main, is increasing its capacity for empathy. The basis of empathy is attention towards others. We shift our attention from our own needs and how to secure them towards others and how we can help them. This attention allows us to sense what others feel and to think about their needs. We become attuned.

The third stage is compassion. Compassion requires thinking. Guided by the emotional experience of another person's situation, we consider how we can act to help. Biologist Frans de Waal calls this targeted helping. He shows how targeted helping happens in primates and a few other species. It is thus totally natural — as is the love a parent feels for an upset child. Yet as humans, with our expanded consciousness, we have vast opportunity to grow and activate the compassion within us. Compassion may help us to relieve suffering and nurture the strength and success of others.

## Training Empathy

Empathy is definitely trainable. Empathy is one of Richard Davidson's six dimensions of mind.[88] As he and others have shown, there is a spectrum of possibility — from psychopath to saint. At the low-empathy side we have people who do not register the feelings or needs of others. Simon Baron-Cohen[89] talks about two forms at this end. The psychopath, narcissist or borderline personality is willing and able to hurt others to secure their own needs — zero negative on the empathy score. Autistic people may have limited ability to understand the feelings of others but seldom try to harm — zero positive. Zero, in my view, is harsh, but he is a renowned expert.

To build empathy we have both the emotional and cognitive pathways. Emotional empathy connects us to the feelings of others. We literally feel the emotions of others (remember the mirror neurons). The emotion we see becomes reality in our consciousness. On the positive side this connects us intimately with the felt world of others.

The downside is that we suffer when we witness the suffering of others. This suffering can be so painful that we take action to relieve our suffering rather than providing the right long-term assistance. For example, we may toss a few coins to the beggar to relieve our discomfort. As a consequence we have wily beggars making good on the street rather than working. Young nurses and doctors, full of kindness, struggle to be firm with patients on the treatments required to make them well.

This is the sympathy trap. It is exhausting and usually does more harm than good. Many people, including our children, staff, friends, family and businesses, actively prey on sympathy. Acting on sympathy leads to bad decisions. Acts of sympathy undermine the other person's resources. Dependency can follow and vulnerability increases. It will exhaust your resources. It is easy to fail in your role as parent or manager, which is to help others be resilient.

Cognitive empathy is conscious understanding and consideration of others. Cognitive empathy is power in today's world. It is a key topic in business, combat and social uplift. As we learn the signals in tones of voice, facial expressions and body language, we gain accurate insight into the experience of another person. We can truly understand their perspective. Further, we can predict how they are likely to act. Many experts now train these skills. Consider:

- A combat officer detecting a facial expression that signals attack or submission.
- A counsellor on the phone recognising suicide risk in tone of voice.
- A negotiator knowing when to press advantage or concede to the other side.
- A judge discerning when a person is lying or telling the truth.
- A loving wife recognising when a grumpy husband needs a hug.

These are examples of people who have learned to become expert at what they do by detecting, understanding and responding to tiny, microsecond signals that most of us miss completely. For more on this topic have a look at www.paulekman.com. Professor Paul Ekman has become world renowned for his work in defining emotional cues and training people to detect them.[90] His work saves lives, guides good justice and shines a light on complex situations.

Cognitive empathy can open the portal to love. By using our minds we can extend ourselves down the empathy curve. The process is clear. Step one is to choose to pay attention to others. We have learned that we can do this far better when we are well rested, relaxed and coherent. Shifting our attention from our own feelings and thoughts to focus fully on what we can learn from another person is a big step. The empathy portal is at least pointed in the right direction. Others respond to attention positively, making it a virtuous loop.

The second step is to study non-verbal signals. Study facial expressions, tone of voice, posture and body language. By working through Ekman's training you will improve your ability to read others accurately at sub-second speed. Untrained, we may recognise only a few cues and it can take half a second or more to read them. Trained, we can learn to detect multiple cues and their variations in less than 0.2 seconds. You have seen what someone is about to feel before they know it. Rich information is streaming through your empathy portal.

The third step is to use information gathered through the empathy portal to understand the perspectives of others. By paying attention you gather the story as it unfolds. Reading non-verbals gives you the accurate signal of what emotions are being felt. We have truly entered the world of another person. We can see how the world looks from their point of view.

You may think this sounds a bit spooky. However, we are quick to make up our minds about others and make judgements. We do this without paying much attention and frequently without accurate non-verbal cues. Would it not be better to collect accurate information first?

........................................................

## Practice

1. Pick one human interaction each day that could benefit from the attention step.
2. During this interaction face the person, remove all distractions and give your full attention.
3. Listen carefully without interruption and stay tuned to the tone of voice.
4. Notice the posture, body movements, eye movements and hands.
5. Watch the face and see if you can detect the different expressions.

Figure 38: The Development Path of Empathy — From Negative to Abundant Skilful Compassion

| Development | Antipathy | Ignorance | Emotional empathy | Cognitive empathy | Compassion |
|---|---|---|---|---|---|
| Neurobiology | Damaged empathy | Tuned into self | Mirror neurons | Spindle cells | Prefrontal active |
| Upside | Avoids powerful | Lucky not to hurt | Sensitive to others | Understands others | Skilful assistance |
| Downside | Preys on weak | Damages on way | Sympathy trap | Manipulative | Fatigue |

6. At a natural pause see if you can relate the point, feelings and thoughts back to the other person.

•••••••••••••••••••••••••••••••••••••••••••••••••••••••••••••••••••••

The empathy portal concept from De Waal is helpful. If we want to connect in a way that makes love skilful and fulfilling, we absolutely must work the empathy portal. Many biologists now believe that it is empathy rather than survival of the fittest that allowed our ancestors to survive and thrive.[91] The advantages of high empathy in a human group include the capacity to recognise who has power and resources, to know when someone is in need versus when they are likely to attack you, and to collaborate skilfully in the hunting, gathering and homemaking that secures survival.

We recognise power of empathy in good leadership, high-performance teams and great customer service. Success is more likely for those who can skilfully understand and serve the needs of others. Building empathy is good business. Empathy enriches family, society, city and nation.

Empathy alone is not enough, although it allows us to understand the needs of others.

Compassion allows us to reflect on the information empathy gives us and then to consider, select and act to achieve constructive outcomes. Compassion is the skilful response to empathy. Brain studies show that when we feel the suffering of others — such as witnessing the plight of war-damaged children — the brain experiences high levels of distress. This distress disables us. If we can maintain our strength and move to a position of compassion, the distress dissolves. In our language, the vagal brake activates and we can deploy more skilful resources.

The common view of compassion is the self-sacrificing work of missionaries and the loving kindness of monks. A contemporary view, as I see it, is a combination of strength and targeted, skilful service to others. A firm, loving (authoritative) parent, a tough but caring manager, and a demanding but supportive coach are good examples of compassion in action. Compassion emerges when we have cultivated strength within in order to respond effectively to the real and long-term needs of others.

To build a good life for ourselves and those we love requires balance. One path of development is power with strength and aggression. We develop a calm physiology, strong body, exploratory positive emotion, sharp mind and a will to lead. This is the hero/heroine theme we love. The balancing path is gentle, caring but firm. We are attuned to the physiology of others, defend them, console, strive to help, and resolve conflict. This is the path of compassion. The desire to love and care must operate in balance with the desire to lead with power.

Figure 39: Balanced Leadership Is Attained When Taking the Dual Path of Compassion and Power Linked to Body, Heart, Mind and Spirit

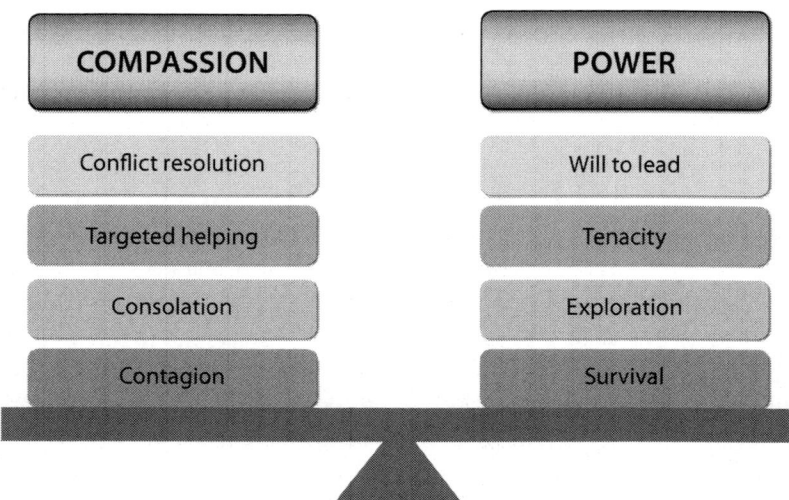

If we lose balance in this development path, we fall into common traps. Working from the bottom up, let's note a few.

1. **Anxiety** Foundation of compassion, super-sensitive, but calming and thinking skill compromised.
2. **Autism** Limited contagion response with low empathy and strongly self-centred.
3. **Sympathy** Strong contagion/consolation overwhelms survival, exploration and thought.
4. **Narcissist** Collapse of compassion and strong development up the power path to tenacity.
5. **Caregiver fatigue** Strong on compassion to high levels, but forgets to strengthen self.

To understand what is possible with compassion, consider those who demonstrate strong development on both paths. In my life the Dalai Lama, Nelson Mandela and Bill Clinton are examples that evidence both compassion and power. Who are your examples?

In the journey to find your power and compassion you are learning to balance your personal resilience with the openness of love. When you are strong and well resourced from the inside you have the energy to attend and contribute to the outside. When we feel anger or sadness, the empathy portal snaps shut (apparently more readily in men than women). There are times when others take advantage of our generosity or threaten our families. In such moments it is quite reasonable to reduce compassion and defend yourself.

## The Scope of Love

Where to direct love? My liver cell, rhinos or the planet?

As we become stronger inside, we feel more energy, curiosity and desire to connect with the outside. Taking our love to others is in our nature. This impulse is good for others and good for us — a win-win. We recognise the value of wisdom. You are moving up the dual path of compassion and power. It is time to direct your love. The choice of where you direct your love defines your life.

Many forget the inside in the rush to save the planet or find a mate. The first target of your love is inward — yourself. It is easy to do this work like an abusive parent. We criticise, punish and imprison ourselves. Some common themes are: 'I am so lazy/fat/stupid/uncaring. I will only eat lettuce/never go shopping/exercise to death. I hate exercise/will never be a good parent/manager.'

Love starts inside. Be attuned to yourself. Recognise when you are tired, distressed and angry. Be kind yet firm to yourself. The practices of bounce, courage and creativity are those of being good to yourself — taking care of your cells, body, emotions and thoughts. This includes being firm when you recognise you need to relax, sleep, eat better, exercise or be positive and mindful. This is the path to power.

When we have the power of inner resilience, we are able to invest in loving others. Home is the next base — parents, children, siblings and partner. When we are connected with love at home, we have so much more resource to consider how we might extend our love to our community, workplace and friends.

Only then do we consider the extended world of charity, nation, other species and the planet. With so much pressure from the challenges facing us 'out there', it is easy to hollow out and despair. We lose love for self and fail in our intimate circles, sometimes desperately struggling to do good somewhere out there. It is not sustainable.

Track the balance between power and compassion. When compassion wavers it is usually because you have slipped down the resilience spiral. It is time to go inward, with compassion, and invest in rebuilding your own resources. As the energy increases, reach out to those close to you, remaining mindful of your balancing act between power and compassion and the scope of love you are endeavouring to cover.

When we get the balance wrong the end result can be compassion fatigue, distress, depression, failed marriage or unhappy family. These are all powerful lessons that take us back to the inside-out process of discovering ourselves and serving our worlds with an open and compassionate heart.

## Summary

- Love is the fuel of connection — physical, emotional, cognitive and spiritual.
- Love is good for us — those who give love and those who receive.
- Empathy is the skill that makes love possible.
- Maintain your balance between power and compassion.
- Love starts with self and widens in ever-increasing circles.

# Chapter 18

# Pray

## Beyond Body, Heart and Mind

Inside-out is a journey of self-discovery during which we understand and master ourselves. We learn who we are — physically, emotionally and cognitively. This understanding helps us know how we want to be in the world. The skills we have covered will support in realising that potential. We have learned how to transcend some thresholds:

1. How to recognise and bounce from adversity and resilience failure.
2. How to move from distressed to calm and coherent.
3. How to build our physical wellbeing, energy and physical presence.
4. How to work from destructive to constructive and positive emotions.
5. How to focus, attend and use the mind to master our thinking.
6. How to connect to our work and those we love.

There are very few educated or wise people who would argue with the need to understand and master body, emotion and mind. The territory we have covered is widely acknowledged as the means for being a good, happy and effective person.

Millions of people will attest to both short-term and long-term benefits when they address the practices covered. We learn who we are and how to be in the situations that make up our lives. What we have covered so far is tangible, concrete and clearly testable. It is believable — albeit demanding to master.

Using the word 'spirit' is immediately less clear. We can document and describe objectively physiology, emotions and thoughts. Physiology can be touched and measured in very concrete ways. Emotions, while less obvious, can be photographed, recorded and matched to a well-described list. Thoughts, even more fleeting and numerous, can be accurately described, communicated and in some ways measured in the brain. There is a progression from tangible and objective to subtle and subjective.

A starting point for spirit is to continue the evolution towards subtlety. Spirit is difficult to observe objectively. Perhaps it is so subtle that we find it hard to believe that it is real. As a consequence many simply ignore the territory.

The standard religions have not kept up with a modern scientific and technological society. They are out of date and disconnected from the realities and needs of our time. The spiritual traditions of Buddhism, Confucianism, Christian mysticism and Sufi wisdom, while attracting plenty of attention from educated folk, remain based in very ancient, patriarchal and impractical codes of conduct.

While respecting spiritual traditions, the intention is to craft a modern framework with practices to make sense of spirit in the 21st century. We know that a life without a body is death, life without positive emotion is bland and miserable, and life without insight into our thoughts can be a torment. What is the difference between a life with and without spirit?

To answer that question we have to have a rough definition at least!

## What is Spirit?

We have a clear sense of body, emotion and mind. We can label them. That is my arm, I am feeling happy, and I am thinking about breakfast. Pause and describe your body, emotion and mind right now. Now, once they are accounted for, are you aware of anything else? The hypothesis to test is whether spirit is that something else.

This is the foundation of spiritual practice. It is the quest that the great mystics undertook. When we are aware of body, emotion and mind — all in their appropriate place but not preoccupied by them — we open ourselves to the question of spirit. So, again, as you sit and push out your awareness, what are you conscious of? A spiritual perspective is first and foremost a state of open, curious and focused awareness.

Once we open to that perspective the next question presents. How do I embrace that vision in my own life? From awareness in our consciousness we try to live in a way that spirit becomes part of who we are. We call this presence. This may be crystallised by asking how others would see us. What do others see in or about us that radiates something beyond a clump of cells, emotions and thoughts?

The third perspective asks us how we would act if we embraced a spiritual perspective. We call this resonance. Body wants food or sleep, emotion wants pleasure or contentedness, and thoughts seek solutions. What does your spirit seek? What are you to do if you wish to act in alignment with your spirit? How do we live in this world and among others in ways that embrace the essence of spirit.

In a previous book I took a more detailed look at the world of spirit and how to work through it.[92] Here we will focus on the foundations of spiritual connection: awareness, presence and resonance.

## Awareness

The practice of awareness takes time and dedication. We have learned to sit quietly with calm physiology, emotion and mind. This is the base of meditation. The benefits to sleep, recovery, wellbeing, positivity and effective mind are well established. The base practice is clearly laid out at the end of the part four, chapter 13 on Mind. In the section 'Witness self, reality and integration' on pages 202–203, we open the door to spirit. From a practical point of view it is important to have a sense of what we are looking for as we peer out from this quiet point of being.

The first search is inward. As we peer into the inner self — deeper than body, emotion and mind — we sense the essence of being we might call spirit (small s). This is the deepest form of love on the inside. We begin with atoms and molecules, all with their own history — some shared with Caesar, Jesus, Buddha and Mohammed. These make up our cells and genetic scripts inherited through generations, from algae to primate to human to parents. Cells make up the organs of life and awareness. The vast humming connectivity across your 40 trillion odd cells is you. Can you feel it?

Brain scientists have shown us that practised meditators trigger a powerful wave of gamma (>30 Hz) across the brain. It appears that the sense of being fully aware and connected is mirrored in wide areas of the brain resonating at the gamma level. Maybe this a clue to the feeling of spirit.

Awareness practice allows us to explore this wonderful miracle that is surging and retreating on each breath. Outside becomes inside and inside becomes outside as oxygen, carbon dioxide and nitrogen exchange between your fluid self and the environment. We can watch body, heart and mind respond and settle with tenderness and curiosity. Awareness opens to fill the space we can call 'spirit'. This is the witness — that part of you that senses all this and embraces the amazing drama. As we breathe in we draw our attention inwards to the source of the witness — or spirit.

The exhalation directs attention outwards. We can become aware of clothing, seat, place, sounds, light and aromas. As we extend further outwards we become aware of sky, clouds, rain, sun, nature and the activity of life around us. Reaching yet further, we can see ourselves as a dot on a map surrounded by mountains, seas, forests and life. As we extend outwards to embrace the planet, solar system, time and the universe the spirit becomes a tiny element of the vast Spirit (big S) of existence.

Some will quickly have a sense of God as awareness expands to embrace the vastness of life and universe. Others may have an awesome sense of nature, cosmology or evolution. Others may simply be able to rest in the recognition that we are a tiny dot in a vast mystery. If we judge too quickly, awareness collapses back to the tangibles of the next e-mail or meal. Relax. Simply rest in this awareness — curious, open and gentle. Every time you get lost, simply follow the breath inwards, back to cells and your life, and then as you exhale embrace the vastness around you.

When you find the quiet, alert awareness that is always present, it is magnificently peaceful, blissful and rejuvenating. Accomplished meditators find this practice so beautiful they acknowledge that it is like a drug that can draw you into a cave of isolation as you liberate your spirit. This is the ascending path of the hermit. While most of us do not intend to retreat to a cave, we can at least acknowledge the wisdom of being more in touch with both spirit inside and Spirit outside.

For those of us in normal lives, awareness is the crown jewel. The mind is quiet, the emotions positive, the body alert yet relaxed, and we are free to allow the spirit a little space in our busy lives. The little distractions and irritations of life drop away for a blissful moment and we experience total freedom. It is a passive expression of flow.

### Practice

1. Meditation remains the base practice for which we have already articulated a strong case.
2. Seek out a meditation practice that works for you and get some base training established.
3. Science supports a practice of between 10 and 30 minutes per day — preferably in the morning.
4. One Minute Meditation[93] on the hour has shown some wonderful benefits. See www.onemomentmeditation.com.
5. Grab gaps to relax, smile, breathe out, open your awareness and invite your spirit back in.
6. Develop quick tools to go inwards (spirit) and outwards (Spirit) and use what works.

## Presence

Most of us come back to the hustle and bustle of daily life. Awareness practice is peaceful and rejuvenating. We strive to become aware of spirit. The next question is: how do we bring spirit back into reality?

Here I am in this chair reading this book. I can sense my body relaxed into the cushion, I feel curious but a little unnerved by what I am reading, and my thoughts keep flicking to that presentation I have to prepare. Here I am in this moment. Is my spirit present? If my partner was watching would he or she see body, heart, mind and spirit? I accept that my body can be seen, and perhaps my curiosity and discomfort, but can my partner really see my thoughts? Surely he or she cannot see spirit? Perhaps we should ask.

Presence is what others experience of us. How are we fronting up? We all know that some people are able to carry a large and spirited presence. They have a memorably positive impact. Others are barely noticed. The practice of presence is taking time and effort to radiate that positive impact.

We have learned how good, open posture pumps up our vitality hormones such as testosterone and reduces cortisol. Researchers at Harvard University[94] have shown how this has a measurably positive impact on leadership. We have seen how positive emotion radiates a feel-good aura that nurtures healthy and happy families and teams. We also understand that the nature of our thoughts can shift us from low- to high-road outcomes.

The first step in presence is to bring spirit into each of these levels of expressing yourself to others — body, heart and mind. How do we bring to life that inner spirit we discover in awareness? We have covered this territory in depth. Your challenge is to find an authentic expression of yourself. If you choose to allow spirit to shine from your physical being you have to find a way to sit and stand that reflects your inner truth. The challenge from Harvard's Professor Amy Cuddy tests us. Are you prepared to fake it until you make it?

The second step is to work on holding that awareness of spirit and Spirit present as we interact during the day. Good posture, positive emotions, attentiveness and an open empathy portal lay the foundations. Can we hold the connection with spirit and Spirit in our active lives in a way that we know it and others sense it? We seal the deal when our actions reflect our presence.

## Practice

1. Stay tuned to your posture. Consider a muscle-balance assessment. Check pictures. Stretch.
2. Work on positivity and spend some time flexing the positive emotions each day.
3. Rest and prepare your mind for meetings so that you can be calm and attentive.
4. Consider hiring a coach and doing some video recording of yourself in action.
5. Use mini meditations to reach both inside and outside to spirit and Spirit.
6. Practise, practise, practise.

## Resonance

Resonance is the final perspective in spiritual connection. The ascending spiritual path of meditation and presence in front of God is liberating, and some choose this as their purpose. The descending spiritual path brings that wisdom and skill back into the world. Resonance is the way in which we connect with others and our world. Once again the foundations are well described.[95] We enter our activities with calm, energy, positivity and mindfulness. We remember the distinction between a happy life, a good life and a meaningful life. Wherever we can, we master situations from the high road. The empathy portal is open. We are kind yet firm.

The journey into resonance takes time. We need lots of practice in the little moments of life — saying hello, taking a moment to be kind, not doing harm, and so on. We must slowly define our talents and sharpen our skills so that we can tackle the challenges of life. Then we begin to look for meaningful challenges. Spirit can be active in all of these.

The goal in resonance is to decide what you are here to do with your life. Some of us choose big hairy goals like saving rhinos and others simply strive to find a good reason to share a smile. There is no right or wrong. This is your life journey. What really matters to you? Some are lucky enough to connect with a life goal early and it becomes a calling. Others work away at defining it and preparing the path. It may take us until 35 or even 70 years of age before we achieve full resonance in our engagement with the world.

The easy way out is to believe that nothing matters — that there is no point in making an effort because it cannot make a difference to a world spinning madly with lots of evil. So why not just grab what little moments of self-indulgence we can — a drink, a party, sex, quick money? This is a collapse and abdication of spirit. Resonance slips away.

Humans are meaning-makers. We search for signals that indicate value. We are equipped with all the resources to know ourselves, make sense of our world and find a way to achieve resonance in our lives. Step up, start the search and be all that you can be. Proudly savour the small moments of bringing joy to another person, and humbly accept the responsibility of making radical constructive change if you have the skills. Be your life: fully, unapologetically and with enthusiasm. Remember that the root of enthusiasm is 'entheos' — God within.

## Practice

1. Enthusiastically live the principles and practices of inside-out.
2. Search for the spiritual essence alive in body, emotion and mind.
3. Take your spiritual depth into the world in which you live.
4. Connect with enthusiasm — live, love and work with body, heart, mind and spirit.
5. Stay alert for situations that call out to you, then seek a meaningful role.
6. Be kind and supportive — nurture body, heart, mind and spirit in others.
7. Define your talents, sharpen your skills and get to work on things that matter.
8. Deepen awareness, cultivate presence and seek resonance.

## Summary

- Push your consciousness from tangible body to subtle emotion and mind.
- Explore what spirit means to you.
- Deepen awareness.
- Cultivate presence.
- Seek resonance.

# Chapter 19

# Discipline

## What is Non-negotiable?

Inside-out is the journey for those ready to search beyond the dash for cash and find out what altitude and quality means in life. The trap is to think, read, talk, and dream, and then go no further. Inside-out can be based only on action and the application of skilful practice. The noise of our thoughts, the push of our emotions and the energy of the body is you seeking to express yourself. The journey can be resourced with knowledge and desire, but can start only with action. We do the best we can to seek the evidence and truth. We search for the best practices to drive growth and development — the journey of self-completion. We have at our disposal the wondrous resources of body, heart, mind and spirit.

This final chapter is a call to action. If you are serious, this must be disciplined action. Armed with knowledge and instructions we must put them to work in practice. There are many paths to choose from and thousands of practices to test and evaluate. Your life will be defined by what you put into practice. Practice must be diligent and regular. It has to fit into the realities of your life.

Inside-out takes a lifetime. The sooner we master the practices and acquire skill, the faster and further we progress. There will be setbacks and aggravations. That is why bounce is critical. We need a healthy body to take us through the journey. That is why we need the courage to take care of ourselves, exercise, sleep well and eat healthily. We have vast scope for creativity. That requires mastering emotion, mind and flow. Ultimately, it is all about connection. A good life is one in which we discover meaningful work, love and the spark of spirit.

Here we invite you to develop your own Integral Daily Practice. This is a framework for action and monitoring. Just as we must diarise the important commitments to our family or work, so it makes sense to diarise the important practices that will fuel our journey. Those who choose the dedicated paths of monastic life, elite forces or world-class sport craft the entire day around the embodiment of these practices. There is a very active science on how to optimise human performance. We can take advantage of this in appropriate ways to fine-tune our practices to match our aspirations.

## Step One: Reality Check

The starting point is to review the actions of your day. If followed with a video recorder, what would be recorded of your day? For example, many tell us they sleep well, but if we look a little deeper:

- they go to bed an hour later than they claim
- they sit on the laptop or iPhone as they lie in bed
- when they fall asleep they drop into a shallow sleep
- by 2 a.m. they are showing signs of sleep apnoea
- shortly thereafter they are awake and worrying
- when the alarm goes they take just a 'short nap'
- they drag themselves out of bed an hour late, missing exercise and breakfast

Basic sleep discipline has failed. First, we must see this accurately for what it is. If we cannot see reality clearly, it is unlikely that we will change. Compounding our tendency to ignore facts is that some of us will not change until we feel pain. Many clients laugh away my suggestions until struck by serious illness. Suddenly they are inspired to take action, but often following the huge inconvenience of surgery, hospitalisation and healthcare costs that could have been avoided. Sometimes it is a trusted friend telling you that you have put on weight.

An essential element of waking up to reality is a preventive health and resilience assessment. Getting this right is a messy job as different experts suggest different approaches. Some often have narrow special interests. Let me do my best to outline what you should check to secure your resilience and guide the practices you choose.

## Annual checks

| | |
|---|---|
| **Review your Distress Questionnaire** | See part two, chapter 2, the Death Spiral. |
| **Resting pulse** | This should be tracked daily with a simple check at wrist or neck. |
| **Blood pressure** | Suggest have your own BP device at home (e.g. Omron). |
| **Waist to Hip ratio** | Specifically check waist circumference at belly button. |
| **Heart rate variability** | Download your family em-wave at www.heartmath.com. |
| **Resilience Diagnostic** | www.resiliencei.com |
| **Positivity Ratio** | www.positivityratio.com |
| **Blood tests (age 15+)** | Once you know your trends, reduce frequency until age 45. |
| **Fasting blood glucose** | Aim for 3.5 mmol/l to 5.5 mmol/l (early detection of pre-diabetes). |
| **Fasting lipids** | Triglyceride to be less than 1.5 mmol/l. HDL to be high as possible — ideally >1.5 mmol/l. LDL and total cholesterol of questionable value. |
| **Vitamin D** | Essential to keep it high, but rarely checked and corrected. |
| **Ferritin** | A test for women to check the level of iron stores. |

## In the case of fatigue and listlessness

Add Vitamin B12 and folate.

Consider insulin and HbA1C (glucose metabolism).

Get a full blood count.

Check thyroid function.

**Over 45**

| | |
|---|---|
| Colonoscopy | Specifically if there is a change in bowel habits or a family history of disease of the bowel. |
| Women | Age-appropriate breast and gynaecological checks. |
| Men | Age-appropriate prostate checks. |
| Key hormones | To be discussed with your doctor or a healthy ageing clinic. |

Some professionals will tell you that this is all bunk. Let me tell you a story close to home.

### Case study: Teenage death spiral

My teenage daughter was completing her final year at school. Always a bright, active and social person, Lauren had become increasingly reclusive, tired, listless and moody. She was doing little in terms of exercise and had chosen to be vegan— mainly for ethical reasons. This meant she was getting 80% of her calories from carbohydrates, including perhaps a bit too much fruit and fruit juice. She was putting on weight and clearly not feeling good about herself. With exams she was staying up later than normal and struggled to get going in the mornings.

No advice from dad was welcome. Recommending that she get out into the sun and exercise a bit led to the exact opposite behaviour. Rather, it escalated into a tense, conflict-laden atmosphere. Advised that this was normal for dad–teenage daughter relationships, I tried to grin and bear it. As a parent, this was very difficult to deal with.

After six months I reached the end of my tolerance and insisted that she see a doctor and get a full set of blood tests completed. With my training telling me there was no need to test a young, healthy person, this was not easy. We got the support of a wellbeing-focused doctor who organised the tests and provided a wonderful explanation to Lauren.

The tests showed a very low and at-risk vitamin D level, low vitamin B12 and low iron stores. With some well-articulated advice, Lauren learned how to improve the way she was eating and started to replace the deficiencies with supplements. She was clearly engaged and, in retrospect, desperate for help.

She went on a low carbohydrate diet with higher fat and protein for a month, and began exercising vigorously daily and going to sleep earlier. The change was nothing short of transformational. Lauren's body shape altered dramatically, her energy increased, and she went back to cracking jokes and jumping around the house again. It had a truly uplifting effect on our household — let alone on her life.

As a parent trying to guide your daughter through school exams and the entry into adulthood, this is hard territory to navigate. It is easy to make mistakes and I am sorry I was not more attentive. I can only imagine how many young people might be struggling through with deficiencies like this. Please check!

•••••••••••••••••••••••••••••••••••••••••••••••••••••••••••••••••

## Step Two: Why?

The second step in the discipline of practice is to select a purpose. What exactly are you trying to achieve? What do you want yourself, your work, your sport, your family, your life to be through the investment you are about to make? This is your personal, creative work. Some of your purpose might be in small goals along the way, such as completing an event, losing x amount of weight or spending more time in flow. Hopefully, an element of this will be a long-term motivating intention for your life. Your smaller goals might be subsets of the longer-term purpose.

## Step Three: Initiation

The third step in developing your practice is to select the one practice — or cluster of practices — that will help you secure your purpose effectively (result) and efficiently (minimum strain). This is not always obvious. There is evidence that any ritualised daily practice supports wellbeing, happiness and success. Be curious and selective in choosing your battles. Time and energy are real constraints, so we need to be sensible about what is effective and efficient.

Below is a simple example of how some of the inside-out practices can be built into a day. These practices are well supported by evidence and the experience of experts. Think of the boxes as simply holding spaces within which you will design your own personal discipline. Take some time to review how your actual practice matches up to the suggestions in each box.

Tick those that you believe are clearly secured, regular and active in your life. Put a question mark in those boxes where you are not certain or where your practice is intermittent. Circle those that you are simply missing out on. Keep in mind that there is no absolute right and wrong. Each of us has a unique biological response to these practices. Getting it right can optimise your biology and transform your life.

The example below is based on some of the well-respected practices that help to accelerate and focus your journey. While the science may be somewhat complex, the practice is very simple. One can study 1776 pages of the current *Sleep Manual* or simply decide to be asleep at 10.00 p.m. and awake by 6 a.m. Some study all the references but never take action. Locking in an agreed practice will take courage. It is also a wonderful journey of creativity. We can try different timing, different practices and combinations. We will learn what works best for our unique situation.

Figure 40: An Example of Integral Daily Practice

| Morning Practice | Daytime Practice | Evening Practice |
| --- | --- | --- |
| Seven to eight hours unbroken sleep (asleep by 10.30 p.m.) | 30 minutes daily, include strength and speed | Smart switch from work or family/private life |
| Wake up at the same time each day, even weekends | Lunch of fish, turkey or chicken with leafy greens, beans and tomatoes | Create some play time and plan an early dinner |
| Spend at least five minutes stretching major muscles | Powernap or relaxation | Light meal: mixed vegies, pasta, stir-fried rice |
| Mindfulness, visualisation, positivity | A mid-afternoon snack: sandwich, nuts or fruit | Engaged family/friendship time |
| Breakfast including oats, fibre, milk, eggs, nuts and some fruit | Periodic rejuvenation: stretch, microbreaks | Gratitude and appreciation, celebration of goodness |
| Intention to make a positive impact | Engage others with full attention and compassion | Relax, body, smooth breath and release into deep sleep |

## Step Four: Establish Rhythm

Identify one change to which you can reasonably commit for a period of six weeks or more. Make it simple and ensure you find it believable that you will get a benefit. In my experience, big winners include stretching on waking, a big breakfast, daily short bursts of exercise, a powernap, two hours of device-free time before bed, a switching activity to prepare for home, and a regular wake-up time. Make sure that you balance the testing moments (getting up early to exercise) with rewarding moments (enjoying a hearty breakfast with friends).

Seek rhythm that is sourced in habit. This saves on the rare resource of willpower.

Key changes may require some help. It can be a lonely job when working on your own. You may have to try a few support systems before you find the one(s) that work for you. Good options include hiring a personal trainer or coach, joining a regular group activity such as a bootcamp, or committing as a family to a regular activity.

Build enjoyment into the activities you select. Avoid activities that do not give you joy. Wherever you can, involve family or friends for more joy and stickiness. Look out for activities that give you a buzz, be it golf, cycling, paddle-boarding, yoga or a meditation class. Keep the interest elevated. Track progress. Look for benefits in your body, emotions, mind or spirit. Stay curious and creative. Commit to three-month modules and then shift things around a bit. Respond and adjust to different seasons.

## Step Five: Learn, Adjust and Provoke Flow

We are unique with a vast range over which we can develop. You cannot do it all. There may be times in your life (for example when you have young children or during illness) when you feel like you can hold to only one lifesaver practice. At other times you will feel like you have a rich rhythm that really works. You are nudging into flow. Stay alert, practise with others, use coaches, read and even study. Look for adjustments that might work. Change your practice environment.

Think about how your home and work enhance or undermine your practice. For some an hour commute would be a nightmare and for others it is relaxation time. We are living in a time of changing jobs and careers.

Stay alert to the environments that reinforce your practices and those that deplete you. At times push yourself out of your comfort zone and try something that might be a bit scary. Even if it does not work out, you will learn important adjustment skills and clarify your true purpose.

Over the course of life you are building biological wisdom. You are maturing through the inside-out journey. Your true self feels like it is being expressed in both practice and purpose. Target flow, control, relaxation and sometimes arousal in your practice.

In my own training, I test each of these zones. High intensity training is 'arousal' and very productive. Don't do it too much. Three times per week is plenty. Other times you seek to enter the flow. Entering flow requires that we enter the situation in a relaxed state, fully embodied, emotionally engaged and deeply focused. Relaxed practice such as an easy activity, massage, meditation or family meal is really important. Turn off devices, drop your worries and agitations and work at being calm, focused and connected.

Over the years spent studying, practising and teaching resilience, I see a tight correlation between flow in your integral daily practice and flow in your life. When you get your own disciplines sorted out they will feel good. You will sense the development of skills that allow you to be playful with the challenges you choose. Engage in your disciplined practices with the intention of finding the joy, curiosity and playfulness that emerge in states of flow. What was once hard work becomes sheer enjoyment. Sometimes your practice is demanding and your day's work is a breeze.

When you have your inside work (integral daily practice) mastered, your outside work (how you fulfil your purpose in life) surges into flow. You are developing skills (horizontal axis) against the challenges (vertical axis) you set in your daily practice. You are learning how to master the challenge-skill relationship. Just as athletes master the elite performance by practising the parts, in the same way you master your life through your integral daily practice.

That integral daily practice will most certainly optimise your biology. It also helps you practise being successful. By learning how to master the performance states below, including being comfortable with the acute strain and distress of arousal, you are practising for life. Biology, skills, attitudes and the disciplines of success lift you towards flow in both the moment and in your life.

Figure 41: Build Your Skill, Lift Your Game and Secure More Flow

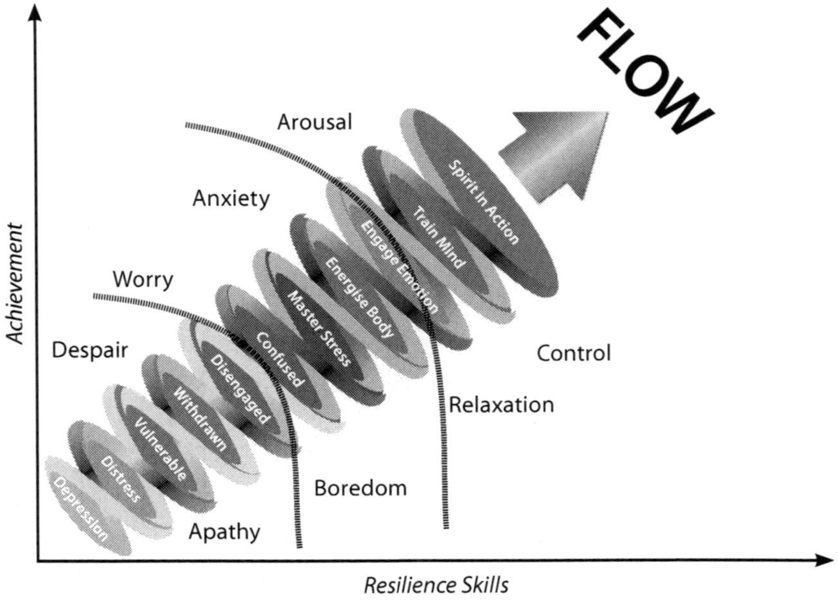

*Achievement* (y-axis) vs *Resilience Skills* (x-axis)

Labels: Arousal, Anxiety, Worry, Despair, Depression, Distress, Vulnerable, Withdrawn, Disengaged, Confused, Master Stress, Energise Body, Engage Emotion, Train Mind, Spirit In Action, Control, Relaxation, Boredom, Apathy, FLOW

## Practice Tipping Points

Over the years there have been a few very practical steps that make a big difference to people's lives. I have listed these from the morning through to the end of the day following the Integral Daily Practice model in figure 40.

**Wake-up Discipline**   Learn what time is the best for you to wake up and get going. Strict discipline in aligning your biology and blue light with your wake-up will bring your entire biology into your service. It will add productivity and energy to your day and deliver you to bed in the evening ready to fall into a deep sleep. Dozing and sleeping in on weekends will make progress much harder.

**Personal exercise routine**   Develop your own exercise routine for every morning. Include a series of stretches, balance exercises, and core strength (yoga, sit-ups, press-ups, squats or lunges). Try to get outdoors for brisk activity at least four days a week — a walk in the dawn, cycle, swim, paddle or the gym if the weather is bad. Ritualising your morning activity is a powerful enabler of all other practices and productive work. A couple of times a week do High Intensity Training (pulse at 85% of maximum).

**Breath/meditation**  Make sure you allocate at least five minutes to go into deep relaxation each day. Simply sitting upright and sinking into the breathing practice we have described in part two, chapter 7, Coherence. Let the mind become quiet and clear in a relaxed, upright posture with an attitude of kindness, joy and gratitude. This is great for distress symptoms, optimising health, focusing the mind and cultivating a calm and responsive attitude to the challenges of the day.

**Enjoy a good breakfast**  Take the time and care to secure your breakfast. The benefits have been known for decades and the research continues to support breakfast. The case for protein, healthy fats and low carbohydrate is clear. Use eggs, whole-fat Greek yoghurt, mushrooms, nuts, blueberries and bacon for taste. Enjoy a high fat (butter and cream) coffee. Make your own nut-based muesli.

**Chunk your day**  Schedule your day into the flow zones. Make sure you have a couple of well-defined and limited times to deal with e-mail. Alternate focused, intense work with short periods of relaxed, fun activity. Keep meetings short and empathy enabled. Take breaks in the sun or fresh air, have walks and snacks. A few minutes' exposure to sunshine without sunscreen each day will improve sleep, lift mood and build your vitamin D stores.

**Secure flow**  Make sure that each day you schedule some time to focus deeply into a challenge that gives you flow. Knowing that a part of your day will be or has been in the flow state will provide real engagement and satisfaction in your day. In the overloaded chaos of information, this is easily forgotten. If you have secured your flow, the hurly-burly of information shunting is tolerable.

**Cultivate joy and positivity**  Given that our default is to activate negative emotions, making space to activate a profound state of positive emotion proves to be a powerful catalyst to resilience. There are many options: watching a funny movie, laughter, playing with your children, loving kindness, meditation, random acts of kindness, or simply soaking in nature or your hot, soapy bath.

**Capture intimate time with friends and family** In our 24/7 always-connected world we can squeeze out highly engaged time with those we love. Ideally, schedule these times over dinner, a walk, evening conversation or a shared activity. Over the past months I have been going for a swim and workout with my son five times a week. This simple ritual has become a highlight of both our days.

**Kill all electronics two hours before bed** This simple discipline secures a raft of benefits for our clients — sleep quality, relaxation, energy, improved relationships. This space will fill with conversation, games, reading and relaxation. Your sleep quality and morning freshness will take off. Complement with low light, a light evening meal and relaxing music.

**Deep relaxation into sleep** Regardless of how your day has been always relax fully when you get into bed. Lie flat on your back, relax your body, specifically your face, neck and tongue. Smooth and slow your breathing to a very gentle inhale and long, relaxing exhale. On each inhalation recall a special moment from your day and as you exhale soak yourself in gratitude. Settle the mind on the rise and fall of your umbilicus until you fall into deep sleep.

## Conclusion

Inside-out is a journey to life fulfilment, joy and connection. This is the meaning of life. It is the wonderful opportunity that life presents. Do we allow ourselves to wallow in the dark or do we reach out to the colours, richness and magic of a life of resilience? Define your talents, refine your skills and seek the challenges that bring you joy and meaning.

This is your life's work. Make it count.

## Summary

- Bounce back regularly.
- Exhale.
- Breathe diaphragmatically.
- Take periodic breaks.
- Lock down your non-negotiables.
- Experiment with your own engage–relax rhythms.

# NOTES

1. Seligman, Martin, *Authentic Happiness*. Free Press, New York, 2002.
2. Fredrickson, Barbara, *Positivity*. Three Rivers Press, New York, 2009.
3. Wilson, Edward O., *The Social Conquest of Earth*. Liveright Publishing Corporation, New York, 2012.
4. Hernstein, Richard; Murray, Charles, *The Bell Curve*. Free Press Paperbacks, New York, 1994.
5. Baron-Cohen, Simon, *The Science of Evil*. Basic Books, New York, 2011.
6. Cooper Ramo, Joshua, *The Age of the Unthinkable*. Little, Brown & Company, New York, 2009.
7. Seligman, Martin, *Authentic Happiness*. Free Press, New York, 2002.
8. Seligman, Martin, *Learned Optimism*. Pocket Book, New York, 1998.
9. Seligman, Martin, *Flourish*. Free Press, New York, 2011.
10. Porges, Stephen W., *The Polyvagal Theory*. W.W. Norton & Company, New York, 2012.
11. Ekman, Paul, *Emotional Awareness*. Times Books, New York, 2008.
12. Davidson, Richard; Begley, Sharon, *The Emotional Life of your Brain*. Hodder & Stoughton, London, 2012.
13. Baumeister, William; Tierney, David, *Willpower*. Penguin Group, New York, 2011.
14. Damasio, Antonio, *Looking for Spinoza*. Harcourt Books, Orlando, 2003.
15. De Waal, Frans, *The Age of Empathy*. Souvenir Press, London, 2009.
16. Cuddy, Amy, 'Connect, then Lead', *Harvard Business Review*, Harvard Business School, July/August 2013.
17. Seligman, Martin, *Authentic Happiness*. Free Press, New York, 2002.
18. Wilson, Edward O., *Consilience*. Vintage Books, New York, 1998.
19. Grossman, Dave, *On Combat*. Warrior Science Group, Millstadt, 2008.
20. Goleman, Daniel, *Focus: the hidden driver of excellence*. Bloomsbury Publishing, London, 2013.
21. Kahneman, Daniel, *Thinking, Fast and Slow*. Farrar, Straus and Giroux, New York, 2011.
22. Redfield Jamieson, Kay, *Exuberance*. Alfred A. Knopf, New York, 2004.
23. Grossman, Dave, *On Combat*. Warrior Science Group, Millstadt, 2008.
24. Shiraldi, Glenn, *The Resilient Warrior*. Resilience Training International, Ashburn, VA, 2011
25. McCaw, Richie, *The Open Side*. Hodder Moa, Hachette NZ Ltd, 2012.
26. Porges, Stephen W., *The Polyvagal Theory*. W.W. Norton & Company, New York, 2012.
27. emWave from www.heartmath.com. This device is readily available for PC, Mac, iPad and iPhone.
28. Grossman, Dave, *On Combat*. Warrior Science Group, Millstadt, 2008.
29. Davidson, Richard; Begley, Sharon, *The Emotional Life of your Brain*. Hodder & Stoughton, London, 2012.
30. These include some of the following well-respected academics: Richard Davidson, Jon Kabat-Zinn, Brian Hanson, Daniel Goleman, Daniel Siegel, Martin Seligman and Paul Ekman.
31. Huffington, Arianna, *Thrive*. Harmony Books, New York, 2014
32. Boutcher, Stephen, 'High Intensity Intermittent Exercise and Fat Loss'. *Journal of Obesity*, Hindawi Publishing

Corporation, Cairo, Egypt, 2011. See more in the Exercise chapter.
33 Baumeister, William; Tierney, David, *Willpower*. Penguin Group, New York, 2011.
34 WHO Global Health Expenditure Atlas, 2012.
35 National Health and Nutrition Examination Study on 3382 adolescents between 1999 and 2008.
36 Fries, J.F., 'Measuring and Monitoring Success in Compressing Morbidity', *Annals of Internal Medicine*, 2 September 2003.
37 Dellara, F. Terry et. al., 'Cardiovasuclar Risk Factors Predictive of Survival in the Oldest-Old Framingham Heart Study Participants', *Journal of the American Geriatric Society*, November, 2005.
38 World Economic Forum and PricewaterhouseCoopers, *Working Toward Wellness Report*, 2007.
39 Pilzner, Paul Zane, *The Wellness Revolution*. John Wiley & Sons, Hoboken, 2007.
40 Life, Jeffry, *Mastering the Life Plan*, Simon & Schuster, New York, 2013.
41 *Annals of Human Biology*, Vol. 40, Nov–Dec 2013. We also carry ten times that number of bacteria — about 10% of our body weight.
42 Fisher-Wellman & Bloomer, 'Acute Exercise and Oxidative Stress', *Dynamic Medicine*, 13 January 2009.
43 Editorial, *Annals of Internal Medicine*, 159: 850–51, 2013.
44 Lieberman, Daniel, *The Story of the Human Body: Evolution, Health and Disease*. The Penguin Group, London, 2013
45 Noakes, Tim, et al, *The Real Meal Revolution*. Quivertree Publications, Cape Town, 2013.
46 www.glycemicindex.com is set up by Professor Jenny Brand-Miller at the University of New South Wales.
47 Davis, William, *Wheat Belly*.

Royale Books, New York, 2011; and Perlmutter, David, *Grain Brain*. Little, Brown and Company, New York, 2013.
48 Volek, Jeff; Phinney, Steve, *The Art and Science of Low Carbohydrate Performance*. Beyond Obesity, Miami, 2012.
49 Esselstyn, Caldwell, *Prevent and Reverse Heart Disease*. Penguin Group, New York, 2007.
50 Tough, Paul, *How Children Succeed*. Random House Books, London, 2012.
51 Lieberman, Daniel, *The Story of the Human Body: Evolution, Health and Disease*. The Penguin Group, London, 2013.
52 Boutcher, Stephen, 'High Intensity Intermittent Exercise and Fat Loss', *Journal of Obesity*, October, 2010.
53 For more, see http://www.bbc.com/news/health-27406987
54 Kryger, Roth and Dement, *Principles and Practice of Sleep Medicine*. Elsevier, St Louis, 2011.
55 Duhigg, Charles, *The Power of Habit*. William Heinemann, London, 2012.
56 Volek, Jeff; Phinney, Steve, *The Art and Science of Low Carbohydrate Living*. Beyond Obesity, Miami, 2011.
57 Noakes, Tim, et. al., *The Real Meal Revolution*. Quivertree Publications, Cape Town, 2013.
58 Djokovic, Novak, *Serve to Win*. Transworld Publishers, London, 2013.
59 Mosley, Michael, *The Fast Diet*. Michael Mosley, 2013; www.thefastdiet.co.uk
60 Darwin, Charles, *The Expression of the Emotions in Man and Animals*. John Murray (Penguin Classics), London, 1872.
61 Ekman, Paul, *Emotions Revealed*. Henry Holt and Company, New York, 2003; www.paulekman.com
62 Davidson, Richard; Begley, Sharon, *The Emotional Life of your Brain*. Hodder & Stoughton, London, 2011.
63 Goleman, Daniel, *The Brain and*

*Emotional Intelligence: New Insights.* More than Sound, Northampton, 2012.
64 Baron-Cohen, Simon, *The Science of Evil.* Basic Books, New York, 2011.
65 Scott, Susan, *Fierce Conversations.* Hachette Digital, London, 2002.
66 Seligman, Martin, *Authentic Happiness.* Free Press, New York, 2002.
67 Fredrickson, Barbara, *Positivity.* One World Publications, Oxford, 2009.
68 Fredrickson, Barbara, *Love 2.* Hudson Street Press, New York, 2013.
69 Gilbert, Daniel; Killingworth, Matthew, 'A wandering mind is an unhappy mind'. *Science*, November 2010.
70 Damasio, Antonio, *Self Comes to Mind.* William Heinemann, London, 2010.
71 De Waal, Frans, *The Age of Empathy.* Souvenir Press, London, 2009.
72 Kahneman, Daniel, *Thinking, Fast and Slow.* Farrar, Straus and Giroux, New York, 2011.
73 Tolle, Eckhart, *A New Earth.* Penguin Group, New York, 2005.
74 Baumeister, William; Tierney, David, *Willpower.* Penguin Group, New York, 2011.
75 Kabat-Zinn, Jon, *Beginners Guide to Mindfulness.* Sounds True, Boulder, 2012.
76 Boroson, Martin, *The One Moment Master.* Rider, Ebury Publishing, London, 2007.
77 Perlow, Leslie, 'Manage your Team's Collective Time'. *Harvard Business Review*, June 2014.
78 Kotler, Steven, *The Rise of Superman.* Amazon Publishing & Quercus Editions, London, 2014.
79 Seligman, Martin, *Authentic Happiness.* Free Press, New York, 2002.
80 Epstein, David, *The Sports Gene: What Makes the Perfect Athlete.* Yellow Jersey Press, London, 2013.
81 Djokovic, Novak, *Serve to Win.* Transworld Publishers, London, 2013.
82 Gardner, Howard, *Multiple Intelligences.* Basic Books, New York, 2008.
83 Isaacson, Walter, *Jobs.* Little, Brown Book Group, London, 2011.
84 Nohria, Nitin; Lawrence, Paul, *Driven.* Jossey Bass, San Francisco, 2002.
85 De Waal, Frans, *The Age of Empathy.* Souvenir Press, London, 2009.
86 Fredrickson, Barbara, *Love 2.* Hudson Street Press, New York, 2013.
87 Pinker, Steven, *The Better Angels of our Nature.* Viking Adult, New York, 2011.
88 Davidson, Richard; Begley, Sharon, *The Emotional Life of your Brain.* Hodder & Stoughton, London, 2012.
89 Baron-Cohen, Simon, *The Science of Evil.* Basic Books, New York, 2011.
90 Ekman, Paul, *Emotions Revealed.* Henry Holt and Company, New York, 2003; www.paulekman.com
91 Wilson, Edward O. *The Social Conquest of Earth.* Liveright Publishing Corporation, New York, 2012.
92 Hansen, Sven, *Spirit in Action.* Bateman, Auckland, 2006.
93 Boroson, Martin, *The One Moment Master.* Rider, Ebury Publishing, London, 2007.
94 *Your Body Language Shapes Who You Are*, Professor Amy Cuddy, www.ted.com/talks/amy_cuddy_your_body_language_shapes_who_you_are
95 Boyatzis, Richard; McKee, Annie, *Resonance.* Harvard Business School Publishing, Boston, 2005.

# GLOSSARY

| | |
|---|---|
| Biology | the study of life from the first cells to complex human society |
| Bounce | the ability to recognise resilience failure and to regain optimal function |
| Circadian Rhythm | the body clock that runs alternating sleep and wakefulness |
| Cognitive | the process of mind and thought, including the ability to watch and direct thoughts |
| Coherence | a rhythmic relationship between breathing and pulse-rate changes |
| Condition Black | state of biological distress that leads to gross failures in performance |
| Condition Grey | state of biological strain that compromises performance and exhausts |
| Condition Yellow | state of biological calm allowing effective performance under challenge |
| Condition Red | state of peak performance that is short and not sustainable |
| Connection | the physical, emotional, cognitive or spiritual union with self, others or nature |
| Consciousness | to reflect on experience, discern patterns and make calculated decisions |
| Courage | the ability to take definitive, purposeful action to improve self, others or nature |
| Creativity | the ability to direct one's talent to an original challenge and secure a novel outcome |
| Death Spiral | a codified model to understand how mind, emotion and body react as resilience fails |
| Emotional | the felt experience of 412 (or thereabouts) emotions through bodily changes |
| Flow | a concept of effective, engaged and skilful response to challenge |
| Glycation | the destructive effects of glucose in the body (also called glycosylation) |

| | |
|---|---|
| Hyperglycyaemia | abnormally high blood-glucose levels after meals |
| Hyperinsulinaemia | abnormally high insulin levels both after a meal and after fasting, indicating diabetes risk |
| Inflammation | the body's response to attack, injury or infection |
| Insulin | a hormone produced in the pancreas that stores glucose and fat |
| Neurobiology | the study of how the brain and nervous system work from an objective perspective |
| Oxidation | the process of cellular damage due to reactive oxygen and nitrogen molecules |
| Physical | of the body: atoms, molecules, cells, organs, skeleton, muscle, brain and skin |
| Plaque | the collection of oxidised cholesterol, blood and inflammation in arteries |
| Positivity | the central theme of positive psychology is to discover, savour and build positive emotions |
| Psychology | the study of how the mind works from an interpretation of the subjective experience |
| Resilience | a learned ability to demonstrate bounce, courage, creativity and connection |
| Response to Challenge Curve | maps how our biology responds to challenge defining performance |
| Ultradian Rhythm | the 90–110 minute cycle defining deep and dreaming sleep |
| Spiritual | what is beyond body, emotion and mind, ranging from core self to creative force |

Made in the USA
Lexington, KY
10 May 2018